The Trinity's Embrace
God's Saving Plan

The Trinity's Embrace
God's Saving Plan

A Catechesis on Salvation History

Pope John Paul II

With a Foreword by
Sister Paula Jean Miller, FSE

Pauline
BOOKS & MEDIA
BOSTON

Library of Congress Cataloging-in-Publication Data

John Paul II, Pope,   1920–
   The Trinity's embrace : God's Saving Plan / John Paul II.
      p.   cm.
Includes index.
  ISBN 0-8198-7408-6
1. Catholic Church — Doctrines. 2. Trinity. 3. Salvation.
4. Lord's Supper — Catholic Church. I. Title.
  BX1751.3 .J64 2002
  252'.02 — dc21

                                 2001003421

Reprinted with permission from *L'Osservatore Romano,* English edition.

Cover photo: *La Trinita,* Andre J. Rublev, Mosca Galleria Tretjakov

Printed and published in the U.S.A. by Pauline Books & Media, 50 Saint Pauls Avenue, Boston MA 02130-3491.

www.pauline.org

Pauline Books & Media is the publishing house of the Daughters of St. Paul, an international congregation of women religious serving the Church with the communications media.

1 2 3 4 5 6   07 06 05 04 03 02

The following abbreviations are used in the text
to indicate certain documents:

Documents of Vatican II

AA   *Apostolicam Actuositatem* (Decree on the
Apostolate of the Laity)

AG   *Ad Gentes* (Decree on the Mission Activity of the
Church)

DV   *Dei Verbum* (Dogmatic Constitution on Divine
Revelation)

GS   *Gaudium et Spes* (Pastoral Constitution on the
Church in the Modern World)

LG   *Lumen Gentium* (Dogmatic Constitution on the
Church)

NA   *Nostra Aetate* (Declaration on the Relation of the
Church to Non-Christian Religions)

SC   *Sacrosanctum Concilium* (Constitution on the
Sacred Liturgy)

UR   *Unitatis Redintegratio* (Decree on Ecumenism)

Documents of Pope John Paul II

DC   *Dominicae Cenae* (On the Mystery and Worship
of the Eucharist)

DViv   *Dominum et Vivificantem* (On the Holy Spirit in
the Life of the Church and the World)

EV   *Evangelium Vitae* (The Gospel of Life)
FC   *Familiaris Consortio* (On the Role of the
      Christian Family in the Modern World)
MD   *Mulieris Dignitatem* (On the Dignity and
      Vocation of Women)
OL   *Orientale Lumen* (Light of the East)
RH   *Redemptor Hominis* (The Redeemer of Man)
RM   *Redemptoris Missio* (Mission of the Redeemer)
RMat *Redemptoris Mater* (Mother of the Redeemer)
RP   *Reconciliatio et Paenitentia* (Reconciliation and
      Penance)
SRS   *Sollicitudo Rei Socialis* (On Social Concern)
TMA   *Tertio Millennio Adveniente* (On Preparation for
      the Jubilee of the Year 2000)
VC   *Vita Consecrata* (Consecrated Life)
VS   *Veritatis Splendor* (The Splendor of Truth)

Other documents and sources

CCC   *Catechism of the Catholic Church*
DP   *Dialogue and Proclamation* (By the Pontifical
      Councils for Interreligious Dialogue and for the
      Evangelization of Peoples)
DS   *Denzinger-Schönmetzer* (A collection of
      Church documents)
EI   *Enchiridion Indulgentiarum* (Handbook on
      Indulgences by the Holy See)
EN   *Evangelii Nuntiandi* (On Evangelization in the
      Modern World by Pope Paul VI)
OP   *Ordo Paenitentiae* (Rite of Penance by the Holy
      See)

Contents

The Holy Spirit

God the Father

The Trinity

The Eucharist and the Kingdom

Foreword

"When God acts, the impossible becomes possible. It is our task to say 'yes' to God's saving will and to accept his mysterious plan with our whole being. The world today needs to be awakened to God's love and to his saving plan" (Pope John Paul II, Syria, May 6, 2001).

John Paul II's historic pilgrimage to Athens and Damascus captures the heartbeat of his pontificate and of this Jubilee collection. This pope has a vision and a goal: he challenges the human community, in the tensions of its diversity, to image the Divine Communion of Love. He speaks, he acts, he travels the globe to "make the impossible possible" — to awaken all human beings to God's love and saving plan, a plan to be progressively revealed and actualized in history by the Holy Spirit, "the bond of love between eternity and time, the Trinity and history" (8/26/98).

History is a key theme of John Paul II. In the first part of his catechesis on the theology of the body, *Original Unity of Man and Woman,* history is the time of redemption. It is the link between the fall from paradise and eschatological fulfillment. History is salvation history, for humanity can never go back to its paradisal beginning, but only move forward into redeemed wholeness. History begins with sin and the expulsion from the garden, but most importantly, it begins with a promise: the promise of a messiah. History is the gradual unfolding of God's saving plan which finds its "key, center and purpose in Jesus Christ" (9/23/98).

In this volume, Pope John Paul emphasizes the historical nature of the human condition. In creating the universe, God created time. "Time, therefore, is God's gift…he guides its unfolding according to his plan" (11/19/97). Creation comes forth *from God* and returns *to God* through the mediation of human beings, who have been mandated to cultivate the earth and take care of it. "The human creature receives a mission to govern creation in order to make all its potential shine" (1/17/01). Time is God's gift, for human beings need time to become like God: to learn how to be God's divine Providence in the world. "By communion with the Body and Blood of Christ, the faithful grow in that mysterious divinization by which the Holy Spirit makes them dwell in the Son as children of the Father" (9/27/00).

In the context of this salvific dimension of time, Pope John Paul celebrates the mystery of Jubilee — 2000 years of grace! "Indeed, for believers the passage from the second to the third millennium is not merely a stage in the relentless march of time, but a significant occasion *to become more aware of God's plan* unfolding in the history of humanity" (11/19/97). Jubilees mark history, creation and humanity as God's own. They call humanity to remember, reverse, restore and recapitulate the universe into Christ. Jubilees awaken consciousness, wresting eternal significance from the inexorable flow of seemingly mundane events and relationships. "The new millennium must not be considered as merely the next step in the course of time, but as *a stage in humanity's journey toward its definitive destiny"* (12/10/97).

The Gospel presents the span of Christ's earthly life as the time of the wedding feast, for Jesus the God-man is the marriage between God and humanity, when time "is impregnated with eternity," when an "hour" creates a new relationship with God, a new form of worship, a new work, a new creation. Christ's life is "the hour of love." His human hours are transparent with the presence of God; *chrónos* is reconstituted as *kairos.* Ordinary time becomes God's *season,* which calls humanity to reject the indifference which equalizes all moral behaviors, which invites man to discern and to allow himself to be challenged, to be transformed into the likeness of the God of Love. "In fact, to have Christ enter one's life means to see one's history and projects disrupted" (8/9/00). "Jesus Christ…bursting onto history's stage, is presented as 'the Lamb of God, who takes away the sins of the world' (Jn 1:29). Here are the first words he says in public: 'Repent, for the kingdom of heaven is at hand!'" (8/30/00).

To illuminate the drama of contemporary history, Pope John Paul slowly turns the spotlight on revealed Truth, letting the light play upon its many faces: *Father, Son, Holy Spirit — Trinity; Jesus, Mary, humanity — salvation history; Reconciliation, Eucharist, divine-human communion — eschaton.* The life of Christ and of the Church is enfolded in the Father and the Holy Spirit even as it is unfolded in the mystery of time. "The whole of the Christian life is like a great *pilgrimage to the house of the Father....* This pilgrimage takes place in the heart of each person, extends to the believing community, and then reaches to the whole of humanity" (8/11/99).

The stage of history is an interplay of darkness and light, of dialogue and silence, of movement and stillness. "On the one hand, humanity strives for the infinite and the eternal, but on the other, it is firmly planted on earth, within the coordinates of time and space" (12/13/00). The Holy Father reminds us in this Jubilee catechesis that the Incarnation, the wedding of earth and heaven, "is not a flash of light dispelling the darkness for a moment, but a seed of divine life sown in the world and in human hearts forever" (4/5/00), that the supreme manifestation of the Trinity in the life of Christ took place in darkness, and the cross "joins humanity and divinity, death and life, suffering and glory" (5/24/00). And so for us, born in time, born for eternity, "God entered the world and human history and proceeds silently, waiting patiently for humanity with its delays and conditioning. He respects its freedom, supports it when it is gripped by desperation, leads it step by step, and invites it to collaborate in the kingdom's project of truth, justice and peace" (1/31/01).

Sister Paula Jean Miller, FSE
University of St. Thomas
Houston, Texas
May 8, 2001

SALVATION HISTORY

God Is the Lord of Creation and History

In the Apostolic Letter *Tertio Millennio Adveniente,* I asked all the Church's members "to open their hearts to the promptings of the Spirit," to prepare to "celebrate the Jubilee with renewed faith and generous participation" (n. 59). This exhortation becomes more and more urgent with the approach of that historic date. In fact the event acts as a *watershed between the past two millennia* and the new phase dawning for the future of the Church and of humanity. We must prepare for it in the light of faith. Indeed, for believers the passage from the second to the third millennium is not merely a stage in the relentless march of time, but a significant occasion *to become more aware of God's plan* unfolding in the history of humanity.

This new cycle of catecheses aims to do precisely this. For a long time we have been conducting a systematic program of reflections on the Creed. Our last theme was Mary in the mystery of Christ and of the Church. Previously we had reflected on revelation, the Trinity, Christ and his saving work, the Holy Spirit, and the Church.

At this point, the profession of faith would invite us to consider the resurrection of the body and life everlasting, which concern *the future of man and of history.* But precisely this

3

eschatological theme coincides naturally with what has been proposed by *Tertio Millennio Adveniente,* which described a path of preparation for the Jubilee *in a Trinitarian key.* The year 1997 was to focus especially on Jesus Christ, 1998 on the Holy Spirit, and 1999 on the Father.

In the light of the Trinity, the "last things" also acquire meaning. It is possible to understand more deeply the journey of man and history toward their *ultimate goal:* the world's return to God the Father, to whom Christ, the Son of God and Lord of history, leads us through the life-giving gift of the Holy Spirit.

This broad horizon of history in motion suggests several basic questions: What is time? What is its origin? What is its goal?

Indeed, as we look at Christ's birth, our attention focuses on the 2000 years of history that separate us from that event. But our gaze also turns *to the millennia that preceded it,* and spontaneously we look back to the origins of man and the world. Contemporary science is involved in formulating hypotheses about the beginning and development of the universe. Nevertheless, what can be grasped by scientific instruments and criteria is not everything. Faith and reason refer, beyond verifiable and measurable data, to the perspective of mystery, which is indicated in the first sentence of the Bible: "In the beginning God created the heavens and the earth" (Gn 1:1).

Everything was created by God. Therefore, nothing existed before creation except God. He is a transcendent God, who created everything by his own omnipotence, without being constrained by any necessity, by an absolutely free and gratuitous act dictated only by love. He is God the Trinity, who reveals himself as Father, Son, and Holy Spirit.

In creating the universe, God created time. From him comes the beginning of time, as well as all its later unfolding. The Bible stresses that living beings depend at every moment on divine action: "When you hide your face they are dismayed; when you take away their breath, they die and return to their dust. When you send forth your Spirit, they are created; and you renew the face of the earth" (Ps 104:29–30).

Time, therefore, is God's gift. Continuously created by God, it is in his hands; he guides its unfolding according to his plan. Every day is a gift of divine love for us. From this standpoint, we also welcome the date of the Great Jubilee as a gift of love.

God is Lord of time not only as Creator of the world, but also as author of the *new creation* in Christ. He intervened to heal and renew the human condition, deeply wounded by sin. He spent much time preparing his people for the splendor of the new creation, especially through the words of the prophets: "For behold, I create new heavens and a new earth, and the former things shall not be remembered or come to mind. But be glad and rejoice forever in that which I create; for behold, I create Jerusalem as a joy and her people as a delight" (Is 65:17–18).

His promise was fulfilled 2000 years ago with the birth of Christ. In this light, the Jubilee is an invitation to celebrate the Christian era as a period of renewal for humanity and the universe. Despite the difficulties and sufferings, the past years have been 2000 years of grace.

The years to come are also in God's hands. The future of man is first of all *God's future,* in the sense that he alone knows it, prepares it, and brings it about. Of course, he calls for and invites human cooperation, but he never ceases to be the transcendent "director" of history.

Only God knows how the future will be. We know, however, that it will be a future of grace; it will be the fulfillment of a divine plan of love for all humanity and for each one of us. That is why, as we look to the future, we are full of hope and are not overcome with fear. The journey to the Jubilee is a great journey of hope.

General audience of November 19, 1997

With Jesus,
Eternity Has Entered Time

The celebration of the Jubilee has us contemplate Jesus Christ as the end point of the time preceding him and the starting point of all that follows him. Indeed, he inaugurated a new history not only for those who believe in him, but also for the entire human community, because the salvation he accomplished is offered to every human being. Henceforth, the fruits of his saving work are mysteriously diffused throughout history. With Christ, eternity has entered time!

"In the beginning was the Word" (Jn 1:1). With these words John begins his Gospel, taking us beyond the beginning of our time, to the divine eternity. Unlike Matthew and Luke, who primarily consider the circumstances of the human birth of the Son of God, John directs his gaze to the mystery of the divine preexistence.

In this sentence, "in the beginning" means the absolute beginning, eternity precisely. The expression echoes that used in the creation account: "In the beginning God created the heavens and the earth" (Gn 1:1). But in creation it was a question of the beginning of time, whereas here, where the Word is mentioned, it is a question of eternity. There is an infinite distance between the two principles. It is the distance between time and eternity, between creature and God.

Existing eternally as the Word, Christ has an origin that goes back far beyond his birth in time. John's assertion is based on Jesus' exact words. To the Jews who rebuked him for claiming to have seen Abraham although he was not yet fifty years old, Jesus replied: "Truly, truly, I say to you, before Abraham was, I AM" (Jn 8:58). The assertion stresses the contrast between the *becoming* of Abraham and the *being* of Jesus. The word *genésthai,* used in the Greek text for Abraham, actually means "to become," or "to come into being"; it is the appropriate verb to designate the mode of being proper to creatures. On the contrary, Jesus alone can say: "I AM," indicating by this expression the *fullness of being* which lies beyond all becoming. Thus, he expresses his awareness of possessing an eternal personal existence.

By applying the expression "I AM" to himself, *Jesus* makes *God's name* his own, the name revealed to Moses in Exodus. After entrusting him with the mission of liberating his people from slavery in Egypt, Yahweh, the Lord, guaranteed him assistance and closeness. As a pledge of his fidelity, he revealed to him the mystery of his name: "I AM WHO I AM" (Ex 3:14). Thus, Moses can say to the Israelites: "I AM has sent me to you" (Ex 3:14). This name expresses God's saving presence for the sake of his people, but also his inaccessible mystery.

Jesus makes this divine name his own. In John's Gospel this expression appears several times on his lips (cf. 8:24, 28, 58; 13:19). With it, Jesus effectively shows us that in his person eternity not only precedes time, but *enters time.*

Although sharing the human condition, Jesus is conscious of his eternal being, which confers a higher value on all his activities. He himself emphasized this eternal value: "Heaven and earth will pass away, but my words will not pass away" (Mk 13:31; Mt 24:35; Lk 29:33). His words, like his actions, have a unique, definitive value, and will continue to call for a response from humanity until the end of time.

Jesus' work involves two closely related aspects: it is a *saving action* that frees humanity from the power of evil, and it is a *new creation* that obtains for humanity participation in the divine life.

Liberation from evil was prefigured in the old covenant, but only Christ can fully achieve it. He alone, as Son, has eternal power over human history: "If the Son makes you free, you will be free indeed" (Jn 8:36). The Letter to the Hebrews forcefully underscores this truth, showing how the one sacrifice of the Son obtained for us "eternal redemption" (Heb 9:12), far exceeding the value of the old covenant sacrifices. The new creation can only be achieved by the One who is all-powerful, because it implies the communication of divine life to human existence.

The perspective of the eternal origin of the Word, especially emphasized in John's Gospel, spurs us to enter more deeply into the mystery. Let us, therefore, profess our faith in Christ ever more forcefully: "God from God, Light from Light, true God from true God." These phrases of the Creed give us access to the mystery; they invite us to approach it. Jesus continues to testify to our generation, as he did 2000 years ago to his disciples and listeners, to his awareness *of his divine identity:* the mystery of the I AM.

Because of this mystery, human history is no longer left to decay, but has a meaning and a direction: it has in a way been *impregnated with eternity*. The consoling promise Christ made to his disciples resounds for everyone: "Lo, I am with you always, to the close of the age" (Mt 28:20).

General audience of November 26, 1997

The True Face of the Messiah
Was Gradually Revealed

"The Word became flesh and dwelt among us" (Jn 1:14). With this forceful and concise statement, the Evangelist John expresses the event of the Incarnation. He had just spoken of the Word, contemplating his eternal existence and describing it with the well-known words: "In the beginning was the Word" (Jn 1:1). This Johannine perspective, linking eternity to time, also includes Christ's mysterious journey *in the history that preceded him.*

His presence in our world began to be announced long before the Incarnation. The Word was in some way present in humanity's history from the very beginning. Through the Spirit, he prepared his coming as Savior, secretly directing hearts to nurture expectation in hope. Traces of a hope of liberation are encountered in the various religious cultures and traditions.

But Christ is present in a particular way in the history of the people of Israel, the people of the covenant. This history is specifically marked by the expectation of a Messiah, an ideal king consecrated by God, who would fulfill the Lord's promise. As this orientation became gradually clearer, Christ progressively revealed the true face of the promised and longed-for

Messiah, also glimpsed against the background of a violent death (cf. Is 53:8). In fact, a certain messianic image, firmly established among some Jewish people who expected a political liberator who would bring national autonomy and material well-being, came to a radical crisis when the prophecies were historically fulfilled in the scandal of the cross.

In his earthly life, Jesus clearly showed his awareness of being the reference point for his people's history. To those who reproached him for claiming to be greater than Abraham, promising that those who kept his word would never see death (cf. Jn 8:51), Jesus replied: "Your father Abraham rejoiced that he was to see my day; he saw it and was glad" (8:56). Abraham was thus oriented to Christ's coming. According to the divine plan, Abraham's joy at the birth of Isaac, and at his rebirth after the sacrifice, was a messianic joy; it announced and prefigured the ultimate joy that the Savior would offer.

Other eminent figures of the Jewish people shine in their full value in the light of Christ. This is the case with Jacob, as can be seen in the Gospel account of Jesus' meeting with the Samaritan woman. According to Christ's words, the well that the ancient patriarch had left to his sons prefigured the water Jesus would give, the water of the Holy Spirit, welling up to eternal life (cf. Jn 4:14).

Moses also announced some of the basic aspects of Christ's mission. As liberator of the people from their slavery in Egypt, Moses symbolically anticipated the true exodus of the new covenant, constituted by the paschal mystery. As legislator of the old covenant, he prefigured Jesus who promulgated the Gospel Beatitudes and guides believers with the interior law of the Spirit. Even the manna that Moses gave the hungry people is a basic figure of God's definitive gift. "Truly, truly, I say to you, it was not Moses who gave you the bread from heaven; my Father gives you the true bread from heaven. For the bread of God is that which comes down from heaven and gives life to the world" (Jn 6:32–33). The Eucharist fulfills the meaning hidden in the gift of manna. Christ thus presents himself as the true and perfect fulfillment of what was symbolically foretold in the old covenant.

Another of Moses' acts had a prophetic value: to quench the thirst of the people in the desert, he made water flow from the rock. On the "feast of Tabernacles," Jesus promised to quench humanity's spiritual thirst: "If anyone thirst, let him come to me and drink. Whoever believes in me, as Scripture says, 'Out of his heart shall flow rivers of living water'" (Jn 7:37–38). The water that Moses gave prefigures the abundant outpouring of the Holy Spirit, whom Jesus announced with the image of rivers of living water. In referring to this messianic event, St. Paul also stresses the mysterious reference to Christ: "All drank the same supernatural drink. For they drank from the supernatural Rock that followed them, and the Rock was Christ" (1 Cor 10:4).

Along with Abraham, Jacob and Moses, David also referred to Christ. He was aware that the Messiah would descend from him and described his ideal image. Christ fulfilled this image at a transcendent level, affirming that David himself mysteriously alluded to his authority when, in Psalm 110, he called the Messiah "my Lord" (cf. Mt 22:45; Lk 20:44). From the Old Testament history several characteristic features of Christ's face emerge, a face that is somehow "sketched" in the features of the persons who prefigured him.

Christ is present not only in these prefigurations, but also in the prophetic texts of the Old Testament that describe his coming and his saving work.

He is foretold in a particular way in the figure of the mysterious "descendant" of which Genesis speaks in the account of original sin, stressing his victory in the struggle with the enemy of humanity. The divine oracle promises to the man, dragged down the path of evil, the coming of another man, descended from the woman, who will bruise the serpent's head (cf. Gn 3:15).

The prophetic poems of the suffering servant put before our eyes a liberator who begins to reveal the face of Christ in its moral perfection (Is 42:1–4; 49:1–6; 50:4–9; 52:13—53:12). It is the face of a man who expresses his messianic dignity in the humble condition of a servant. He offers himself in sacrifice to free humanity from the oppression of sin. He behaves in an exemplary way in his physical and especially his moral sufferings, generously enduring injustices. As the fruit of his sacrifice, he receives a new life and obtains universal salvation. His sublime conduct will be found again in Christ, the Son of God made man, whose humility reaches an unsurpassable height in the mystery of the cross.

General audience of December 3, 1997

Eternity Now Pervades Time

In inviting us to commemorate 2000 years of Christianity, the Jubilee takes us back to the event that inaugurates the Christian era: the birth of Jesus. Luke's Gospel tells us of this extraordinary event in simple and moving words: Mary "gave birth to her firstborn son, wrapped him in swaddling clothes and laid him in a manger, because there was no place for them in the inn" (2:7).

Jesus' birth makes visible the mystery of the Incarnation, already realized in the Virgin's womb at the annunciation. As the docile and responsible instrument of the divine plan, she gave birth to the child whom she had conceived by the power of the Holy Spirit. Through the humanity assumed in Mary's womb, the eternal Son of God began to live as a child and grew "in wisdom and stature and favor with God and man" (Lk 2:52). Thus, he manifested himself as true man.

John stresses this truth in the prologue of his Gospel, when he says *"The Word became flesh* and dwelt among us" (1:14). By saying, "became flesh," the evangelist is alluding to Jesus' human nature not only in its mortal condition, but also in its entirety. The Son of God assumed all that is human, except sin. The Incarnation is the fruit of an immense love, which spurred God to willingly share our human condition to the full. In becoming man, the Word of God brought about a fundamental change in the very condition of time. We can say that in Christ *human time was filled with eternity.*

This transformation touches the destiny of all humanity, since "by his Incarnation the Son of God has united himself in some fashion with every man" (*GS* 22). He came to offer everyone participation in his divine life. The gift of this life includes sharing in his eternity. Jesus said so especially with regard to the Eucharist: "Whoever eats my flesh and drinks my blood has eternal life" (Jn 6:54). Through the effect of the Eucharistic banquet, we already possess this life. Elsewhere Jesus indicated the same possibility with the symbol of the living water that could quench thirst, the living water of his Spirit given in view of eternal life (cf. Jn 4:14). The life of grace thus reveals a dimension of eternity that lifts up our earthly existence and directs it, with true continuity, to our entrance into heavenly life.

The communication of Christ's eternal life also means that we share in his attitude of filial love for the Father. In eternity, "the Word was with God" (Jn 1:1), that is, in a perfect bond of communion with the Father. When the Word became flesh, this bond began to be expressed in all Jesus' human behavior. On earth the Son lived in constant communion with the Father, in an attitude of perfect loving obedience.

The entry of eternity into time is the entrance, in Jesus' earthly life, of the eternal love that unites the Son to the Father. The Letter to the Hebrews alludes to this when it speaks of Christ's inner attitude at the moment he entered the world: "I have come to do your will, O God" (10:7). The immense "leap" from the heavenly life of the Son of God into the abyss of human existence is motivated by his will to fulfill the Father's plan in total self-giving.

We are called to assume this same attitude, walking on the way opened by the Son of God made man, so that we can share his journey to the Father. The eternity that enters into us is a sovereign power of love that seeks to guide our whole life to its ultimate purpose, hidden in the mystery of the Father. Jesus himself indissolubly linked the two movements, descent and ascent, which define the Incarnation: "I came from the Father and have come into the world; again, I am leaving the world and going to the Father" (Jn 16:28). Eternity has entered human life. Now human life is called to make the journey with Christ from time to eternity.

If in Christ time is raised to a higher level, receiving access to eternity, this implies that the new millennium must not be considered as merely the next step in the course of time, but as *a stage in humanity's journey toward its definitive destiny.* The year 2000 is not only the door to another millennium; it is the door to eternity that, in Christ, continues to open onto time to give it its true direction and authentic meaning.

This discloses to our mind and our heart a far broader perspective in which to consider the future. Time is often unappreciated. It seems to disappoint us with its precariousness, its rapid flow, which makes all things futile. But if eternity has entered time, then time itself must be recognized as rich in value. Its inexorable flow is not a journey to nothingness, but a journey to eternity.

The real danger is not the passing of time, but using it badly, rejecting the eternal life offered by Christ. The desire for life and eternal happiness must be ceaselessly reawakened in the human heart. The celebration of the Jubilee is meant precisely to increase this desire, helping believers and the people of our time to open their hearts to an unbounded life.

General audience of December 10, 1997

Jesus' Life Is a
Reference Point for Our Faith

The entrance of eternity into time through the mystery of the Incarnation makes Christ's whole life on earth an exceptional period. The span of this life was a unique time, a time for the fullness of revelation, in which the eternal God spoke to us in his incarnate Word through the veil of his human existence.

That time will remain forever as a normative point of reference: *the time of the Gospel.* All Christians recognize it as the time from which their faith began. It was the time of a human life that changed all human lives. Christ's life was rather short, but its intensity and value are beyond compare. We stand before the greatest wealth for human history, an inexhaustible richness, because it is the wealth of eternity and divinity.

Those who lived in Jesus' time and had the joy of being close to him, seeing him, and hearing him were especially fortunate. Jesus himself called them blessed: "Blessed are the eyes which see what you see! For I tell you that many prophets and kings desired to see what you see but did not see it, and to hear what you hear but did not hear it" (Lk 10:23–24).

The formula "I tell you" makes it clear that the affirmation goes beyond mere observation of a historical fact. Jesus says a *word of revelation* that sheds light on the profound meaning of history. In the past that preceded him, Jesus not only saw the external events that prepared his coming, he looked at the deep aspirations of hearts that were at the basis of those events and anticipated their final outcome.

The majority of Jesus' contemporaries were unaware of their privilege. They saw and heard the Messiah without recognizing him as the Savior for whom they hoped. They addressed him without realizing they were speaking to God's Anointed foretold by the prophets.

In saying "what you see," "what you hear," Jesus invited them to perceive the mystery, going beyond the veil of the senses. He helped his disciples especially to penetrate it: "To you has been given the secret of the kingdom of God" (Mk 4:11).

Our faith, based precisely on the disciples' witness, is rooted in their gradual discovery of the mystery. We do not have the privilege of seeing and hearing Jesus, as was possible during his earthly life, but with faith we receive the immeasurable grace of entering into the mystery of Christ and his kingdom.

The time of the Gospel opened the door to a deep knowledge of Christ's person. In this regard, we can recall Jesus' sad rebuke to Philip: "Have I been with you so long and yet you do not know me, Philip?" (Jn 14:9). Jesus expected a penetrating knowledge full of love from the one who, as an apostle, lived in a very close relationship with the Teacher. Precisely because of this intimacy, Philip should have understood that the Father's face was revealed in Jesus: "He who has seen me has seen the Father" (Jn 14:9). With the eyes of faith the disciple is called to discover the invisible face of the Father in Christ's face.

The Gospel presents the span of Christ's earthly life as the *time of the wedding feast.* It is a time made for spreading joy. "Can the wedding guests fast while the bridegroom is with them? As long as they have the bridegroom with them, they cannot fast" (Mk 2:19). Here Jesus used a simple and evocative image. He is the bridegroom who announces his wedding feast, the wedding feast of love between God and humanity. He is the bridegroom who wants to communicate his joy. The bridegroom's friends are invited to share it by coming to the wedding feast.

Precisely in this wedding context, however, Jesus announced the time when he would no longer be present: "The days will come when the bridegroom is taken away from them, and they will fast in that day" (Mk 2:20). This is a clear reference to his sacrifice. Jesus knew that the joy would be followed by sadness. Then the disciples would "fast," that is, they would suffer as they participated in his passion. Christ's coming on earth, with all the joy it involves for humanity, is inseparably linked to suffering. The wedding feast is marked by the drama of the cross, but it will culminate in paschal joy.

This drama results from Christ's inevitable conflict with the power of evil: "The light shines in the darkness and the darkness has not overcome it" (Jn 1:5). The sins of all humanity play an essential part in this drama. But the failure of a certain group of his own people to recognize him was especially distressing for Christ. Addressing the city of Jerusalem, he reproached her: "You did not know the time of your visitation" (Lk 19:44).

The time of Christ's earthly presence was the time of God's visitation. Of course, some persons gave a positive response, the response of faith. Before recounting Jesus' tears over the rebellious city (cf. Lk 19:41–44), Luke describes for us his "royal," "messianic" entry into Jerusalem, when "the whole multitude of the disciples began to rejoice and praise God with a loud voice for all the mighty works that they had seen, saying, 'Blessed is the king who comes in the name of the Lord! Peace in heaven and glory in the highest'" (19:37–38). But in Jesus' eyes, this enthusiasm could not conceal the bitter fact of being rejected by the leaders of his people and by the crowd they had incited.

Moreover, before his triumphal entry into Jerusalem, Jesus had foretold his sacrifice: "For the Son of Man also came not to be served but to serve, and to give his life as a ransom for many" (Mk 10:45; cf. Mt 20:28).

The time of Christ's earthly life was thus marked by his redeeming sacrifice. It was the time of the paschal mystery of his death and resurrection, from which flows the salvation of the human family.

General audience of December 17, 1997

Jesus' Hour Is the
Time of Human Salvation

The celebration of the Jubilee invites us to focus our attention on the hour of salvation. On various occasions Jesus used the word "hour" to indicate the moment the Father had determined for the fulfillment of the work of salvation. Jesus spoke of it from the start of his public life, at the wedding feast of Cana, when he received a request from his mother on behalf of the bride and groom who were in difficulty because of the lack of wine. To indicate the reason why he was opposed to answering the request, Jesus said to his mother: "My hour has not yet come" (Jn 2:4).

This certainly means the hour for the first manifestation of Jesus' messianic power. The Gospel account informs us that it is an especially important hour, for it presents the miracle as "the beginning" or the "start" of his signs (cf. Jn 2:11). But on the horizon appears the hour of Jesus' passion and glorification (cf. Jn 7:30; 8:20; 12:23–27; 13:1; 17:1; 19:27), when he will complete the work of human redemption. By working this "sign" through the efficacious intercession of Mary, Jesus manifests himself as the messianic Savior. While he goes to meet the wedding couple, it is really he himself who is beginning his work as the Bridegroom, inaugurating the wedding feast that is an image of God's kingdom (cf. Mt 22:2).

With Jesus the hour has come for a new relationship with God, the hour for a *new form of worship:* "The hour is coming, and now is here, when true worshipers will worship the Father in spirit and truth" (Jn 4:23). The basis for this universal worship is the fact that, by becoming incarnate, the Son has enabled men and women to share in his filial worship of the Father.

The "hour" is also the time when the *work of the Son* is made manifest: "Truly, truly, I say to you, the hour is coming, and now is, when the dead will hear the voice of the Son of God, and those who hear will live. For as the Father has life in himself, so he has granted the Son also to have life in himself" (Jn 5:25–26). The great hour in world history occurs when the Son gives his life, making his saving voice heard to those who are under the power of sin. It is the hour of redemption.

All of Jesus' earthly life was directed to this hour. At an agonizing moment shortly before his passion, Jesus said: "Now my soul is troubled. And what shall I say? 'Father, save me from this hour?' No, for this purpose I have come to this hour" (Jn 12:27). With these words Jesus revealed the inner drama that was oppressing his soul in view of his approaching sacrifice. He had the possibility of asking the Father that this terrible trial might pass. On the other hand, he did not wish to flee from this painful destiny. "For this purpose I have come." He came to offer the sacrifice that would bring salvation to humanity.

This crucial hour was *willed and determined by the Father*. Before the hour chosen by the divine plan, his enemies had no power over Jesus. Many attempts were made to stop Jesus or to kill him. In relating one of these attempts, John's Gospel highlights the impotence of his adversaries: "They sought to arrest him, but no one laid hands on him, because his hour had not yet come" (7:30).

When the hour came, it also appeared as the *hour of his enemies.* Jesus said to "the chief priests and captains of the temple and elders, who had come out against him.... This is your hour, and the power of darkness" (Lk 22:52–53). In that dark hour it seemed that no one could stop the raging power of evil. Nevertheless, this hour also remained under the Father's power. He allowed Jesus' enemies to capture him. Their work was mysteriously included in the plan established by God for the salvation of all.

More than the hour of his enemies, the hour of his passion was thus *Christ's hour,* the hour when his mission was fulfilled. John's Gospel lets us perceive Jesus' state of mind at the beginning of the Last Supper: "When Jesus knew that his hour had come to depart from this world to the Father, having loved his own who were in the world, he loved them to the end" (13:1). It is thus the *hour of love,* which wants to go "to the end," that is, to the supreme gift. In his sacrifice Christ revealed perfect love to us; he could not have loved us more deeply!

This decisive hour was both the hour of passion and the *hour of glorification.* According to John's Gospel, it was the hour when the Son of Man was "lifted up from the earth" (12:32). The lifting up on the cross was the lifting up to heavenly glory. Then the phase of the new relationship with humanity began, especially with the disciples, as Jesus himself announced: "I have said this to you in figures; the hour is coming when I shall no longer speak to you in figures but tell you plainly of the Father" (Jn 16:25). The supreme hour was ultimately the moment when the Son returned to the Father. It clarified the meaning of his sacrifice and shed full light on the value of this sacrifice for humanity, redeemed and called to be united with the Son in his return to the Father.

General audience of January 14, 1998

Jesus Gave His Life
As a Ransom for Many

Christ revealed himself throughout his earthly life as the Savior whom the Father sent for the salvation of the world. The very name "Jesus" expresses this mission. It actually means "God saves." Jesus was given this name as a result of heavenly instruction: both Mary and Joseph received the order to call him by this name (cf. Lk 1:31; Mt 1:21). The message to Joseph explains the meaning of the name: "You are to name him Jesus, for he will save his people from their sins."

Christ defined his saving mission as a service whose highest expression would be the sacrifice of his life for mankind: "For the Son of Man also came not to be served but to serve, and to give his life as a ransom for many" (Mk 10:45; Mt 20:28). These words, spoken to counter the disciples' tendency to seek the first place in the kingdom, were primarily meant to awaken in them a new mentality that conforms more closely to that of the Teacher.

In the Book of Daniel, the figure described as "one like a son of man" is shown surrounded by the glory due to leaders who receive universal veneration: "All peoples, nations and languages should serve him" (7:14). Jesus contrasted this figure with the Son of Man who put himself at the service of all. As a divine Person, he would be fully entitled to be served. But in saying he had "come to serve," he showed a disturbing aspect of God's behavior: although he has the right and the power to make himself served, he puts himself "at the service" of his creatures. Jesus expressed this desire to serve in an eloquent and moving way at the Last Supper when he washed his disciples' feet. This symbolic act would be impressed as a rule of life on their memory forever: "You also ought to wash one another's feet" (Jn 13:14).

In saying that the Son of Man came to give his life as a ransom for many, Jesus was referring to the prophecy of the suffering servant who "makes himself an offering for sin" (Is 53:10). It is a personal sacrifice, very different from the animal sacrifices used in ancient worship. It is a life given "as a ransom for many," that is, for the immense multitude of humanity, for "all." Jesus thus appears as the *universal Savior:* all human beings, according to the divine plan, are ransomed, freed and saved by him. Paul says: "Since all have sinned and fall short of the glory of God, they are justified by his grace as a gift, through the redemption which is in Christ Jesus" (Rom 3:24). Salvation is a gift that can be received by each one to the extent of his free consent and voluntary cooperation.

As universal Savior, Christ is the *only Savior.* Peter affirmed this clearly: "There is salvation in no one else, for there is no other name under heaven given among men by which we must be saved" (Acts 4:12). At the same time, he is also proclaimed as the *only mediator* between God and men, as the First Letter to Timothy affirms: "For there is one God, and there is one mediator between God and men, the man Christ Jesus, who gave himself as a ransom for all" (2:5–6). As the God-man, Jesus is the perfect mediator who unites men with God, obtaining for them the goods of salvation and divine life. This is a unique mediation that excludes any competing or parallel mediation, although it is compatible with participated forms of mediation (cf. *Redemptoris Missio,* 5).

Consequently, any other autonomous sources or ways of salvation cannot be admitted apart from Christ. Thus in the great religions, which the Church considers with respect and esteem in the way indicated by the Second Vatican Council, Christians recognize the presence of saving elements, which nevertheless operate in dependence on the influence of Christ's grace. Therefore, by virtue of the mysterious action of the Holy Spirit who "blows where he wills" (Jn 3:8), these religions can contribute to helping men on their way to eternal happiness. But this role is also the fruit of Christ's redemptive activity. Thus, with regard to other religions, Christ the Savior is also mysteriously at work. In this task he unites to himself the Church, which is in a way the "sacrament of communion with God and of unity among all men" (*Lumen Gentium,* 1).

I would like to conclude with a wonderful passage from the *Treatise on True Devotion to the Blessed Virgin,* by St. Louis de Montfort, which proclaims the Christological faith of the Church:

> Jesus Christ is *the Alpha and the Omega, the beginning and the end* of everything.... He is the only teacher from whom we must learn, the only Lord on whom we should depend, the only Head to whom we should be united, and the only model that we should imitate. He is the only Physician who can heal us, the only Shepherd who can feed us, the only Way who can lead us, the only Truth that we can believe, the only Life that can animate us. He alone is everything to us and he alone can satisfy all our desires.... Each one of the faithful who is not united to him is like a branch broken from the stem of the vine. It falls and withers and is fit only to be burnt. If we live in Jesus and Jesus lives in us, *we need not fear damnation.* Neither angels in heaven, nor men on earth, nor devils in hell, no creature whatever can harm us, for no creature *can separate us from the love of God which is in Christ Jesus.*

Through him, with him and in him we can do all things and render *all honor and glory* to the Father in the unity of the Holy Spirit; we can become perfect and be for our neighbor a fragrance of eternal life (n. 61).

General audience of February 4, 1998

The Son of God Brings
the Fullness of Salvation

In the programmatic speech Jesus gave in the synagogue of Nazareth at the beginning of his ministry, he applied to himself the prophecy of Isaiah in which the Messiah appears as the one sent to proclaim "release to the captives" (Lk 4:18; cf. Is 61:1–2). Jesus came to offer us a salvation which, although primarily a liberation from sin, also involves the totality of our being with its deepest needs and aspirations. Christ frees us from this burden and threat, and opens the way to the complete fulfillment of our destiny. Jesus reminds us in the Gospel that sin puts man in a state of slavery: "Truly, truly I say to you, everyone who commits sin is a slave to sin" (Jn 8:34).

Jesus' listeners thought of freedom primarily in external terms, proudly relying on the privilege of being the people of the covenant: "We are descendants of Abraham, and have never been in bondage to anyone" (Jn 8:33). Jesus was anxious to draw their attention to another more basic freedom, threatened not so much from the outside as from the snares found in the human heart itself. Whoever is oppressed by the dominating, destructive power of sin cannot accept Jesus' message, much less his person, the only source of true freedom: "If the Son makes you free, you will be free indeed" (Jn 8:36). It is only the Son of God who, by communicating his divine life, can make men share in his filial freedom.

The liberation offered by Christ removes, in addition to sin, the obstacles preventing friendship and a covenant relationship with God. From this standpoint it is *a reconciliation.* Paul wrote to the Christians of Corinth: "God...through Christ reconciled us to himself" (2 Cor 5:18). This reconciliation is obtained by the sacrifice of the cross. From it flows that peace which consists in the fundamental agreement of the human will with the divine. This peace not only affects relations with God, but also concerns relations between human beings. Christ "is our peace," because he unites all who believe in him, reconciling them "to God in one body" (cf. Eph 2:14–16).

It is comforting to think that Jesus does not limit himself to freeing the heart from the prison of selfishness, but communicates divine love to each person. At the Last Supper he gave the new commandment that must characterize the community he founded: "Love one another as I have loved you" (Jn 13:34; 15:12). The newness of this precept of love consists in the words "as I have loved you." The "as" points to the Teacher as the model whom his disciples must imitate, but at the same time it points to the origin or source of mutual love in him. Christ communicates to his disciples the power to love as he loved. He raises their love to the superior level of his own and urges them to tear down the barriers that divide people.

His desire to put an end to all discrimination and exclusion can be powerfully seen in the Gospel. He overcame the obstacles preventing contact with lepers, who were subjected to a painful segregation. He violated the customs and rules that tended to isolate those considered "sinners." He did not accept the prejudices that put women in an inferior position but accepted them among his followers and had them serve his kingdom. The disciples must imitate his example. The entry of God's love into human hearts is expressed in a special way in the obligation to love our enemies: "I say to you, love your enemies and pray for those who persecute you, so that you may be sons of your Father who is in heaven; for he makes his sun rise on the evil and on the good, and sends rain on the just and on the unjust" (Mt 5:44–45).

Starting from the heart, the salvation Jesus brought is extended to the various areas of human life: spiritual and physical, personal and social. By defeating sin with his crucifixion, Christ inaugurates a movement of integral liberation. In his public life he healed the sick, freed people from demons, and alleviated every kind of suffering, thereby showing a sign of God's kingdom. He told the disciples to do the same when they preach the Gospel (cf. Mt 10:8; Lk 9:2; 10:9). If not by miracles, which depend on divine consent, then certainly by works of fraternal charity and a commitment to promoting justice, Christ's disciples are called to actively contribute to eliminating the causes of suffering which humiliate and sadden humanity.

Of course it is impossible to entirely overcome pain in this way. The anguish of death remains on every human being's path. But everything receives new light from the paschal mystery. Suffering endured with love and united to Christ's passion bears fruits of salvation; it becomes "salvific pain." Even death, if faced with faith, takes on the reassuring aspect of a passage to eternal life, in expectation of the resurrection of the flesh. We can thus understand how rich and deep is the salvation Christ brought. He came to save not only *every* person but also the *whole* person.

General audience of February 18, 1998

God Intervenes in History When He Wills

After considering the total salvation accomplished by Christ the Redeemer, we would now like to reflect on its progressive realization in human history. In a certain sense, it is precisely this problem that the disciples asked Jesus about before the ascension: "Lord, will you at this time restore the kingdom to Israel?" (Acts 1:6). Put this way, the question shows how they were still influenced by the prospect of a hope that conceived of God's kingdom as an event closely linked to Israel's destiny as a nation. During the forty days between the resurrection and the ascension, Jesus had spoken to them of "the kingdom of God" (Acts 1:3). But they were able to grasp its profound aspects only after the great outpouring of the Spirit at Pentecost. In the meantime, Jesus corrected their impatience, spurred by their desire for a kingdom still too political and earthly, by inviting them to trust in God's mysterious designs: "It is not for you to know the times or seasons which the Father has fixed by his own authority" (Acts 1:7).

Jesus' admonition concerning "God's times" proves more significant than ever after 2000 years of Christianity. As we face the rather slow growth of God's kingdom in the world, we are asked to trust in the plan of the merciful Father who guides all things with transcendent wisdom. Jesus invites us to admire the "patience" of the Father, who adapts his transforming action to the slowness of human nature wounded by sin. This patience was already revealed in the Old Testament, in the long history which prepared Jesus' coming (cf. Acts 3:25). It continues to be revealed after Christ, in the growth of his Church (cf. 2 Pt 3:9).

In his response to the disciples, Jesus speaks of "times" *(chrónoi)* and "seasons" *(kairoí)*. In biblical language, these two words for time have two nuances that are worth recalling. *Chrónos* is time in its ordinary course; it is under the influence of divine Providence, which governs everything. But into this ordinary flow of history God makes his special interventions, which give a particular saving value to specific moments. These are precisely the *kairoí,* God's seasons, which man is called to discern, and by which he must allow himself to be challenged.

Biblical history is full of these special moments. The most fundamentally important was the time of Christ's coming. In the light of this distinction between *chrónoi* and *kairoí,* it is also possible to reread the Church's 2000 years of history. Sent to all humanity, the Church experiences different moments in her growth. In some places and periods she encounters special problems and obstacles; in others her progress is much faster. Long periods of waiting are recorded in which her intense missionary efforts seemed ineffective. These times test the power of hope, directing it to a more distant future. Nevertheless, there are also favorable moments when the Good News is warmly welcomed and conversions increase. The first and fundamental moment of the most abundant grace was Pentecost. Many others have followed and still more are to come.

When one of these moments occurs, those who have a special responsibility for evangelization are called to recognize it, to make the best use of the opportunities offered by grace. But it is impossible to know their date in advance. Jesus' reply (cf. Acts 1:7) is not limited to restraining the disciples' impatience, but emphasizes their responsibility. They are tempted to expect that Jesus will take care of everything. Instead, they receive a mission that calls them to make a generous commitment: "You shall be my witnesses" (Acts 1:8). Although at the ascension he disappeared from their sight, Jesus still wants to continue his presence in the world precisely through the disciples.

To them he entrusted the task of spreading the Gospel throughout the world, spurring them to abandon their narrow vision limited to Israel. He broadened their horizons, inviting them to be his witnesses "in Jerusalem and in all Judea and Samaria and to the end of the earth" (Acts 1:8). Thus, everything will happen in Christ's name, but everything will also come to pass through the personal work of these witnesses.

The disciples could have shrunk from this demanding mission, judging themselves incapable of assuming such a serious responsibility. But Jesus showed them the secret that enabled them to fulfill this task: "You shall receive power when the Holy Spirit has come upon you" (Acts 1:8). With this power the disciples would succeed, despite human weakness, in being authentic witnesses of Christ throughout the world.

At Pentecost the Holy Spirit filled each of the disciples and the entire community with the abundance and diversity of his gifts. Jesus revealed the importance of the gift of power *(dýnamis),* which would sustain their apostolic work. The Holy Spirit came upon Mary at the annunciation as "the power of the Most High" (cf. Lk 1:35), and brought about the miracle of the Incarnation in her womb. The very power of the Holy Spirit will work new marvels of grace in the task of evangelizing the nations.

General audience of March 11, 1998

We Respond in Faith to Revealed Truth

The primary objective of the Jubilee is the "strengthening of faith and of the witness of Christians" (*Tertio Millennio Adveniente,* 42). After outlining in previous catecheses the basic characteristics of the salvation Christ offers, today we pause to reflect on the faith he expects of us. "The obedience of faith," *Dei Verbum* teaches, "is to be given to God who reveals" (n. 5). God revealed himself in the Old Covenant, asking of the people he had chosen a fundamental response of faith. In the fullness of time, this faith is called to be renewed and increased, to respond to the revelation of the incarnate Son of God. Jesus expressly asked for it when he spoke to his disciples at the Last Supper: "Believe in God, believe also in me" (Jn 14:1).

Jesus had already asked the twelve apostles to profess their faith in his person. At Caesarea Philippi, after questioning his disciples about people's opinion of his identity, he asked: "But who do you say that I am?" (Mt 16:15). The reply came from Simon Peter: "You are the Christ, the Son of the living God" (16:16). Jesus immediately confirmed the value of this profession of faith, stressing that it stems not only from human thought but from heavenly inspiration: "Blessed are you, Simon Bar-Jona! For flesh and blood has not revealed this to you, but my Father who is in heaven" (Mt 16:17). In strongly Semitic tones, these statements indicate the total, absolute and supreme revelation: the one that concerns the person of Christ, Son of God. Peter's profession of faith would remain as the definitive expression of Christ's identity. Mark uses this same expression to begin his Gospel (cf. 1:1), and John refers to it at the end of his, saying that he has written his Gospel "so that you may come to believe that Jesus is the Christ, the Son of God, and that through believing you may have life in his name" (20:31).

In what does faith consist? The Constitution *Dei Verbum* explains that by faith, "man commits his whole self freely to God, offering 'the full submission of intellect and will to God who reveals'" (n. 5). Thus faith is not only the intellect's adherence to the truth revealed, but also a submission of the will and a gift of self to God revealing himself. It is a stance that involves one's entire existence.

The Council also recalls that this faith requires "the grace of God and the interior help of the Holy Spirit [which] must precede and assist, moving the heart and turning to God, opening the eyes of the mind and giving 'joy and ease to everyone in assenting to the truth and believing it'" (*DV* 5). In this way we can see how, on the one hand, faith enables us to welcome the truth contained in revelation and proposed by the magisterium of those who, as pastors of God's people, have received the "sure gift of truth" (*DV* 8). On the other hand, faith also spurs us to true and deep consistency, which must be expressed in all aspects of a life modeled on that of Christ.

As a fruit of grace, faith influences events. This is wonderfully seen in the exemplary case of the Blessed Virgin. Her faith-filled acceptance of the angel's message at the annunciation was decisive for Jesus' coming into the world. Mary is the Mother of Christ because she first believed in him. At the wedding feast in Cana, Mary obtained the miracle through her faith. Despite Jesus' reply, which did not seem very favorable, she kept her trustful attitude, thus becoming a model of the bold and constant faith that overcomes obstacles.

The Canaanite woman also had a bold and insistent faith. She had come to seek the cure of her daughter. Jesus countered this woman with the Father's plan that restricted his mission to the lost sheep of the house of Israel. The Canaanite replied with the full force of her faith and obtained the miracle. Jesus said, "O woman! Great is your faith! Be it done for you as you desire" (Mt 15:28).

In many other cases the Gospel witnesses to the power of faith. Jesus expressed his admiration for the centurion's faith: "Truly, I say to you, not even in Israel have I found such faith" (Mt 8:10). And he said to Bartimaeus: "Go your way; your faith has made you well" (Mk 10:52). He said the same thing to the woman with a hemorrhage (cf. Mk 5:34).

His words to the father of the epileptic who wanted his son to be cured are no less striking: "All things are possible to him who believes" (Mk 9:23).

The role of faith is to cooperate with this omnipotence. Jesus asked for this cooperation to the point that upon returning to Nazareth, he worked almost no miracles because the inhabitants of his village did not believe in him (cf. Mk 6:5–6). For Jesus, faith has a decisive importance for the purposes of salvation.

St. Paul developed Christ's teaching when, in conflict with those who wished to base the hope of salvation on observance of the Jewish law, he forcefully affirmed that faith in Christ is the only source of salvation: "We hold that a man is justified by faith apart from works of law" (Rom 3:28). However, it must not be forgotten that St. Paul was thinking of that authentic and full faith which "works through love" (Gal 5:6). True faith is animated by love of God, which is inseparable from love for our brothers and sisters.

General audience of March 18, 1998

Faith and Baptism
Are the Way to Salvation

According to Mark's Gospel, Jesus' final instruction to his disciples presents faith and Baptism together as the only way to salvation: "He who believes and is baptized will be saved, but he who does not believe will be condemned" (16:16). In recounting the missionary mandate Jesus gave the apostles, Matthew stresses the connection between Baptism and preaching the Gospel: "Go and make disciples of all nations, baptizing them in the name of the Father, and of the Son, and of the Holy Spirit" (28:19).

In conformity with these words of Christ, Peter addressed the people on the day of Pentecost to exhort them to conversion, inviting his listeners to receive Baptism: "Repent and be baptized, every one of you, in the name of Jesus Christ for the forgiveness of your sins, and you shall receive the gift of the Holy Spirit" (Acts 2:38). Conversion involves not only an interior attitude but also entry into the Christian community through Baptism, which takes away sins and makes one a member of Christ's Mystical Body.

To grasp the deep meaning of Christian Baptism, we must meditate again on the mystery of Jesus' baptism at the beginning of his public life. At first sight this is a surprising episode, because

John's baptism, which Jesus received, was a baptism of "repentance" that prepared man to receive the forgiveness of sins. Jesus knew well that he had no need of that baptism, since he was completely innocent. One day he would challenge his enemies, saying: "Can any one of you convict me of sin?" (Jn 8:46).

Actually, in submitting to John's baptism, Jesus did not receive it for his own purification but as a sign of redemptive solidarity with sinners. His baptismal act contains a *redemptive intention,* since he is "the Lamb of God, who takes away the sin of the world" (Jn 1:29). Later he would call his passion a "baptism," describing it as a kind of immersion in suffering redemptively accepted for the salvation of all: "I have a baptism to receive. What anguish I feel until it is over!" (Lk 12:50).

At his baptism in the Jordan, Jesus not only foretold the task of redemptive suffering, but also received a special outpouring of the Holy Spirit, who descended in the form of a dove, that is, as the Spirit of reconciliation and divine goodwill. This descent prefigured the gift of the Holy Spirit, which would be imparted to Christians in Baptism. A heavenly voice also proclaimed: "You are my beloved Son; with you I am well pleased" (Mk 1:11). The Father acknowledged his own Son and expressed the bond of love between them. Christ is actually united with the Father in a unique relationship, because he is the eternal Word "of one being with the Father." However, through the divine sonship conferred by Baptism, it can be said that the Father's words, "You are my beloved son," apply to every person baptized and grafted onto Christ. Thus, the source of Christian Baptism and its spiritual riches are found in Christ's baptism.

St. Paul explained Baptism primarily as a sharing in the fruits of Christ's redemptive work, stressing the need to renounce sin and to begin a new life. He wrote to the Romans: "Do you not know that all of us who have been baptized into Christ Jesus were baptized into his death? We were indeed buried with him by baptism into death, so that as Christ was raised from the dead by the glory of the Father, we too might walk in newness of life" (6:3–4). Because it is an immersion into Christ's paschal mystery, Christian Baptism has a much greater value than Jewish and pagan baptismal rites, which were ablutions symbolizing purification, but incapable of taking away sins. Christian Baptism, however, is an effective sign that really purifies consciences and forgives sins. It also bestows a much greater gift: the new life of the risen Christ, which radically transforms the sinner.

Paul revealed the essential effect of Baptism when he wrote to the Galatians: "All of you who have been baptized into Christ have clothed yourselves with him" (3:27). The Christian bears a fundamental likeness to Christ, which involves the gift of divine adoptive sonship. Precisely because they have been "baptized into Christ," Christians are "children of God" in a special way. Baptism causes a true "rebirth."

Paul's reflection is linked to the doctrine transmitted by John's Gospel, especially to Jesus' conversation with Nicodemus: "Unless one is born of water and the Spirit, he cannot enter the kingdom of God. That which is born of the flesh is flesh, and that which is born of the Spirit is spirit" (3:5–6). "Born of water" is a clear reference to Baptism, which is thus seen as a true rebirth by the Spirit. In it man receives the Spirit of life, who "consecrated" Christ's humanity from the moment of the Incarnation, and whom Christ himself poured out through his redeeming work.

The Holy Spirit brings about the birth and growth of a divine, "spiritual" life in Christians. This life animates and elevates their being. Through the Spirit, the very life of Christ bears its fruit in Christian existence. What a great gift and mystery is Baptism! It is to be hoped that all the Church's children will become more deeply aware of it.

General audience of April 1, 1998

Baptism Is the
Foundation of Communion

Today we consider again the sacrament of Baptism, which by immersing man in the mystery of Christ's death and resurrection, makes him a child of God and incorporates him into the Church. Baptism is essential for the Christian community. In particular, the Letter to the Ephesians includes Baptism among the foundations of the communion which binds the disciples to Christ: "There is one body and one Spirit, just as you were called to the one hope that belongs to your call, one Lord, one faith, one baptism, one God and Father of us all" (4:4–6).

The affirmation of one Baptism in the context of the other foundations of ecclesial unity has particular significance. In fact, it refers to the one Father, who in Baptism offers everyone divine sonship. It is intimately linked to Christ, the one Lord, who unites the baptized in his Mystical Body, and to the Holy Spirit, the principle of unity in the variety of his gifts. A sacrament of faith, Baptism transmits a life that gives access to eternity, and thus refers to the hope that waits with certainty for the fulfillment of God's promises. The one Baptism, therefore, expresses the unity of the whole mystery of salvation.

When Paul wanted to show the Church's unity, he compared her to a body, the Body of Christ, built up precisely through Baptism: "For by one Spirit we were all baptized into one body — Jews or Greeks, slaves or free — and all were made to drink of one Spirit" (1 Cor 12:13). The Holy Spirit is the principle of the Body's unity, since he animates both Christ the head and his members. In receiving the Spirit, all the baptized, despite their differences of origin, nationality, culture, sex and social status, are united in the Body of Christ, so that Paul can say: "There is neither Jew nor Greek, there is neither slave nor free, there is neither male nor female; for you are all one in Christ Jesus" (Gal 3:28).

On the basis of Baptism, the First Letter of Peter urges Christians to gather round Christ to help build the spiritual edifice founded by and on him: "Come to him [Christ], to that living stone, rejected by men but in God's sight chosen and precious, and like living stones be yourselves built into a spiritual house, to be a holy priesthood, to offer spiritual sacrifices acceptable to God through Jesus Christ" (2:4–5). Thus Baptism unites all the faithful in the one priesthood of Christ, enabling them to take part in the Church's worship and to make their lives a spiritual offering acceptable to God. In this way they grow in holiness and influence the development of the entire community.

Baptism is also a source of apostolic dynamism. The missionary task of the baptized, in conformity with their own vocation, is extensively considered by the Council, which teaches: "The obligation of spreading the faith is imposed on every disciple of Christ, according to his state" (*LG* 17). In the Encyclical *Redemptoris Missio,* I stressed that by virtue of Baptism all lay people are missionaries (cf. n. 71).

Baptism is also a fundamental point of departure for ecumenical dialogue. Concerning our separated brethren, the *Decree on Ecumenism* says: "For men who believe in Christ and have been truly baptized are put in communion with the Catholic Church, even though this communion is imperfect" (n. 3). In reality, validly conferred Baptism brings about an effective incorporation into Christ and makes all the baptized truly brothers and sisters in the Lord, regardless of their denomination. This is what the Council teaches: "Baptism, therefore, establishes a sacramental bond of unity which links all who have been reborn by it" (*UR* 22.)

It is an initial communion that needs to be developed in the direction of full unity, as the Council itself urges: "But of itself Baptism is only a beginning, an inauguration wholly directed toward the fullness of life in Christ. Baptism, therefore, envisages a complete profession of faith, complete incorporation in the system of salvation such as Christ willed it to be, and finally complete ingrafting in Eucharistic communion" (*UR* 22).

In the perspective of the Jubilee, this ecumenical aspect of Baptism deserves to be given special emphasis (cf. *TMA* 41). 2000 years after Christ's coming, Christians unfortunately present themselves to the world without the full unity he desired and for which he prayed. But at the same time we must not forget everything that already unites us. Doctrinal dialogue must be promoted at all levels, as well as mutual openness, cooperation, and, above all, the spiritual ecumenism of prayer and the commitment to holiness. The grace of Baptism itself is the foundation on which to build that full unity to which the Spirit continually spurs us.

General audience of April 15, 1998

The End of History
Began with Christ's Coming

While the path to the Jubilee recalls the first historical coming of Christ, it also invites us to look forward with expectation to his second coming at the end of time. This eschatological perspective, which shows the fundamental orientation of Christian life toward the ultimate realities, is a continual call to hope and to involvement in the Church and in the world. We must not forget that for Christians the *eschaton,* that is, the final event, is to be understood not only as a future goal, but as a reality that has already begun with the historical coming of Christ. His passion, death and resurrection are the supreme event in the history of humanity, which has now entered its final phase, making a qualitative leap, so to speak. The horizon of a new relationship with God is unfolding for humanity, marked by the great offer of salvation in Christ.

This is why Jesus can say: "The hour is coming, and now is, when the dead will hear the voice of the Son of God, and those who hear will live" (Jn 5:25). The resurrection of the dead expected at the end of time already receives its first, decisive realization in spiritual resurrection, the primary objective of the work of salvation. It consists in the new life given by the risen Christ as the fruit of his redemptive work. It is a mystery of rebirth in water and the Spirit (cf. Jn 3:5), which deeply marks the present and future of all humanity, even if its effectiveness at the moment is shown only in those who totally accept God's gift and radiate it in the world. This twofold dimension, present and future, of Christ's coming is apparent in his words. In the eschatological discourse that immediately precedes the paschal drama, Jesus predicts: "They will see the Son of Man coming in clouds with great power and glory. And then he will send out the angels, and gather his elect from the four winds, from the ends of the earth to the ends of heaven" (Mk 13:26–27).

In apocalyptic language, clouds signify a *theophany:* they indicate that the second coming of the Son of Man will not take place in the weakness of flesh, but in divine power. These words of the discourse suggest the ultimate future that will bring history to an end.

However, in the answer he gave to the high priest during his trial, Jesus repeated the eschatological prophecy, formulating it in terms of an imminent event: "I tell you, *hereafter* you will see the Son of Man seated at the right hand of Power and coming on the clouds of heaven" (Mt 26:64). By comparing these words with those of the previous discourse, one can grasp the dynamic sense of Christian eschatology as a historical process that has already begun and is moving toward its fullness.

On the other hand, we know that the apocalyptic images of the eschatological discourse about the end of all things should be interpreted in the light of their intense symbolism. They express the precariousness of the world and the sovereign power of Christ, in whose hands has been placed the destiny of humanity. History advances toward its goal, but Christ has not specified any chronological date. Attempts to predict the end of the world are therefore deceptive and misleading. Christ has assured us only that the end will not come before his saving work has reached a universal dimension through the preaching of the Gospel: "This Gospel of the kingdom will be preached throughout the whole world, as a testimony to all nations, and then the end will come" (Mt 24:14).

Jesus says these words to his disciples who are anxious to know the date of the end of the world. They would have been tempted to think of a date close at hand. Jesus makes them realize that many events and upheavals must occur first and will be only "the beginning of sufferings" (Mt 13:8). Therefore, as Paul says, all creation is "groaning in travail," waiting impatiently for the revelation of the sons of God (cf. Rom 8:19–22).

The evangelization of the world involves the profound transformation of the human person under the influence of Christ's grace. Paul pointed out that the goal of history lies in the Father's plan to "unite all things in him [Christ], things in heaven and things on earth" (Eph 1:10). Christ is the center of the universe, who draws all people to himself to grant them an abundance of grace and eternal life.

The Father gave Jesus "authority to execute judgment, because he is the Son of Man" (Jn 5:27). If judgment obviously foresees the possibility of condemnation, it is nevertheless entrusted to the One who is the "Son of Man," that is, to a person full of understanding and in solidarity with the human condition. Christ is a divine judge with a human heart, a judge who wants to give life. Only unrepentant attachment to evil can prevent him from offering this gift, for which he did not hesitate to face death.

General audience of April 22, 1998

We Must Love Mary As Christ Loved Her

In directing our gaze to Christ, the Jubilee also invites us to turn our eyes toward Mary. We cannot separate the Son from the mother, because "being born of Mary" belongs to Jesus' personal identity. In the very first formulas of faith, Jesus is acknowledged as the Son of God and Son of Mary. Tertullian, for example, recalls this when he states: "We must believe in one God, the Almighty, the Creator of the world, and in his Son, Jesus Christ, born of the Virgin Mary" (*De virginibus velandis*, 1, 3).

As mother, Mary was the first human person to rejoice over the birth that marked a new era in the religious history of humanity. From the angel's message she knew what her child's extraordinary destiny would be in the plan of salvation. Mary's joy lies at the root of all jubilees to come. The Jubilee we are going to celebrate was thus prepared in her maternal heart. For this reason, the Blessed Virgin must be "indirectly" present, so to speak, in dealing with the themes planned throughout the preparatory phase (cf. *TMA* 43). Our Jubilee will have to be a sharing in her joy.

The inseparability of Christ and Mary comes from the Father's sovereign will in carrying out the plan of the Incarnation. As St. Paul says, "When the time had fully come, God sent his Son, born of woman" (Gal 4:4). The Father wanted a mother for his incarnate Son, so that he would be born in a truly human way. At the same time, he wanted a virginal mother as a sign of the child's divine sonship. To make this motherhood a reality, the Father asked Mary for her consent. The angel explained the divine plan to her and waited for an answer, which had to come from her free will. This can be clearly seen in the annunciation account, which stresses that Mary posed a question that reveals her intention to remain a virgin. When the angel explained to her that the obstacle would be overcome through the action of the Holy Spirit, she gave her consent.

"Behold, I am the handmaid of the Lord; let it be to me according to your word" (Lk 1:38). Mary's acceptance of the divine plan had an immense effect on the entire future of mankind. We can say that the "yes" she expressed at the time of the annunciation changed the face of the world. It was a "yes" to the coming of the One who was to free human beings from the slavery of sin and win for them the divine life of grace. A future of happiness for the universe was made possible by this "yes" from the young woman of Nazareth. A wondrous event! The praise that wells up from Elizabeth's heart in the story of the visitation aptly expresses the joy of all humanity: "Blessed are you among women, and blessed is the fruit of your womb!" (Lk 1:42).

From the moment of Mary's consent, the mystery of the Incarnation became a reality. The Son of God entered our world and began to live as a man, while remaining fully God. From that moment Mary became the *Mother of God*. This is the highest title that can be given to a creature. It is totally justified in Mary's case, because a mother is mother of the person of her son in the complete fullness of his humanity. Mary is the "Mother of God" inasmuch as she is the Mother of the "Son of God," even if this motherhood is defined in the context of the mystery of the Incarnation.

Precisely this insight gave rise to the title of *Theotókos,* Mother of God, in the hearts and on the lips of Christians from the third century. The most ancient prayer addressed to Mary originated in Egypt and asks for her help in difficult circumstances, invoking her as "Mother of God." Later, when some challenged the legitimacy of this title, the Council of Ephesus solemnly approved it in 431, and its truth has prevailed in doctrinal language and in prayer.

By her divine motherhood Mary fully opened her heart to Christ, and in him to all humanity. Mary's total dedication to the work of the Son is especially shown by her participation in his sacrifice. According to John's testimony, the Mother of Jesus "stood by the cross" (19:25). She thus united herself to all the sufferings that Jesus endured, and shared in the generous offering of his sacrifice for the salvation of mankind.

This association with Christ's sacrifice brought about a new motherhood in Mary. She who suffered for all men became the mother of all men. Jesus himself proclaimed this new motherhood, when he said to her from the height of the cross: "Woman, behold your son" (Jn 19:26). Mary thus became the mother of the beloved disciple, and in Jesus' intention, the mother of every disciple, every Christian.

Mary's universal motherhood, intended to foster life according to the Spirit, is an extraordinary gift to humanity from Christ crucified. Jesus said to the beloved disciple: "Behold, your mother." And from that hour he "took her to his own home" (Jn 19:27), or better, "among his possessions," among the precious gifts left him by the crucified Master. The words, "Behold your mother," are addressed to each of us. We are invited to love Mary as Christ loved her, to welcome her into our lives as our mother, to let her lead us along the ways of the Holy Spirit.

General audience of April 29, 1998

Mary Is Our Model and Guide in Faith

The first beatitude cited in the Gospel is that of faith, and it refers to Mary: "Blessed is she who believed" (Lk 1:45). These words, spoken by Elizabeth, highlight the contrast between Zechariah's disbelief and Mary's faith. On receiving the message about the future birth of his son, Zechariah had found it hard to believe, judging it impossible since both he and his wife were advanced in age.

At the annunciation Mary was confronted with an even more surprising message, the proposal that she become the mother of the Messiah. She did not react with doubt to this prospect, but limited herself to asking how the virginity to which she felt called could be reconciled with the vocation to motherhood. To the reply of the angel, who pointed out the divine omnipotence working through the Spirit, Mary gave her humble and generous consent. At that unique moment in human history, faith played a decisive role. St. Augustine rightly states: "Christ is believed and conceived through faith. First, the coming of faith takes place in the Virgin's heart, followed by fruitfulness in the mother's womb" (*Sermon* 293, *PL* 38, 1327).

If we wish to contemplate the depth of Mary's faith, the Gospel account of the wedding feast at Cana is a great help. Faced with the lack of wine, Mary could have sought some human solution to the problem at hand, but she did not hesitate to turn to Jesus: "They have no wine" (Jn 2:3). She knew that Jesus had no wine available; it is therefore likely that she was asking for a miracle. Her request was even more daring since, until that moment, Jesus had not worked any miracles. By acting in this way, she was doubtless obeying an inner inspiration, since according to the divine plan, Mary's faith must precede the first manifestation of Jesus' messianic power, as it preceded his coming to earth. She already embodied the attitude that Jesus praised for true believers in every age: "Blessed are those who have not seen and yet believe" (Jn 20:29).

The faith Mary was called to was not an easy one. Even before Cana, while meditating on the words and behavior of the Son, she had to draw on a deep faith. The episode of the twelve-year-old Jesus lost in the temple was symbolic, when she and Joseph, in distress, heard the answer: "How is it that you sought me? Did you not know that I must be in my Father's house?" (Lk 2:49). But in Cana, Jesus' response to his mother's request seemed even clearer and far from encouraging: "O woman, what have you to do with me? My hour has not yet come" (Jn 2:4). In the intention of the fourth Gospel, it is not the hour of Christ's public manifestation so much as an anticipation of the significance of Jesus' supreme hour (cf. 7:30; 12:23; 13:1; 17:1). The wine as a symbol of prosperity and joy effectively represent that supreme hour's messianic fruits of redemption and of the Spirit. But the fact that this hour had not yet occurred chronologically is an obstacle that, coming from the sovereign will of the Father, seemed insurmountable.

Yet Mary did not withdraw her request, to the point of involving the servants in accomplishing the expected miracle: "Do whatever he tells you" (Jn 2:5). With her docility and the depth of her faith, she looked beyond the immediate sense of Jesus' words. She intuited the unfathomable abyss and infinite resources of divine mercy and did not doubt her Son's loving response. The miracle was an answer to the perseverance of her faith. Mary is thus presented as the model of a faith in Jesus that rises above all obstacles.

Jesus' public life also tested Mary's faith. On the one hand, it gave her joy to know that Jesus' preaching and miracles caused admiration and approval in so many people. On the other, she sadly noted the increasingly harsh opposition of the Pharisees, the doctors of the law, and the priestly hierarchy. One can imagine how much Mary suffered from this disbelief, which she observed even in her relatives. Those who were called "the brethren of Jesus," that is, his relatives, did not believe in him and interpreted his behavior as inspired by ambition (cf. Jn 7:2–5). Although Mary was sad to hear the family disagreement, she did not break off relations with these relatives, whom we find with her in the first community waiting for Pentecost (cf. Acts 1:14). With her kindness and love, Mary helped others to share her faith.

In the drama of Calvary, Mary's faith remained unwavering. For the disciples' faith, this tragedy was overwhelming. Only through the effectiveness of Christ's prayer was it possible for Peter and the others, who were also put to the test, to continue on the path of faith in order to become witnesses to the resurrection.

In saying that Mary stood at the foot of the cross, the Evangelist John (cf. 19:25) shows us that Mary remained full of courage at that critical moment. It was certainly the hardest stage in her "pilgrimage of faith" (cf. *LG* 58). But she could stand there because she had remained firm in her faith. Put to the test, Mary continued to believe that Jesus was the Son of God, and that by his sacrifice he would transform the destiny of mankind. The resurrection was the definitive confirmation of Mary's faith. In her heart, more than in any other, faith in the risen Christ acquired its most complete and authentic aspect, that of joy.

THE HOLY SPIRIT

The Spirit Is Gradually Revealed in Scripture

In preparation for the Great Jubilee of the Year 2000, the current year is dedicated particularly to the Holy Spirit. Continuing on the path marked out for the whole Church, and after concluding the Christological theme, today we begin a systematic reflection on the One who is the "Lord and Giver of life." I have spoken extensively about the Third Person of the Blessed Trinity on various occasions. I recall in particular the Encyclical *Dominum et Vivificantem* and the catechesis on the Creed.[1] The imminent prospect of the Jubilee gives me the opportunity to reflect once again on the Holy Spirit, to examine with an adoring heart his action in the flow of time and history.

In fact, reflection is not easy, unless the Spirit himself comes to aid us in our weakness (cf. Rom 8:26). How can we discern the presence of God's Spirit in history? We can answer this question only by turning to the Holy Scriptures, which, being inspired by the Paraclete, gradually reveal his action and identity to us. They express to us, in a certain way, the Spirit's

---

1. These catecheses are collected in the volume *The Spirit: Giver of Life and Love,* Boston: Pauline Books & Media, 1996. *Ed.*

"language," "style" and " logic." With eyes that penetrate beyond mere external observation, it is also possible to interpret
the reality in which he works to discern traces of his presence
behind things and events. Scripture itself, beginning with the
Old Testament, helps us understand that nothing of what is
good, true and holy in the world can be explained without
reference to the Spirit of God.

A first, veiled allusion to the Spirit is found in the very first
lines of the Bible, in the hymn to God the Creator which opens
the Book of Genesis: "The Spirit of God was moving over the
face of the waters" (1:2). Here the Hebrew word *rûãh* is used
for "spirit," which means "breath," and can designate either the
wind or the breath. As we know, this text belongs to the so-
called "priestly source" that dates back to the period of the
Babylonian exile (sixth century B.C.), when Israel's faith had
explicitly reached a monotheistic conception of God. As Israel
became aware of the creative power of the one God through the
light of revelation, it came to realize that God created the
universe by the power of his Word. The role of the Spirit
appears in conjunction with the latter. This perception is encouraged by the very analogy of language, which by association combines the word with the breath of the lips: "By the
word of the Lord the heavens were made, and all their host by
the breath *(rûãh)* of his mouth" (Ps 33:6). God's vital and life-
giving breath is not limited to the initial moment of creation,
but keeps all creation in existence and gives it life by continuously renewing it: "When you send forth your Spirit, they are
created, and you renew the face of the earth" (Ps 104:30).

The most original feature of biblical revelation is to have
recognized history as the privileged realm for the action of
God's Spirit. In about 100 passages of the Old Testament, the
rûãh YHWH indicates the action of the Lord's Spirit guiding his
people, especially at important turning points in their journey.
Thus, in the period of the judges, God sent his Spirit upon frail

men and changed them into charismatic leaders invested with divine energy. This is what happened to Gideon, to Jephthah, and in particular to Samson (cf. Jgs 6:34; 11:29; 13:25; 14:6, 19).

With the arrival of the Davidic monarchy this divine force, which until then had been manifested unpredictably and sporadically, acquired a certain stability. This can be clearly seen in the royal consecration of David, of which Scripture says: "The Spirit of the Lord came mightily upon David from that day forward" (1 Sam 16:13).

During and after the Babylonian exile, Israel's whole history is reread as a long dialogue between God and the people chosen "by his Spirit through the former prophets" (Zech 7:12). The prophet Ezekiel explains the link between the Spirit and prophecy when he says, for example: "And the Spirit of the Lord fell upon me, and he told me to say: 'Thus says the Lord...'" (11:5).

But the prophetic vision looks above all to that privileged time in the future when the promises will be fulfilled under the sign of the divine *rûâh.* Isaiah foretells the birth of a descendant on whom "the Spirit of the Lord shall rest...the spirit of wisdom and understanding, the spirit of counsel and might, the spirit of knowledge and the fear of the Lord" (11:2–3). "This text," as I wrote in the encyclical *Dominum et Vivificantem,* "is important for the whole pneumatology of the Old Testament, because it constitutes a kind of bridge between the ancient biblical concept of *'spirit,'* understood primarily as a 'charismatic breath of wind,' and the *'Spirit' as a person and as a gift, a gift for the person.* The Messiah of the lineage of David ('from the stump of Jesse') is precisely that person on whom the Spirit 'shall rest'" (n. 15).

Two marks of the mysterious identity of the Holy Spirit can already be seen in the Old Testament and are then amply confirmed by the revelation of the New Testament. The first mark is the absolute *transcendence* of the Spirit, who is therefore called "holy," (Is 63:10, 11; Ps 51:13). The Spirit of God is in every respect "divine." He is not a reality which man can acquire with his strength, but a gift that comes from on high; he can only be invoked and received. Infinitely "other" with regard to man, the Spirit is communicated with total gratuitousness to those who are called to cooperate with him in the history of salvation. When this divine energy finds humble and ready acceptance, man is stripped of his selfishness and freed from his fears; truth and love, freedom and peace, flourish in the world.

Another mark of God's Spirit is the *dynamic* power he reveals when intervening in history. At times there is a risk of projecting onto the biblical image of the Spirit concepts tied to other cultures, for example, the concept of "spirit" as something evanescent, static and inert. The biblical concept of *rûăh,* however, indicates a supremely active, powerful and irresistible energy: the Spirit of the Lord, we read in Isaiah, "is like an overflowing stream" (30:28). Therefore, when the Father intervenes with his Spirit, chaos is transformed into cosmos; the world comes alive and history is set in motion.

General audience of May 13, 1998

The Spirit Is the Source
of New and Eternal Life

The revelation of the Holy Spirit as a person distinct from the Father and the Son, foreshadowed in the Old Testament, becomes clear and explicit in the New. It is true that the New Testament writings do not offer us a systematic teaching on the Holy Spirit. However, by gathering the many statements found in the writings of Luke, Paul, and John, it is possible to perceive the convergence of these three great currents of New Testament revelation concerning the Holy Spirit.

Compared to the other two synoptic Gospels, the Evangelist Luke offers us a far more developed pneumatology. In the Gospel he intends to show us that Jesus alone possesses the fullness of the Holy Spirit. Of course, the Spirit also comes upon Elizabeth, Zechariah, John the Baptist, and especially Mary herself, but only Jesus, throughout his earthly life, fully possesses God's Spirit. Jesus is conceived by the work of the Holy Spirit (cf. Lk 1:35). The Baptist will say of him: "I baptize you with water, but he who is mightier than I is coming.... He will baptize you with the Holy Spirit and with fire" (Lk 3:16).

Before being baptized with the Holy Spirit and with fire, Jesus was baptized in the Jordan and "the Holy Spirit de-

scended upon him in bodily form, as a dove" (Lk 3:22). Luke
stresses that Jesus not only went into the wilderness "led by the
Spirit," but that he went there "full of the Holy Spirit" (Lk 4:1)
and was victorious there over the tempter. He undertook his
mission "in the power of the Spirit" (Lk 4:14). In the synagogue
at Nazareth, when he officially began his mission, Jesus applied
to himself the prophecy of the book of Isaiah (cf. 61:1–2): "The
Spirit of the Lord is upon me, because he has anointed me to
preach good news to the poor" (Lk 4:18). The Spirit thus
guided all of Jesus' evangelizing activity.

This same Spirit will sustain the Church's evangelizing
mission, as the Risen One had promised his disciples: "Behold,
I send the promise of my Father upon you; but stay in the city,
until you are clothed with power from on high" (Lk 24:49).
According to the Book of Acts, the promise was fulfilled on the
day of Pentecost: "They were all filled with the Holy Spirit and
began to speak in other tongues, as the Spirit gave them utterance" (2:4). Joel's prophecy was thus realized: "In the last days
it shall be, God declares, that I will pour out my Spirit upon all
flesh, and your sons and your daughters shall prophesy" (Acts
2:17). Luke sees the apostles as representing the People of God
of the last days, and rightly emphasizes that this Spirit of
prophecy involves the whole People of God.

St. Paul in turn highlights the aspect of renewal and the
eschatological dimension of the Spirit's work: the Spirit is seen
as the source of the new and eternal life that Jesus communicates to his Church. In the First Letter to the Corinthians, we
read that Christ, the new Adam, by virtue of the resurrection
became "a life-giving spirit" (15:45). He was transformed by
the vital power of God's Spirit to become, in turn, a principle of
new life for believers. Christ communicates this life precisely
through the outpouring of the Holy Spirit.

Believers no longer live as slaves under the law, but as
sons, because in their hearts they have received the Spirit of the

Son and can cry out: "*Abba,* Father!" (cf. Gal 4:5–7; Rom 8:14–16). It is a life "in Christ," that is, a life of belonging exclusively to him and of incorporation into the Church: "For by one Spirit we were all baptized into one body" (cf. 1 Cor 12:13). The Holy Spirit gives rise to faith (1 Cor 12:3), pours love into our hearts (cf. Rom 5:5), and guides the prayer of Christians (cf. Rom 8:26).

As the principle of a new existence, the Holy Spirit also produces a new and active dynamism in the believer: "If we live by the Spirit, let us also walk by the Spirit" (Gal 5:25). This new life is opposed to that of the "flesh," whose desires displease God and enclose the person in the suffocating prison of an ego turned in on itself (cf. Rom 8:5–9). Instead, by opening himself to the Holy Spirit, the Christian can taste the fruits of the Spirit: love, joy, peace, patience, kindness, goodness, faithfulness, etc. (cf. Gal 5:16–24).

According to Paul, however, what we now possess is only a "down payment" or the first fruits of the Spirit (cf. Rom 8:23; cf. also 2 Cor 5:5). In the final resurrection, the Spirit will complete his masterpiece by bringing about, for believers, the full "spiritualization" of their bodies (cf. 1 Cor 15:43–44), and in some way involve the whole universe in salvation as well (cf. Rom 8:20–22).

In the Johannine perspective, the Holy Spirit is above all *the Spirit of truth, the Paraclete.* As Jesus completed his earthly work, he announced the gift of the Spirit: "When the Paraclete comes, the Spirit of truth who comes from the Father — and whom I myself will send from the Father — he will bear witness on my behalf. You must bear witness as well, for you have been with me from the beginning" (Jn 15:26 ff.). In further explaining the Spirit's role, Jesus added: "He will guide you into all the truth; for he will not speak on his own authority, but whatever he hears he will speak, and he will declare to you the things that are to come. He will glorify me, for he will take what is mine and declare it to you" (Jn 16:13–14). Thus, the Spirit will not bring a new revelation, but will guide the faithful to an interiorization and deeper penetration of the truth revealed by Jesus.

What does it mean to call the Spirit of truth the *Paraclete?* The Johannine perspective views Jesus' trial as one that continues in the disciples who will be persecuted because of his name. Bearing this in mind, the Paraclete is the one who defends the cause of Jesus, convincing the world "of sin, of righteousness and of judgment" (Jn 16:7 f.). The fundamental sin, which the Paraclete will make known, is not to have believed in Christ. The justice he indicates is that which the Father gave his crucified Son by glorifying him in the resurrection and ascension into heaven. In this context, the judgment consists in revealing the sin of those who, dominated by Satan, the prince of this world (cf. Jn 16:11), rejected Christ (cf. *DViv* 27). With his inner assistance, the Holy Spirit is therefore the defender and supporter of Christ's cause, the One who leads the minds and hearts of disciples to full acceptance of the "truth" of Jesus.

General audience of May 20, 1998

The Spirit Enables Us to Share in the Divine Nature

From the first moment of his existence in time, Jesus was linked with the Holy Spirit, as the *Nicene-Constantinopolitan Creed* recalls: *"Et incarnatus est de Spiritu Sancto ex Maria Virgine."* The Church's faith in this mystery is based on the word of God. "The Holy Spirit," the Angel Gabriel announced to Mary, "will come upon you and the power of the Most High will overshadow you; therefore, the child to be born will be called holy, the Son of God" (Lk 1:35). Joseph was told: "That which is conceived in her is of the Holy Spirit" (Mt 1:20). The Holy Spirit's direct intervention in the Incarnation brings about the supreme grace, the "grace of union," in which human nature is united to the Person of the Word. This union is the source of every other grace, as St. Thomas explains (*Summa Theol.,* III, q. 2, a. 10–12; q. 6, a. 6; q. 7, a. 13).

For a deeper understanding of the Holy Spirit's role in the Incarnation, it is important to return to what the word of God tells us. St. Luke says that the Holy Spirit will come upon Mary and overshadow her as power from on high. From the Old Testament, we know that every time God decides to bring forth life, he acts through the "power" of his creative breath: "By the word of the Lord the heavens were made, and all their host by the breath of his mouth" (Ps 33:6). This is true for every living being, to the point that if God "should take back his spirit to himself, and gather to himself his breath, all flesh [that is, every human being] would perish together, and man would return to dust" (Jb 34:14–15). God has his Spirit intervene especially at the moments when Israel feels powerless to raise itself by its own strength alone. The prophet Ezekiel suggests this in his dramatic vision of the immense valley filled with skeletons: "The breath came into them, and they lived, and stood upon their feet" (37:10).

The virginal conception of Jesus is "the greatest work accomplished by the Holy Spirit in the history of creation and salvation" (*DViv* 50). In this event of grace, a virgin is made fruitful; a woman, redeemed since her conception, conceives the Redeemer. Thus a new creation is prepared, and the new and everlasting covenant initiated: a man who is the Son of God begins to live. Never before this event had it been said that the Holy Spirit descended directly upon a woman to make her a mother. Whenever miraculous births occurred in Israel's history, wherever they are mentioned, the divine intervention is related to the newborn child, not the mother.

If we ask ourselves what the Holy Spirit's purpose was in bringing about the Incarnation, the word of God gives us a succinct reply in the Second Letter of Peter, telling us that it happened so that we might become "partakers of the divine nature" (2 Pt 1:4). "In fact," St. Irenaeus of Lyons explains, "this is the reason why the Word became flesh and the Son of God became the Son of Man: so that man, by entering into communion with the Word and thus receiving divine sonship, might become a son of God" (*Adv. Haer.,* III 19, 1). St. Athanasius adopts the same line: "When the Word came upon the Blessed Virgin Mary, the Spirit entered her together with the Word; in the Spirit the Word formed a body for himself and adapted it to himself, desiring to unite all creation through himself and lead it to the Father" (*To Serapion,* 1, 31). St. Thomas repeats these assertions: "The Only-begotten Son of God, wanting us to be partakers of his divinity, assumed our human nature so that, having become man, he might make men gods" (*Opuscula 57 for Corpus Christi,* 1), that is, partakers through grace of the divine nature.

The mystery of the Incarnation reveals God's astonishing love, whose highest personification is the Holy Spirit, since he is the Love of God in person, the Person-Love: "In this the love of God was made manifest among us, that God sent his only Son into the world, so that we might live through him" (1 Jn 4:9). The glory of God is revealed in the Incarnation more than in any other work. Quite rightly we sing in the *Gloria in excelsis:* "We praise you, we bless you...we give you thanks for your great glory." These statements can be applied in a special way to the action of the Holy Spirit who, in the First Letter of Peter, is called "the Spirit of glory" (4:14). This glory is pure gratuitousness: it does not consist of taking or receiving, but only of giving. In giving us his Spirit, who is the source of life, the Father manifests his glory, making it visible in our lives. In this regard St. Irenaeus says that "the glory of God is man fully alive" (*Adv. Haer.,* IV, 20, 7).

If now we try to look more closely at what the Incarnation reveals to us of the mystery of the Spirit, we can say that this event shows us primarily that he is the *gracious power of God who brings forth life.* The power that "overshadows" Mary recalls the cloud of the Lord that covered the tent in the desert (cf. Ex 40:34) or filled the temple (cf. 1 Kgs 8:10). Thus, it is the friendly presence, the saving closeness of God who comes to make a covenant of love with his children. It is power in the service of love, which is exercised under the sign of humility. Not only does it inspire the humility of Mary, the handmaid of the Lord, but it is almost hidden behind her, to the point that no one in Nazareth can foresee that what "is conceived in her is of the Holy Spirit" (Mt 1:20). St. Ignatius of Antioch marvelously describes this paradoxical mystery: "Mary's virginity and her birth were hidden from the prince of this world, as was the death of the Lord. These are the three resounding mysteries that were accomplished in the quiet stillness of God" (*To the Ephesians*, 19, 1).

The mystery of the Incarnation, seen from the perspective of the Holy Spirit who brought it about, also sheds light on the mystery of man. If the Spirit works in a unique way in the mystery of the Incarnation, he is also present at the origin of every human being. Our being is a "received being," a reality thought of, loved and given. Evolution does not suffice to explain the origin of the human race, just as the biological causality of the parents alone cannot explain a baby's birth. Even in the transcendence of his action, God is ever respectful of "secondary causes" and creates the spiritual soul of a new human being by communicating the breath of life to him (cf. Gn 2:7) through his Spirit who is "the giver of life." Thus every child should be seen and accepted as a gift of the Holy Spirit.

The chastity of celibates and virgins is a unique reflection of that love "poured into our hearts through the Holy Spirit" (Rom 5:5). The Spirit, who gave the Virgin Mary a share in the divine fruitfulness, also ensures that those who have chosen virginity for the kingdom of heaven will have many descendants in the spiritual family formed of all those who "were born, not of blood, nor of the will of the flesh, nor of the will of man, but of God" (Jn 1:13).

General audience of May 27, 1998

The Spirit Accompanied Jesus' Public Life

After the Incarnation, another significant intervention by the Holy Spirit in the life of Jesus took place during his baptism in the Jordan River. Mark's Gospel gives the following account of the event: "In those days Jesus came from Nazareth of Galilee and was baptized by John in the Jordan. And when he came up out of the water, immediately he saw the heavens opened and the Spirit descending upon him like a dove; and a voice came from heaven, 'You are my beloved Son; with you I am well pleased'" (1:9–11; cf. Mt 3:13–17; Lk 3:21–22; Jn 1:29–34). In the fourth Gospel there is a reference to the witness given by John: "I saw the Spirit descend as a dove from heaven, and it remained on him" (Jn 1:32).

In the concordant testimony of the Gospels, the Jordan event marks the beginning of Jesus' public mission and of his revelation as the Messiah, the Son of God. John preached "a baptism of repentance for the forgiveness of sins" (Lk 3:3). We find Jesus among the crowd of sinners coming to be baptized by John. He recognized Jesus and proclaimed him the innocent lamb who takes away the sin of the world (cf. Jn 1:29), to lead humanity back to communion with God. The Father expressed his pleasure with his beloved Son, who became an obedient servant unto death, and gave him the Spirit's power so that he could carry out his mission as the Messiah-Savior.

Jesus had certainly possessed the Spirit since his conception (cf. Mt 1:20; Lk 1:35), but in baptism he received a new outpouring of the Spirit, an anointing of the Holy Spirit, as St. Peter attested in his speech at Cornelius' house: *"God anointed* Jesus of Nazareth *with the Holy Spirit* and with power" (Acts 10:38). This anointing was an *elevation* of Jesus in "the eyes of Israel as the Messiah, that is to say, the *'One Anointed'* with the Spirit" (*DViv* 19); it was a true *exaltation* of Jesus as Christ and Savior.

While Jesus lived in Nazareth, Mary and Joseph were able to observe his growth in years, wisdom and grace (cf. Lk 2:40, 51) under the guidance of the Holy Spirit, who was working in him. Now, instead, the messianic age was being inaugurated; a new phase in the historical existence of Jesus was beginning. His baptism in the Jordan was like a "prelude" to what would happen later. Jesus began to stand by sinners, to reveal the Father's merciful face to them. His immersion in the Jordan River prefigured and anticipated his "baptism" in the waters of death, while the voice of the Father, proclaiming him his beloved Son, foretold the glory of the resurrection.

After his baptism in the Jordan, Jesus began to exercise his threefold mission: *a royal* mission, which involved him in fighting the spirit of evil; *a prophetic* mission, which made him the tireless preacher of the Good News; and *a priestly* mission, which spurred him to praise the Father and to offer himself to him for our salvation.

All three synoptic Gospels stress that, immediately after his baptism, Jesus was "led" by the Holy Spirit into the wilderness "to be tempted by the devil" (Mt 4:1; cf. Lk 4:1; Mk 1:12). Satan suggested a triumphal messianism to him, consisting in such spectacular wonders as turning stones into bread, throwing himself down from the pinnacle of the temple without suffering injury, achieving instantaneous political control over all the kingdoms of the world. But Jesus' choice, in total obedience to the Father's will, was clear and unequivocal: he accepted being the suffering, crucified Messiah who would give his life for the world's salvation.

Jesus' struggle with Satan, which began in the wilderness, continued throughout his life. One of his typical activities was precisely that of exorcist, which is why the crowds cried out in amazement: "With authority he commands even the unclean spirits and they obey him" (Mk 1:27). Anyone who dares to say that Jesus' power derives from Satan is blaspheming against the Holy Spirit (Mk 3:22–30). It is "by the Spirit of God" that Jesus cast out demons (Mt 12:28). As St. Basil of Caesarea states, with Jesus "the devil lost his power in the presence of the Holy Spirit" (*On the Holy Spirit,* 19).

According to the Evangelist Luke, after the temptation in the desert, "Jesus returned to Galilee *with the power of the Holy Spirit...and taught* in their synagogues" (Lk 4:14–15). The Holy Spirit's powerful presence was also found in Jesus' evangelizing activity. He himself stressed it in his inaugural address at the synagogue of Nazareth (Lk 4:16–30), applying the passage of Isaiah to himself. "The Spirit of the Lord is upon me" (Is 61:1). In a certain sense we can say that Jesus was the "missionary of the Spirit," sent by the Father to proclaim the Gospel of mercy with the power of the Spirit. Enlivened by the power of the Spirit, what Jesus said truly expressed his mystery as the Word made flesh (Jn 1:14). It was therefore the word of someone with "authority," unlike the scribes (Mk 1:22). It was "a new teaching," as those who heard his first address in Capernaum were amazed to recognize (Mk 1:27). These words fulfill and surpass the Mosaic law, as becomes apparent in the Sermon on the Mount (Mt 5–7). These words extend divine forgiveness to sinners, offer healing and salvation to the sick and even bring the dead back to life. They are the words of the

One who was "sent by God," in whom the Spirit dwells in such a way that he can give that Spirit "without measure" (Jn 3:34).

The presence of the Holy Spirit was particularly prominent in Jesus' prayer. The Evangelist Luke says that at the moment of his baptism in the Jordan, "when Jesus...was praying, the heaven was opened, and the Holy Spirit descended upon him" (3:21–22). This connection between Jesus' prayer and the presence of the Spirit returns explicitly in the hymn of exultation: "Jesus rejoiced *in the Holy Spirit* and said: 'I thank you, Father, Lord of heaven and earth...'" (Lk 10:21).

Thus, the Spirit was present in Jesus' most intimate experience, that of his divine sonship, which prompted him to call God "Abba" (Mk 14:36) with a *unique trust* that is not evidenced in the way any other Jew addressed the Most High. Precisely through the gift of the Spirit, Jesus would enable believers to share in his filial communion and intimacy with the Father. As St. Paul assures us, the Holy Spirit makes us cry out to God, "Abba, Father!" (Rom 8:15; cf. Gal 4:6). This filial life is the great gift we receive in Baptism. We must rediscover and constantly nurture it, making ourselves docile to the work that the Holy Spirit accomplishes in us.

General audience of June 3, 1998

The Spirit's Presence
in the Paschal Mystery

Christ's whole life was lived *in the Holy Spirit.* St. Basil states that the Spirit was Jesus' "inseparable companion in everything" (*De Spiritu Sancto,* 16) and offers us this marvelous summary of Christ's history: "Christ's coming: the Holy Spirit precedes; the Incarnation: the Holy Spirit is present; miraculous works, graces and healings: through the Holy Spirit; demons are expelled, and the devil is chained: through the Holy Spirit; forgiveness of sins, union with God: through the Holy Spirit; resurrection of the dead: by the power of the Holy Spirit" (*On the Holy Spirit,* 19). After meditating on Jesus' baptism and his mission carried out in the power of the Holy Spirit, we now wish to reflect on the revelation of the Spirit in Jesus' supreme "hour," the hour of his death and resurrection.

The Holy Spirit's presence at the moment of Jesus' death was already presupposed by the simple fact that on the cross, the Son of God died in his human nature. If *"Unus de Trinitate passus est"* (*DS* 401), that is, if "one Person of the Trinity suffered," the whole Trinity was present in his passion; thus the Father and the Holy Spirit were present as well. However, we have to ask ourselves: what was the Holy Spirit's precise role in Jesus' supreme hour? This question can only be answered if the mystery of redemption is understood as a *mystery of love*.

Sin, which is the creature's rebellion against the Creator, had interrupted the dialogue of love between God and his children. In the Incarnation of the Only-begotten Son, God expressed his faithful and passionate love for sinful humanity, to the point of making himself vulnerable in Jesus. Sin, for its part, revealed on Golgotha its nature as an "attack on God," so that whenever human beings fall back into serious sin, as the Letter to the Hebrews says, "they crucify the Son of God on their own account and hold him up to contempt" (6:6). In handing his Son over for our sins, God revealed to us that his loving plan precedes our every merit and abundantly surpasses all our infidelities. "In this is love, not that we loved God but that he loved us, and sent his Son to be the expiation for our sins" (1 Jn 4:10).

The passion and death of Jesus is an ineffable mystery of love in which the three divine Persons were involved. The Father took the free and absolute initiative: he loved us first, and in delivering the Son into our murderous hands, exposed his dearest possession. As St. Paul says, he "did not spare his own Son," that is, he did not keep him for himself as a jealously held treasure, but "gave him up for us all" (Rom 8:32). The Son fully shared the Father's love and his plan of salvation: "he gave himself for our sins...according to the will of our God and Father" (Gal 1:4).

And the Holy Spirit? As in the intimacy of Trinitarian life, so too in this exchange of love that took place between the Father and the Son in the mystery of Golgotha, the Holy Spirit is the Person-Love in whom the love of the Father and the Son converge. The Letter to the Hebrews develops the image of sacrifice, stating that Jesus offered himself "through the eternal Spirit" (Heb 9:14). In the Encyclical *Dominum et Vivificantem,*

I showed that in this passage "eternal Spirit" means precisely the Holy Spirit: as fire consumed the sacrificial victims of the old ritual sacrifices, so "the Holy Spirit acted in a special way in this absolute self-giving of the Son of Man in order to transform this suffering into redemptive love" (n. 40). "The Holy Spirit as Love and Gift *comes down, in a certain sense, into the very heart of the sacrifice* which is offered on the cross. Referring here to the biblical tradition we can say: *he consumes this sacrifice with the fire of the love* that unites the Son with the Father in Trinitarian communion. And since the sacrifice of the cross is an act proper to Christ, also in this sacrifice he 're- ceives' the Holy Spirit" (*DViv* 41). In the Roman liturgy, the priest rightly prays before Communion in these significant words: "Lord Jesus Christ, Son of the living God, by the will of the Father *and the work of the Holy Spirit,* your death brought life to the world."

Jesus' history did not end in death but led to the glorious life of Easter. "By his resurrection from the dead, Jesus Christ our Lord" was "designated Son of God in power according to the Spirit of holiness" (cf. Rom 1:4). The resurrection is the fulfillment of the Incarnation and it took place, like the Son's birth in the world, "by the work of the Holy Spirit." St. Paul said at Antioch in Pisidia: "We bring you the good news that what God promised to the fathers, this he has fulfilled to us their children *by raising Jesus;* as is also written in the second psalm, 'You are my Son, today I have begotten you'" (Acts 13:32).

The gift of the Holy Spirit, which the Son received in its fullness on Easter morning, is poured out in abundance by him on the Church. Jesus said to his disciples gathered in the upper room: "Receive the Holy Spirit" (Jn 20:22), and he gave this Spirit to them "as it were through the wounds of his crucifixion: 'He showed them his hands and his side'" (*DViv* 24). Jesus' saving mission is summed up and fulfilled in communicating the Spirit to human beings, to lead them back to the Father.

If the Holy Spirit's "masterpiece" is the paschal mystery of the Lord Jesus, a mystery of suffering and glory, through the gift of the Spirit Christ's disciples can also suffer and make the cross the path to light: *"per crucem ad lucem."* The Spirit of the Son gives us the grace to have the same sentiments as Christ and to love as he loved, to the point of offering our life for the brethren: "He laid down his life for us, and we ought to lay down our lives for the brethren" (1 Jn 3:16).

By communicating his Spirit to us, Christ enters our life, so that each of us can say, like Paul: "It is no longer I who live, but Christ who lives in me" (Gal 2:20). Our whole life thus becomes a continual Passover, a constant passing from death to life, until the final Passover, when we too will pass with Jesus and like Jesus "from this world to the Father" (Jn 13:1). In fact, St. Irenaeus of Lyons says, "those who have received and bear the Spirit of God are led to the Word, that is, to the Son, and the Son welcomes them and presents them to the Father, and the Father gives them incorruptibility" (*Proof of the Apostolic Preaching,* 7).

General audience of June 10, 1998

The Holy Spirit Gives Birth to the Church

At the Last Supper Jesus said to the apostles: "Neverthe-less, I tell you the truth; it is to your advantage that I go away, for if I do not go away, the Counselor will not come to you; but if I go, I will send him to you" (Jn 16:7). On the evening of Easter, Jesus kept his promise. He appeared to the Eleven gathered in the upper room, breathed on them and said: "Re-ceive the Holy Spirit" (Jn 20:22). Fifty days later, on Pentecost, occurred "the definitive manifestation of what had already been accomplished in the same upper room on Easter Sunday" (*DViv* 25). The Acts of the Apostles has preserved a description of the event for us (cf. Acts 2:1–4). By reflecting on this text, we can discern some features of the Holy Spirit's mysterious identity.

First, it is important to see the connection between the Jewish feast of Pentecost and the first Christian Pentecost. Initially, Pentecost was the feast of seven weeks (cf. Tob 2:1), the harvest feast (cf. Ex 23:16), when the new grain was offered to God (cf. Num 28:26; Dt 16:9). Later the feast acquired a new meaning: it became the feast of the covenant God had made with his people on Sinai, when he gave Israel his law.

St. Luke describes the Pentecost event as a theophany, a manifestation of God similar to the one on Mt. Sinai (cf. Ex 19:16–25): a roaring sound, a mighty wind, tongues of fire. The message is clear: Pentecost is the new Sinai; the Holy Spirit is the new covenant; it is the gift of the new law. St. Augustine keenly grasped this connection: "Here is a great and wondrous mystery, brethren: if you observe closely, on the day of Pentecost [the Jews] received the law written by the finger of God, and on the same day of Pentecost the Holy Spirit came" (*Sermon Mai.,* 158, 4). And an Eastern Father, Severian of Gabala, notes: "It was fitting that the grace of the Holy Spirit should be given on the same day that the old law was given" (*Cat. in Act. Apost.,* 2, 1).

The promise made to the fathers is thus fulfilled. We read in the prophet Jeremiah: *"This is the covenant which I will make with the house of Israel after those days, says the Lord: I will put my law within them, and I will write it upon their hearts"* (31:33). And in the prophet Ezekiel: *"A new heart I will give you, and a new spirit I will put within you; and I will take out of your flesh the heart of stone and give you a heart of flesh. And I will put my Spirit within you, and cause you to walk in my statutes and be careful to observe my ordinances"* (36:26–27).

In what way is the Holy Spirit the new and eternal covenant? By taking away sin and pouring the love of God into the human heart: "The law of the Spirit of life in Christ Jesus has set me free from the law of sin and death" (Rom 8:2). The Law of Moses pointed out obligations, but could not change the human heart. A new heart was needed, and that is precisely what God offers us by virtue of the redemption accomplished by Jesus. The Father removes our heart of stone and gives us a heart of flesh like Christ's, enlivened by the Holy Spirit who enables us to act out of love (cf. Rom 5:5). On the basis of this gift, a new covenant is established between God and humanity.

St. Thomas Aquinas says with keen insight that the Holy Spirit himself is the New Covenant, producing love in us, the fullness of the law (cf. *Comm. on 2 Cor.,* 3, 6).

On Pentecost the Holy Spirit descended and the Church was born. The Church is the community of those who are "begotten from above," "by water and the Spirit," as we read in John's Gospel (cf. 3:3, 5). The Christian community is not primarily the result of the free decision of believers; at its origin there is first and foremost the gratuitous initiative of the Love of God, who offers the gift of the Holy Spirit. The assent of faith to this gift of love is a "response" to grace and is itself motivated by grace. Therefore, between the Holy Spirit and the Church there exists a deep and indissoluble bond. St. Irenaeus says in this regard: "Wherever the Church is, the Spirit of God is also there; and wherever the Spirit of the Lord is, the Church is there and every grace" (*Adv. Haer.,* III, 24, 1). Then we can understand St. Augustine's daring expression: "The Holy Spirit is possessed insofar as one loves the Church" (*On John,* 32, 8).

The account of Pentecost emphasizes that the Church is *universal* at her birth: this is the significance of the list of peoples — Parthians, Medes, Elamites, etc. (cf. Acts 2:9–11) — who hear the first proclamation Peter made. The Holy Spirit is given to all people of every race and nation, and accomplishes in them the new unity of Christ's Mystical Body. St. John Chrysostom highlights the communion brought about by the Holy Spirit with the vivid observation; "He who dwells in Rome knows those in the Indies to be his members" (*On John,* 65, 1; *PG* 59, 361).

Since the Holy Spirit is "the New Covenant," the work of the Third Person of the Holy Trinity consists in making the risen Lord present and, with him, God the Father. The Spirit carries out his saving action by making God's presence *imme- diate.* The new and eternal covenant consists in this: God can now be reached by each one of us. Everyone, "from the least to the greatest" (cf. Jer 31:34), is given in a certain sense a *direct* knowledge of the Lord: "The anointing which you received from him abides in you, and so you have no need that anyone should teach you. But as his anointing teaches you about everything, and is true and is not a lie, and just as it has taught you, abide in him" (1 Jn 2:27). Thus, the promise Jesus made to his disciples at the Last Supper is fulfilled: "The Counselor, the Holy Spirit, whom the Father will send in my name, will teach you all things, and bring to your remembrance all that I have said to you" (Jn 14:26).

Through the Holy Spirit, our meeting with the Lord occurs in the ordinary context of *filial* life, in the "face to face" encounter of friendship, in the experience of God as Father, Brother, Friend and Bridegroom. This is Pentecost. This is the New Covenant.

General audience of June 17, 1998

The Gospel Is Preached
in the Power of the Spirit

As soon as the Holy Spirit had come down upon the apostles on the day of Pentecost, they "began to speak in other tongues, as the Spirit gave them utterance" (cf. Acts 2:4). Thus we can say that the Church, at the moment of her birth, received as a gift from the Spirit the ability to "tell [of] the mighty works of God" (Acts 2:11); this is the gift of *evangelizing.*

This fact implies and reveals a basic law of salvation history: it is impossible to evangelize or prophesy, or indeed to speak of the Lord and in the Lord's name, without the grace and power of the Holy Spirit. Using a biological analogy, we could say that just as human words are carried by the human breath, so the Word of God is transmitted by God's breath, by his *rûăh* or his *pneuma,* which is the Holy Spirit.

This connection between God's Spirit and the divine word can already be noted in the experience of the ancient prophets. Ezekiel's call is described as a "spirit" *entering into* his person: "[The Lord] said to me: 'Son of man, stand upon your feet, and I will speak with you.' And when he spoke to me, the Spirit entered into me and set me upon my feet; and I heard him speaking to me" (2:1–2). In the Book of Isaiah we read that the future servant of the Lord will proclaim justice to the nations precisely because the Lord has put his Spirit upon him (cf. 42:1). According to the prophet Joel, the messianic age will be marked by a universal outpouring of the Spirit: "And it shall come to pass afterward, that I will pour out my Spirit on all flesh"; as a result of this communication of the Spirit, "your sons and your daughters shall prophesy" (2:28).

The Spirit-Word relationship reaches its summit in Jesus: he is the very Word made flesh "through the work of the Holy Spirit." He began to preach "in the power of the Spirit" (cf. Lk 4:14 ff.). The very first time he preached in Nazareth, he applied to himself the passage from Isaiah: "The Spirit of the Lord is upon me, because he has anointed me to preach good news to the poor" (Lk 4:18). As the fourth Gospel stresses, the mission of Jesus, "he whom God has sent" and who "utters the words of God," is the fruit of the gift of the Spirit, whom he has received and gives "not by measure" (cf. Jn 3:34). Appearing to his disciples in the upper room on Easter evening, Jesus performed the expressive act of "breathing" upon them, saying: "Receive the Holy Spirit" (cf. Jn 20:21–22). The Church's life unfolds beneath that breath. "The Holy Spirit is indeed the principal agent of the whole of the Church's mission" (*RM* 21). The Church proclaims the Gospel through his presence and saving power. Addressing the Christians of Thessalonica, St. Paul says: "Our Gospel came to you not only in word, but also in power and in the Holy Spirit and with full conviction" (1 Thes 1:5). St. Peter describes the apostles as "those who preached the good news to you through the Holy Spirit sent from heaven" (1 Pt 1:12). But what does "preach the good news through the Holy Spirit" mean? Briefly one can say: it means *evangelizing in the power, in the newness, and in the unity* of the Holy Spirit.

Evangelizing in the power of the Spirit means being invested with that power which was supremely manifested in Jesus' evangelizing activity. The Gospel tells us that those who listened to him were astonished at his teaching because "he taught them as one who had authority, and not as the scribes" (Mk 1:22). Jesus' word drives out demons, calms storms, heals the sick, forgives sinners and raises the dead.

The Spirit bestowed Jesus' authority on the Church as an Easter gift. Thus, we see the apostles filled with *parrhesia,* that is, the boldness that enabled them to speak fearlessly about Jesus. Their adversaries were filled with wonder "when they ...perceived that they were uneducated, common men" (Acts 4:13). Thanks to the gift of the Spirit of the New Covenant, Paul too can say in all truth: "Since we have such a hope, we are very bold" (2 Cor 3:12). This power of the Spirit is more necessary than ever for the Christians of our time, who are asked to bear witness to their faith in a world which is often indifferent, if not hostile and deeply marked by relativism and hedonism. It is a power essential to all preachers who must offer the Gospel anew without yielding to compromises and false shortcuts, by proclaiming the truth about Christ "in season and out of season" (2 Tim 4:2).

The Holy Spirit also guarantees that the message is always fresh and timely, so that preaching does not fall into an empty repetition of formulas and a cold application of methods. Indeed, preachers must be at the service of the "New Covenant," which is not "in a written code" that kills, but "in the Spirit" who gives life (cf. 2 Cor 3:6). It is not a question of spreading a service under the "old written code," but the "new life of the Spirit" (cf. Rom 7:6). This requirement is especially vital today for the "new evangelization," which will truly be "new" in its ardor, method and expression, if those who proclaim the marvels of God and speak in his name have first listened to God and have become docile to the Holy Spirit. Contemplation consisting of listening and prayer is thus fundamental. If the preacher does not pray, he will end up "preaching himself" (cf. 2 Cor 4:5), and his words will be reduced to "godless chatter" (cf. 2 Tim 2:16).

Lastly, the Spirit accompanies and encourages the Church to evangelize in unity and to build unity. Pentecost occurred when the disciples "were all together in one place" (Acts 2:1), and "all with one accord devoted themselves to prayer" (Acts 1:14). After receiving the Holy Spirit, Peter spoke to the crowd for the first time, "standing *with the Eleven*" (Acts 2:14). He is the icon of a unanimous proclamation that must continue to be such even when preachers are scattered throughout the world. For all Christians, preaching Christ under the impetus of the one Spirit in the third millennium involves a concrete and generous effort toward full communion. It is the great task of ecumenism, which should be supported with ever renewed hope and active commitment, even if the times and results are in the hands of the Father, who asks us for humble readiness in accepting his plan and the inner inspirations of the Spirit.

General audience of July 1, 1998

The Holy Spirit Enlivens
and Animates the Church

"If Christ is the head of the Church, the Holy Spirit is her soul." So said my venerable Predecessor Leo XIII in the Encyclical *Divinum Illud Munus* (1897: *DS* 3328). After him, Pius XII explained that in the Mystical Body of Christ the Holy Spirit is "the principle of every vital and truly salvific action in each of the Body's various members" (Encyclical *Mystici Corporis,* 1943: *DS* 3808). Today we would like to reflect on the mystery of Christ's Body, which is the Church, inasmuch as she is enlivened and animated by the Holy Spirit.

After Pentecost, the group that gave rise to the Church profoundly changed. At first it was a closed, static group of "about a hundred and twenty" (Acts 1:15); later it was an open, dynamic group to which, after Peter's address, "were added about three thousand souls" (Acts 2:41). The true newness did not consist so much in this numerical growth, however extraordinary, but in the presence of the Holy Spirit. A group of people is not enough to form a Christian community. The Holy Spirit brings the Church to birth. She appears — to use a happy phrase of the late Cardinal Congar — "entirely suspended from heaven" (*La Pentecoste,* Brescia: 1986, p. 60).

This birth in the Spirit, which occurred for the whole Church on Pentecost, is renewed for every believer at Baptism, when we are immersed "in one Spirit" to become members of "one body" (1 Cor 12:13). We read in St. Irenaeus: "Just as flour cannot become one loaf without water, so we who are many cannot become one in Christ Jesus without the water that comes from heaven" (*Adv. Haer.*, III, 17, 1). The water that comes from heaven and transforms the water of Baptism is the Holy Spirit. St. Augustine states: "What our spirit, i.e., our soul, is for our members, the Holy Spirit is for Christ's members, for the Body of Christ which is the Church" (*Sermon* 267, 4). The Second Vatican Ecumenical Council returns to this image, develops it and explains it: Christ "has shared with us his Spirit who, existing as one and the same being in the head and in the members, gives life to, unifies and moves through the whole body. This he does in such a way that his work could be compared by the holy Fathers with the function which the principle of life, that is, the soul, fulfills in the human body" (*LG* 7). This relationship between the Spirit and the Church guides us in understanding her, without falling into the two opposite errors already pointed out by *Mystici Corporis:* ecclesiological naturalism, which is limited to the visible aspect and so regards the Church as a merely human institution; or the opposite error of ecclesiological mysticism, which emphasizes the Church's unity with Christ and the Church as a sort of physical person. These two errors are analogous — as Leo XIII had already stressed in the Encyclical *Satis Cognitum* — to two Christological heresies: Nestorianism, which separated the two natures in Christ, and Monophysitism, which confused them. The Second Vatican Council offered us a synthesis that helps us grasp the true meaning of the Church's mystical unity by presenting her as "one complex reality that coalesces from a divine and a human element" (*LG* 8).

The Holy Spirit's presence in the Church enables her, despite being marked by the sin of her members, to be preserved from defect. Holiness not only replaces sin, but overcomes it. In this sense, too, we can say with St. Paul that where sin abounds, grace even more abounds (cf. Rom 5:20).

The Holy Spirit dwells in the Church not as a guest who still remains an outsider, but as the soul who transforms the community into "God's holy temple" (1 Cor 3:17; cf. 6:19; Eph 2:21), and makes it more and more like himself through his specific gift, which is love (cf. Rom 5:5; Gal 5:22). The Second Vatican Council teaches that love "rules over all the means of attaining holiness and gives life to these same means" (*LG* 42). Love is the "heart" of Christ's Mystical Body, as we read in a beautiful autobiographical passage of St. Thérèse of the Child Jesus:

> I understood that if the Church had a body composed of different members, the most necessary and noble of all could not be lacking to it, and so I understood that the Church had a heart and that this heart was burning with Love. I understood that it was Love alone that made the Church's members act, that if Love were ever extinguished, apostles would not proclaim the Gospel and martyrs would refuse to shed their blood.... I understood that Love was everything, that it embraced all times and places...in a word, that it was eternal! (*Autobiographical Manuscript* B, 3v°).

The Spirit who dwells in the Church also abides in the heart of every member of the faithful: he is the *dulcis hospes animae* [sweet guest of the soul]. Following a path of conversion and personal sanctification, then, means allowing ourselves to be "led" by the Spirit (cf. Rom 8:14), letting him act, pray and love in us. "Becoming holy" is possible if we allow ourselves to be made holy by him who is the Holy One, by docilely cooperating with his transforming action. For this reason, since the primary objective of the Jubilee is to strengthen the faith and witness of Christians, "it is necessary to inspire in all the faithful *a true longing for holiness,* a deep desire for conversion and personal renewal in a context of ever more intense prayer and of solidarity with one's neighbor, especially the most needy" (*TMA* 42). We can think of the Holy Spirit as the *soul* of our soul, and thus the secret of our sanctification. Let us dwell in his powerful and discreet, intimate and trans-forming presence!

St. Paul teaches us that the indwelling of the Holy Spirit within us is closely connected with Jesus' resurrection and is also the basis of our final resurrection: "If the Spirit of him who raised Jesus from the dead dwells in you, he who raised Christ Jesus from the dead will give life to your mortal bodies also through his Spirit who dwells in you" (Rom 8:11). In eternal happiness we will live in the joyful fellowship that is now prefigured and anticipated by the Eucharist. Then the Spirit will bring to full maturity all the seeds of communion, love and brotherhood that have blossomed during our earthly pilgrim-age. As St. Gregory of Nyssa says, "surrounded by the unity of the Holy Spirit as the bond of peace, all will be one Body and one Spirit" *(Homily 15 on Cant.).*

General audience of July 8, 1998

The Holy Spirit Sanctifies Us

Jesus' act of "breathing" on the apostles, which communicated the Holy Spirit to them (cf. Jn 20:21–22), recalls the creation of man, described by Genesis as the communication of the "breath of life" (Gn 2:7). The Holy Spirit is the "breath" as it were of the Risen One, who instills new life in the Church represented by the first disciples. The most obvious sign of this new life is the power to forgive sins. Jesus says: "Receive the Holy Spirit. If you forgive the sins of any, they are forgiven" (Jn 20:22–23). Wherever "the Spirit of holiness" (Rom 1:4) is poured out, whatever is opposed to holiness, that is, sin, is destroyed. According to Jesus' word, the Holy Spirit is the one who "will convince the world of sin" (Jn 16:8). He makes us aware of sin, but at the same time he himself forgives sin. St. Thomas comments in this regard: "Since it is the Holy Spirit who establishes our friendship with God, it is normal for God to forgive sins through him" (*Contr. Gent.,* IV, 21, 11).

The Spirit of the Lord not only destroys sin, but also accomplishes the sanctification and divinization of man. "God chose" us, St. Paul says, "from the beginning to be saved, through sanctification by the Spirit and belief in the truth" (2 Thes 2:13). Let us look more closely at what this "sanctification-divinization" consists of.

The Holy Spirit is "Person-Love; he is Person-Gift" (*DViv* 10). This love given by the Father, received and reciprocated by the Son, is communicated to the one redeemed, who thus becomes a "new man" (Eph 4:24), a "new creation" (Gal 6:15). We Christians are not only purified from sin, but are also reborn and sanctified. We receive a new life, since we have become "partakers of the divine nature" (2 Pt 1:4); we are "called children of God; and so we are!" (1 Jn 3:1). It is the life of grace, the free gift by which God makes us partakers of this Trinitarian life.

In their relationship with the baptized, the three divine Persons should be neither separated — because each always acts in communion with the others — nor confused, because each Person is communicated as a Person. In reflecting on grace, it is important not to think of it as a "thing." It is "first and foremost the gift of the Spirit who justifies and sanctifies us" (*CCC* 2003). It is the gift of the Holy Spirit, who makes us like the Son and puts us in a filial relationship with the Father; in the one Spirit through Christ we have access to the Father (cf. Eph 2:18).

The Holy Spirit's presence truly and inwardly transforms man: it is *sanctifying or deifying grace,* which elevates our being and our acting, enabling us to live in relationship with the Holy Trinity. This takes place through the theological virtues of faith, hope and charity, "which adapt man's faculties for participation in the divine nature" (*CCC* 1812). Thus, by faith the believer considers God, his brethren and history not merely from the standpoint of reason, but from the viewpoint of divine revelation. By hope man looks at the future with trusting, vigorous certitude, hoping against hope (cf. Rom 4:18), with his gaze fixed on the goal of eternal happiness and the full achievement of God's kingdom. By charity the disciple is obliged to love God with his whole heart and to love others as Jesus loved them, that is, to the total giving of self.

The sanctification of the individual believer always takes place through *incorporation into the Church*. "The life of the individual child of God is joined in Christ and through Christ by a wonderful link to the life of all his other Christian brethren. Together they form the supernatural unity of Christ's Mystical Body so that, as it were, a single mystical person is formed" (Paul VI, Apostolic Constitution *Indulgentiarum Doctrina,* 5).

This is the mystery of the communion of saints. An everlasting bond of charity joins all the "saints," those who have already reached the heavenly homeland or are being purified in purgatory, as well as those who are still pilgrims on earth. There is also an abundant exchange of gifts among them, to the point that the holiness of one helps all the others. St. Thomas states: "Whoever lives in charity participates in all the good that is done in the world" *(On the Apostles' Creed);* and again: "The act of one is accomplished through the charity of another, that charity by which we are all one in Christ" (*Comm. on the Sentences, IV,* d. 20, a. 2; q. 3 *ad* 1).

The Council recalled that "all the faithful of Christ, of whatever rank or status, are called to the fullness of the Christian life and to the perfection of charity" (*LG* 40). Concretely, the way for the faithful to become saints is that of fidelity to God's will, as it is expressed to us in his word, the commandments and the inspirations of the Holy Spirit. As it was for Mary and for all the saints, so for us too, the perfection of charity consists in trusting abandonment into the Father's hands, following Jesus' example. Once again this is possible because of the Holy Spirit, who, even in the most difficult moments, enables us to repeat with Jesus: "I have come to do your will" (cf. Heb 10:7).

This holiness is reflected in a special way in religious life, in which one's baptismal consecration is lived by the commitment to radically follow the Lord through the evangelical counsels of chastity, poverty and obedience.

Like the whole of Christian life, the call to the consecrated life is closely linked to the working of the Holy Spirit. In every age, the Spirit enables new men and women to recognize the appeal of such a demanding choice.... It is the Spirit who awakens the desire to respond fully; it is he who guides the growth of this desire, helping it to mature into a positive response and sustaining it as it is faithfully translated into action; it is he who shapes and molds the hearts of those who are called, configuring them to Christ, the chaste, poor and obedient One, and prompting them to make his mission their own (*Vita Consecrata,* 19).

An eminent expression of holiness, made possible by the power of the Holy Spirit, is *martyrdom,* the supreme witness given in blood to the Lord Jesus. But the Christian commitment is already a significant and fruitful form of witness, when it is lived — day by day, in the various states of life — in radical fidelity to the commandment of love.

General audience of July 22, 1998

The Spirit Is the Source of Communion

A strong bond of fraternal communion united the first Christian community: "All who believed were together and had all things in common; and they sold all their possessions and goods and distributed them to all, as any had need" (Acts 2:44–45). There is no doubt that the Holy Spirit is at the root of this demonstration of love. His outpouring at Pentecost laid the foundations of the New Jerusalem, the city built on love, quite the opposite of the ancient Babel. According to the text of Genesis (ch. 11), the builders of Babel had decided to build a city with a great tower whose top would reach the heavens. The sacred author sees in this project a foolish pride that flows into division, discord and lack of communication. On the day of Pentecost, on the other hand, Jesus' disciples did not want to climb arrogantly to the heavens, but were humbly open to the gift that comes down from above. While in Babel all spoke the same language, but they ended up not understanding each other; on the day of Pentecost different languages were spoken, yet they were very clearly understood. This is a miracle of the Holy Spirit.

The Holy Spirit's proper and specific action already within the Trinity is communion. "It can be said that in the Holy Spirit the intimate life of the Triune God becomes totally gift, an exchange of mutual love between the divine Persons, and that through the Holy Spirit God exists in the mode of gift. It is the Holy Spirit who is *the personal expression* of this self-giving, of this being-love" (*DViv* 10). The third Person — we read in St. Augustine — is "the supreme love that unites both the Persons" (*The Trinity,* 7, 3, 6). Indeed the Father begets the Son by loving him; the Son is begotten by the Father, letting himself be loved and receiving from him the capacity to love; the Holy Spirit is love given in total gratuitousness by the Father, received with full gratitude by the Son, and returned by him to the Father.

The Spirit is also the love and the personal gift that contains every created gift: life, grace and glory. The mystery of this communion shines forth in the Church, the Mystical Body of Christ, enlivened by the Holy Spirit. The Spirit himself makes us "one in Christ Jesus" (Gal 3:28), and thus integrates us within the same unity that binds the Son to the Father. We are left in wonder at this intense and intimate communion between God and us!

The Acts of the Apostles presents several symbolic situations that let us understand how the Spirit helps the Church to live communion in practice, enabling her to overcome the problems she will encounter from time to time. When persons who do not belong to the people of Israel entered the Christian community for the first time, a dramatic moment was experienced. The Church's unity was put to the test. However, at this moment the Spirit descended on the house of the first pagan to be converted, Cornelius, the centurion. The Spirit renewed the miracle of Pentecost and worked a sign favoring unity between the Jews and the Gentiles (cf. Acts 10–11). We can say that this is the *direct* manner of building communion: the Spirit intervenes with the full power of his grace and creates a new, utterly unforeseeable situation.

But the Spirit frequently acts using human mediation. This is what happened — again, according to the narrative of the Acts — when a discussion arose within the community of

Jerusalem about the daily distribution among the widows (cf. 6:1ff.). Unity was then reestablished thanks to the intervention of the apostles, who asked the community to elect seven men "full of the Spirit" (6:3; cf. 6:5). They appointed this group of seven to serve tables.

A critical moment was also experienced by the community at Antioch, which consisted of Christians who had formerly been Jews or pagans. Several Jewish-Christian converts insisted that the latter be circumcised and observe the law of Moses. Regarding this, St. Luke writes that "the apostles and the elders were gathered together to consider this matter" (Acts 15:6), and after "there had been much debate," they reached an agreement, formulated in the solemn words: "For it has seemed good to the Holy Spirit and to us..." (Acts 15:28). Here it can clearly be seen how the Spirit acts through the mediation of the Church's "ministers."

Between the Spirit's two great paths: the *direct* one, more unpredictable and charismatic, and the *mediated* one, more permanent and institutional, there can be no real conflict. Both come from the same Spirit. In cases where human weakness might see causes for tension and conflict, it is necessary to abide by the discernment of authority, with the assistance of the Holy Spirit (cf. 1 Cor 14:37).

Thanks to the "grace of the Holy Spirit" (*UR* 4) there is a desire for full unity among Christians. In this regard, it must never be forgotten that the Spirit is the first common gift to divided Christians. As "the principle of the Church's unity" (*UR* 2), he urges us to rebuild it through conversion of heart, common prayer, mutual knowledge, ecumenical formation, theological dialogue, and cooperation in the various contexts of social service inspired by love.

Christ gave his life so that all his disciples might be one (cf. Jn 17). The celebration of the Jubilee of the third millennium must represent a new phase in overcoming the divisions of the second millennium. Since unity is a gift of the Paraclete, it comforts us to recall that precisely on the doctrine of the Holy Spirit significant steps have been made toward unity among the various Churches, especially among the Catholic Church and the Orthodox Churches. In particular, on the specific problem of the *Filioque*, concerning the relationship between the Holy Spirit and the Word who proceeds from the Father, it is possible to maintain that the difference between the Latin and Eastern traditions does not affect the identity of the faith "in the reality of the same mystery confessed" but its expression, constituting a "legitimate complementarity," which does not jeopardize but indeed can enrich communion in the one faith.[1]

Lastly, the Jubilee must also see fraternal love grow *within* the Catholic Church. That effective love which must prevail in every community "especially [for] those who are of the household of faith" (Gal 6:10), involves every member of the Church, every parish and diocesan community, every group, association and movement in a serious examination of conscience, which will dispose hearts to accept the unifying action of the Holy Spirit.

St. Bernard's words are still timely: "We all need one another: from others I receive the spiritual good which I do not have and do not possess.... And all our differences, which express the riches of God's gifts, will hold good in the one house of the Father, which includes so many mansions. Now there is a division of graces; then there will be a distinction of glories. Unity, both here and there, consists in one and the same love."[2]

General audience of July 29, 1998

---

1. Cf. *CCC* 248; Apostolic Letter *Orientale Lumen,* May 2, 1995, n. 5; Note of the Pontifical Council for Promoting Christian Unity, June 29, 1995: "The Greek and Latin Traditions Regarding the Procession of the Holy Spirit," *L'Osservatore Romano,* English edition, September 20, 1995, p. 3.

2. *Apology to William of St. Thierry,* IV, 8: *PL* 182, 9033–9044.

The Spirit Is the Source of Ministries

The New Testament testifies to the presence of charisms and ministries inspired by the Holy Spirit in the various Christian communities. For example, the Christian community of Antioch is described in this way: "In the church at Antioch there were prophets and teachers, Barnabas, Symeon who was called Niger, Lucius of Cyrene, Manaen, who was a member of the court of Herod the tetrarch, and Saul" (Acts 13:1).

The community of Antioch appears as a living reality in which two distinct roles emerge: that of *prophets,* who discern and announce God's ways, and that of *doctors* or teachers, who properly examine and expound the faith. In the former, one might recognize a more charismatic aspect, in the latter a more institutional tone, but in both cases the same obedience to God's Spirit. Moreover, this interweaving of the charismatic and institutional elements can be perceived at the very origins of the Antioch community — which came into being after the death of Stephen and the dispersion of the Christians — where several brothers had even preached the Good News to pagans, bringing about many conversions. Hearing of this event, the mother community of Jerusalem had delegated Barnabas to pay a visit to the new community. Furthermore, says Luke, when he saw the grace of the Lord, "he was glad, and he exhorted them all to remain faithful to the Lord with steadfast purpose; for he was a good man, full of the Holy Spirit and of faith" (Acts 11:23–24).

In this episode the twofold method clearly emerges with which the Spirit of God governs the Church: on the one hand, he directly encourages the activity of believers by revealing new and unprecedented ways to proclaim the Gospel; on the other hand, he provides an authentication of their work through the official intervention of the Church, represented here by the work of Barnabas, who was sent by the mother community of Jerusalem.

St. Paul, in particular, reflects deeply on charisms and ministries, especially in chapters 12–14 of his First Letter to the Corinthians. On the basis of this text, one can gather certain elements in order to set out a correct theology of charisms. Paul primarily establishes the *fundamental criterion of discernment,* a criterion that could be described as "Christological": a charism is not genuine unless it leads to proclaiming that Jesus Christ is Lord (cf. 12:1–3).

Paul then goes on immediately to stress the *variety* of charisms, and the *unity* of their origin: "There are varieties of gifts, but the same Spirit" (12:4). The gifts of the Spirit, which he distributes "as he wills" (12:11), can be numerous. Paul provides a list of them (cf. 12:8–10), which obviously does not claim to be complete. The Apostle then teaches that the diversity of charisms must not create divisions, and for this reason compares them to the various members of the one body (cf. 12:12–27). The Church's unity is dynamic and organic, and all the gifts of the Spirit are important for the vitality of the Body as a whole.

Paul teaches, on the other hand, that God has established a hierarchy in the Church (cf. 12:28): first come the "apostles," then the "prophets," then the "teachers." These three positions are fundamental and are listed in order of importance. The Apostle then warns that the distribution of gifts is diversified: not everyone has this or that charism (cf. 12:29–30). Each has his own (cf. 7:7) and must accept it with gratitude, generously putting it at the service of the community. This search for communion is dictated by love, which continues to be the "best way" and the greatest gift (cf. 13:13), without which charisms lose all their value (cf. 13:1–3).

Therefore, charisms are graces bestowed by the Holy Spirit on certain members of the faithful to prepare them to contribute to the common good of the Church. The variety of charisms corresponds to the variety of services, which can be temporary or permanent, private or public. The ordained ministries of bishops, priests and deacons are permanent and publicly recognized services. The lay ministries, founded on the sacraments of Baptism and Confirmation, can receive from the Church, through the bishop, official or only *de facto* recognition.

Among the lay ministries we recall those *instituted* with a liturgical rite: the offices of lector and acolyte. Then there are the extraordinary ministers of Eucharistic Communion and those responsible for ecclesial activities, starting with catechists. But we should also remember the "leaders of prayer, song and liturgy, leaders of basic ecclesial communities and Bible study groups, those in charge of charitable works, administrators of church resources, leaders in the various forms of the apostolate, religion teachers in schools" (*RM* 74).

In accordance with the message of Paul and of the New Testament, often recalled and illustrated by the Second Vatican Council (cf. *LG* 12), there is no such thing as one Church according to a "charismatic model" and another according to an "institutional model." As I have had the opportunity to stress on other occasions, opposition between charism and institution is "extremely harmful."[1] Pastors have the task to discern the au-

---

1. Cf. "Address to Participants in the Second International Conference of Ecclesial Movements," March 12, 1987, *L'Osservatore Romano,* English edition, March 16, 1987, p. 12).

thenticity of charisms and to regulate their exercise in an attitude of humble obedience to the Spirit, of disinterested love for the Church's good, and of docile fidelity to the supreme law of the salvation of souls.

General audience of August 5, 1998

The Spirit Acts in
All Creation and History

In view of the Great Jubilee of the Year 2000, ever since the Encyclical *Dominum et Vivificantem* I have invited you to see "with the eyes of faith the 2000 years of the action of the Spirit of truth, who down the centuries has drawn from the treasures of the redemption achieved by Christ and given new life to human beings, bringing about in them adoption in the Only-begotten Son, sanctifying them, so that they can repeat with St. Paul: 'We have received...the Spirit which is from God' (cf. 1 Cor 2:12)" (n. 53).

In our previous catecheses, we have described the manifestation of God's Spirit in the life of Christ, at Pentecost, from which the Church came into being, and in the personal and community life of believers. Our gaze now extends to the horizons of the world and the whole of human history. Thus we are moving within the plan outlined by this same encyclical on the Holy Spirit, which stresses that it is impossible for us to limit ourselves to the 2000 years that have passed since the birth of Jesus Christ. Indeed, we need "to go further back, to embrace the whole of the action of the Holy Spirit even before Christ — from the beginning, throughout the world, and especially in the economy of the Old Covenant" (*DViv* 53). At the same time "we need to look farther and go farther afield, knowing that 'the wind blows where it wills,' according to the image used by Jesus in his conversation with Nicodemus (cf. Jn 3:8)" (*DViv* 53).

Moreover, the Second Vatican Council, focusing on the Church's mystery and mission in the world, offered this breadth of vision. The Council holds that the Holy Spirit's action cannot be limited to the institutional dimension of the Church, where the Spirit also works in a unique and full manner, but should be recognized outside the visible frontiers of Christ's Body as well (cf. *Gaudium et Spes* 22; *LG* 16).

For its part, the *Catechism of the Catholic Church* recalls with the whole of Tradition: "The Word of God and his Breath are at the origin of the being and life of every creature" (n. 703). And a meaningful text of the Byzantine liturgy says: "It belongs to the Holy Spirit to rule, sanctify, and animate creation, for he is God, consubstantial with the Father and the Son.... Power over life pertains to the Spirit, for being God he preserves creation in the Father through the Son" (*CCC* 703). Thus, there is no corner of creation and no moment of history in which the Spirit is not at work.

It is true that all things were created by God the Father through Christ and in Christ (cf. Col 1:16), so that the meaning and the ultimate purpose of creation is to "unite all things in him" (Eph 1:10). However, it is just as true that all this happens through the power of the Holy Spirit. Illustrating this Trinitarian "rhythm" of salvation history, St. Irenaeus says that "the Spirit prepares man beforehand for the Son of God, the Son leads him to the Father, and the Father gives him incorruptibility and eternal life" (*Adv. Haer.,* IV, 20, 5).

Present in creation and active in all the phases of salvation history, the Spirit of God directs all things toward the definitive event of the Incarnation of the Word. Obviously, this Spirit is no different from the one who was given "not by measure" (cf. Jn 3:34) by the crucified and risen Christ. The same identical Holy Spirit prepares the advent of the Messiah in the world, and through Jesus Christ, is communicated by God the Father to the Church and to all humanity. The Christological and pneumatological dimensions are inseparable and not only run through the history of salvation, but the entire history of the world.

Therefore, we can legitimately think that the way to salvation is open wherever there are elements of truth, goodness, genuine beauty and true wisdom, wherever generous efforts are made to build a more human society in conformity with God's plan. Even more so, wherever there is a sincere expectation of God's revelation and a hope open to the saving mystery, we can recognize the hidden and effective work of the Spirit of God, who spurs man to the encounter with Christ, "the Way, the Truth and the Life" (Jn 14:6). When we turn over certain wonderful pages of literature and philosophy, justly admire some masterpiece of art or listen to passages of sublime music, we spontaneously recognize in these expressions of human genius a radiant reflection of God's Spirit. Of course, these reflections are on a different plane from those interventions that make the human being, raised to the supernatural order, a temple in which the Holy Spirit dwells together with the other Persons of the Blessed Trinity (cf. St. Thomas, *Summa Theol.,* I-II, q. 109, a. 1, *ad* 1). Thus the Holy Spirit, directly or indirectly, orients man to his integral salvation.

For this reason we would like to pause in the next catecheses to contemplate the Spirit's action in the vast arena of humanity's history. This vision will also help us grasp the deep relationship that unites the Church and the world, the overall history of man and the particular history of salvation. The latter is not actually a "separate" history, but rather plays a role with regard to the former that we could describe as "sacramental," that is, as a sign and instrument of the one great offer of salvation that reached humanity through the Incarnation of the Word and the outpouring of the Spirit.

With this as the key, it is easy to understand several marvelous pages of the Second Vatican Council on the solidarity that exists between the Church and humanity. In this pneumatological perspective I am pleased to reread the preface of *Gaudium et Spes:*

> The joys and the hopes, the griefs and the anxieties of the men of this age, especially those who are poor or in any way afflicted, are the joys and hopes, the griefs and anxieties of the followers of Christ. Indeed, nothing genuinely human fails to raise an echo in their hearts. For theirs is a community composed of men. United in Christ, they are led by the Holy Spirit in their journey to the kingdom of their Father, and they have welcomed the news of salvation that is meant for every man. That is why this community realizes that it is truly linked with mankind and its history by the deepest bonds (n. 1).

It can be clearly seen here how the Church's solidarity with the world and her mission to it must be understood as starting from Christ, in the light and power of the Holy Spirit. The Church thus experiences herself at the service of the Spirit who works mysteriously in hearts and in history. And we feel we are sent to transmit to all humanity the fullness of the Spirit received on the day of Pentecost.

General audience of August 12, 1998

Creation Must Be a Dwelling Place of Peace

In the eighth chapter of his Letter to the Romans, St. Paul explains the action of the Holy Spirit, who makes us sons of the Father in Christ Jesus (cf. Rom 8:14–16). The Apostle here introduces the theme of the world's path toward its fulfillment according to the divine plan. As we have already explained in previous catecheses, the Holy Spirit is present and active in creation and in the history of salvation. We could say that he enfolds the cosmos in God's love and mercy, and thus directs human history toward its definitive goal.

God created the cosmos as the dwelling place of man and the theater of his adventure of freedom. In the dialogue with grace, every human being is called to accept responsibly the gift of divine sonship in Jesus Christ. For this reason, the created world acquires its true significance in man and for man. He cannot, of course, dispose as he pleases of the cosmos in which he lives, but must, through his intelligence, consciously bring the Creator's work to completion.

Gaudium et Spes teaches: "Man, created to God's image, received a mandate to subject to himself the earth and all it contains, and to govern the world with justice and holiness (cf. Gn 1:26–27; 9:2–3; Wis 9:2–3), a mandate to relate himself and the totality of things to him who was to be acknowledged as the Lord and Creator of all. Thus, by the subjection of all things to man, the name of God would be wonderful in all the earth (cf. Ps 8:7, 10)" (n. 34).

For the divine plan to be fulfilled, man must use his freedom in harmony with God's will, and overcome the disorder that sin has introduced into human life and the world. Without the gift of the Holy Spirit, this twofold achievement cannot occur. The prophets of the Old Testament put great stress on this. The prophet Ezekiel says: "A new heart I will give you, and a new spirit I will put within you; and I will take out of your flesh the heart of stone and give you a heart of flesh. And I will put my spirit within you, and cause you to walk in my statutes and be careful to observe my ordinances.... You shall be my people, and I will be your God" (36:26–28).

This profound personal and community renewal, awaited in the "fullness of time" and brought about by the Holy Spirit, will to some extent involve the whole cosmos. Isaiah writes: "Until the Spirit is poured upon us from on high, and the wilderness becomes a fruitful field.... Then justice will dwell in the wilderness, and righteousness will abide in the fruitful field. And the effect of righteousness will be peace, and the result of righteousness, quietness and trust forever. My people will abide in a peaceful habitation" (32:15–18).

For the Apostle Paul, this promise is fulfilled in Christ Jesus, crucified and risen. Through the Spirit, Christ redeems and sanctifies whoever accepts his word of salvation in faith, transforming his heart and consequently social relations. Through the gift of the Holy Spirit, the world of men becomes a *"spatium verae fraternitatis,"* a place of true brotherhood (cf. GS 37). This transformation of human behavior and of social relations is expressed in ecclesial life, in the commitment to temporal realities, and in dialogue with all people of goodwill. This witness becomes a prophetic sign and leaven in history toward the advent of the kingdom, overcoming everything that prevents communion among men.

In a mysterious but real way, the cosmos is also called to participate in this newness of life, in building up universal peace through justice and love. As the Apostle Paul teaches:

> The creation waits with eager longing for the revealing of the sons of God. For the creation was subjected to futility, not of its own will but by the will of him who subjected it in hope, because the creation itself will be set free from its bondage to decay and obtain the glorious liberty of the children of God. We know that the whole creation has been groaning in travail together until now, and not only the creation, but we ourselves, who have the first fruits of the Spirit, groan inwardly as we wait for adoption as sons, the redemption of our bodies (Rom 8:19–23).

Given life by the presence of the Creator Spirit, creation is called to become "a dwelling place of peace" for the entire human family. Creation achieves this goal by means of the freedom of man, whom God has appointed as its guardian. If man selfishly withdraws into himself, through a false conception of freedom, he fatally involves creation itself in this perversion.

On the contrary, through the gift of the Holy Spirit that Jesus Christ pours out upon us from his side pierced on the cross, man acquires the true freedom of a son in the Son. He can thus understand the true meaning of creation and work to make it a "dwelling place of peace." In this sense, Paul can say that creation is groaning and awaiting the revelation of the sons of God. Only if man, enlightened by the Holy Spirit, recognizes himself as a Son of God in Christ and looks at creation with fraternal sentiment, can the whole cosmos be set free and redeemed in accordance with the divine plan.

The consequence of these reflections is truly comforting: the Holy Spirit is the true hope of the world. Not only does he work in human hearts, into which he introduces that wonderful participation in the filial relationship that Jesus Christ lives with the Father, but he exalts and perfects human activities in the world.

As the Second Vatican Council teaches:

> All human activity...must be purified and perfected by the power of Christ's cross and resurrection. For redeemed by Christ and made a new creature in the Holy Spirit, man is able to love the things themselves created by God, and ought to do so. He can receive them from God and respect and reverence them as flowing constantly from the hand of God. Grateful to his benefactor for these creatures, using and enjoying them in detachment and liberty of spirit, man is led forward into a true possession of them, as having nothing, yet possessing all things (cf. 2 Cor 6:10). "All are yours, and you are Christ's, and Christ is God's" (1 Cor 3:22–23) (*GS* 37).

General audience of August 19, 1998

God Invites Us to Communion with Him

The history of salvation is God's gradual communication of himself to humanity, which reaches its summit in Jesus Christ. God the Father, in the Word made man, wishes to share his own life with everyone; in short, he wants to communicate himself. This divine self-communication takes place in the Holy Spirit, the bond of love between eternity and time, the Trinity and history.

If God opens himself to man in his Spirit, man, on the other hand, is created as a subject capable of accepting the divine self-communication. As the tradition of Christian thought maintains, man is *capax Dei:* capable of knowing God and of receiving the gift he makes of himself. Created in the image and likeness of God (cf. Gn 1:26), man is able to live a personal relationship with him and to respond with loving obedience to the covenant relationship his Creator offers to him.

Against the background of this biblical teaching, the gift of the Spirit, promised to man and bestowed upon him "without measure" by Jesus Christ, therefore means a "call to friendship, in which the transcendent 'depths of God' become in some way opened to participation on the part of man" (*DViv* 34). In this regard, the Second Vatican Council teaches: "The invisible God (cf. Col 1:15; 1 Tim 1:17) out of the abundance of his love speaks to men as friends (cf. Ex 33:11; Jn 15:14–15) and lives among them (cf. Bar 3:38), so that he may invite and take them into fellowship with himself" (*DV* 2).

Therefore, if God, through his Spirit, communicates himself to man, man is continuously called to give himself to God with his whole being. This is his deepest vocation. He is constantly asked to do so by the Holy Spirit, who, enlightening his mind and sustaining his will, brings him into the mystery of divine sonship in Jesus Christ and invites him to live it consistently.

Down the centuries, the Holy Spirit inspires all the generous and sincere efforts of human intelligence and freedom to draw close to the ineffable and transcendent mystery of God. Particularly in the history of the Old Covenant that Yahweh made with the people of Israel, we see this meeting between God and man gradually taking place within the communion disclosed by the Spirit.

For example, there is the striking and intensely beautiful account of the prophet Elijah's encounter with God in the breath of the Spirit:

> And [the Lord] said: "Go forth and stand upon the mount before the Lord." The Lord passed by and a great and strong wind rent the mountains and broke in pieces the rocks before the Lord, but the Lord was not in the wind; and after the wind an earthquake, but the Lord was not in the earthquake; and after the earthquake a fire, but the Lord was not in the fire; and after the fire a still small voice. When Elijah heard it, he wrapped his face in his mantle and went out and stood at the entrance of the cave. Then there came a voice to him that said, "What are you doing here, Elijah?" (1 Kgs 19:11–13).

But the complete and definitive meeting between God and man — awaited and contemplated in hope by the patriarchs and prophets — is Jesus Christ. He, true God and true man, "by the revelation of the mystery of the Father and his love, fully reveals man to man himself and makes his supreme calling clear" (*GS* 22). Jesus Christ accomplished this revelation with his whole life. Indeed, under the impulse of the Holy Spirit, he always strove to fulfill the Father's will, and on the wood of the cross offered himself "once for all" to the Father, "through the eternal Spirit" (Heb 9:12, 14).

Through the paschal event, Christ teaches us that "man, who is the only creature on earth which God willed for itself, cannot fully find himself except through a sincere gift of himself" (*GS* 24). The Holy Spirit, communicated in fullness to the Church of Jesus Christ, ensures that man, by recognizing himself in Christ, will increasingly "find himself through a sincere gift of himself."

This eternal truth about man revealed to us by Jesus Christ has a particular timeliness in our day. Even amid sharp contradictions, the world today is experiencing a season of intense "socialization" (cf. *GS* 6), both with regard to interpersonal relationships within various human communities and with regard to relations among peoples, races, different societies and cultures.

Throughout this journey toward communion and unity, the Holy Spirit's action is also necessary for us to overcome the obstacles and dangers that threaten humanity's progress.

As the Year 2000 since the birth of Christ draws near, it is a question of ensuring that an ever-greater number of people "may fully find themselves...through a sincere gift of self...." Through the action of the Spirit-Paraclete, may there be accomplished in our world a process of true growth in humanity, in both individual and community life. In this regard Jesus himself, "when he prayed to the Father, 'that all may be one...as we are one' (Jn 17:21–22)...implied a certain likeness between the union of the divine persons and the union of the children of God in truth and charity" (*DViv* 59, quoting *GS* 24).

General audience of August 26, 1998

The Holy Spirit Is the Source of True Freedom

The *Catechism of the Catholic Church* teaches that "the human person participates in the light and power of the divine Spirit. By his reason, he is capable of understanding the order of things established by the Creator. By free will, he is capable of directing himself toward his true good. He finds his perfection 'in seeking and loving what is true and good' (cf. *GS* 15)" (n. 1704). The Holy Spirit, who "searches the depths of God," is at the same time the light that illumines man's conscience, and the source of his true freedom (cf. *DViv* 36). In the sanctuary of his conscience, man's most secret core, God makes his voice heard and his law known, that law which reaches its perfection in the love of God and neighbor as Jesus taught (cf. *GS* 16). By following this law in the light and power of the Holy Spirit, man achieves his full freedom.

Jesus Christ is the fully realized truth of God's plan for man, who has received the highest gift of freedom. God wished "that man remain 'under the control of his own decisions' (cf. Sir 15:14) so that he can seek his Creator spontaneously, and come freely to utter and blissful perfection through loyalty to him" (*GS* 17; cf. *CCC* 1730). Adhering to God's plan for man

revealed in Christ Jesus and fulfilling it in one's own life means
discovering the authentic vocation of human freedom, as Jesus
promised his disciples: "If you continue in my word, you are
truly my disciples, and you will know the truth, and the truth
will make you free" (Jn 8:31–32). It is not only a question of
listening to a message and obediently accepting a commandment. "More radically, it involves holding fast to the very
person of Jesus, partaking of his life and his destiny, sharing in
his free and loving obedience to the will of the Father"
(*Veritatis Splendor,* 19).

The Gospel of John emphasizes that it is not Christ's enemies who take his life with the brutal necessity of violence,
but he who gives it freely (cf. Jn 10:17–18). By fully comply-
ing with the Father's will, "the crucified Christ reveals the
authentic meaning of freedom; he lives it fully in the total gift
of himself and calls his disciples to share in his freedom" (*VS*
85). Indeed, with the absolute freedom of his love, he forever
redeems man who, by abusing his freedom, had turned away
from God. He frees man from the slavery of sin, and by granting him a share in his Spirit, gives him the gift of authentic
freedom (cf. Rom 8:2; Gal 5:1, 13).

"Where the Spirit of the Lord is, there is freedom," the
Apostle Paul tells us (2 Cor 3:17). By the outpouring of his
Spirit, the risen Jesus creates the vital space where human
freedom can be fully realized. Through the power of the Holy
Spirit, Jesus' gift of himself to the Father in his death and
resurrection becomes the source and model of every authentic
human relationship with God and with one's brethren. "God's
love," St. Paul writes, "has been poured into our hearts through
the Holy Spirit who has been given to us" (Rom 5:5).

By living in Christ through faith and the sacraments, the
Christian also "freely commits his entire self" to God the Father
(cf. *DV* 5). The act of faith by which he makes a responsible

decision for God, believes in his love revealed in the crucified and risen Christ, and abandons himself responsibly to the influence of the Holy Spirit (cf. 1 Jn 4:6–10) is the highest expression of freedom. By joyfully fulfilling the Father's will in every circumstance of life, after Christ's example and in the power of the Spirit, the Christian advances on the path of authentic freedom and looks with hope to the time when he will enter into the "full life" of the heavenly homeland. "By the working of grace," the *Catechism of the Catholic Church* teaches, "the Holy Spirit educates us in spiritual freedom in order to make us free collaborators in his work in the Church and in the world" (n. 1742).

This new horizon of freedom created by the Spirit also guides our relationship with the brothers and sisters we meet on our way. Precisely because Christ has freed us by his love and given us his Spirit, we can and must give ourselves freely in love to our neighbors. This profound truth is stated in the First Letter of the Apostle John: "By this we know love, that he laid down his life for us, and we ought to lay down our lives for the brethren" (3:16). Jesus' "new" commandment sums up the law of grace; the person who accepts it realizes his freedom to the full: "This is my commandment, that you love one another as I have loved you. Greater love has no man than this, that a man lay down his life for his friends" (Jn 15:12–13). No one can reach this height of love achieved by Christ crucified without the help of the Paraclete. Indeed, St. Thomas Aquinas could write that the "new law" is the grace itself of the Holy Spirit, given to us through faith in Christ (cf. *Summa Theol.,* I-II, q. 105, a. 1, conclus. and *ad* 2).

This "new law" of freedom and love is personified in Jesus Christ, but at the same time, in total dependence on him and his redemption, it is expressed in the Mother of God. The fullness of freedom, which is the Spirit's gift, "was manifested in a sublime way precisely through the faith of Mary, through the 'obedience of faith' (cf. Rom 1:5): truly, 'Blessed is she who believed'!" (*DViv* 51). May Mary, the Mother of Christ and our Mother, guide us to an ever deeper and more joyful discovery of the Holy Spirit as the source of true freedom in our life!

General audience of September 2, 1998

Seeds of Truth Are
Found in Other Religions

In the Declaration on the Relation of the Church to Non-Christian Religions, the Second Vatican Council teaches: "The Catholic Church rejects nothing that is true and holy in these religions. She regards with sincere reverence those ways of conduct and of life, those precepts and teachings which, though differing in many aspects from the ones she holds and sets forth, nonetheless often reflect a ray of that Truth which enlightens all men" (*Nostra Aetate,* 2).

Taking up the Council's teaching in the first encyclical letter of my pontificate, I wished to recall the ancient doctrine formulated by the Fathers of the Church, which says that we must recognize "the seeds of the Word" present and active in the various religions (cf. *Ad Gentes*, 11; *LG* 17). This doctrine leads us to affirm that, though the routes taken may be different, "there is but a single goal to which is directed the deepest aspiration of the human spirit as expressed in its quest for God and also in its quest, through its tending toward God, for the full dimension of its humanity, or in other words, for the full meaning of human life" (*Redemptor Hominis,* 11).

The "seeds of truth" present and active in the various religious traditions are a reflection of the unique Word of God, who "enlightens every man coming into the world" (cf. Jn 1:9) and who became flesh in Christ Jesus (cf. Jn 1:14). They are together an "effect of the Spirit of truth operating outside the visible confines of the Mystical Body" and which "blows where it wills" (Jn 3:8; cf. *RH* 6, 12). Keeping this doctrine in mind, the celebration of the Jubilee of the Year 2000 "will provide a great opportunity, especially in view of the events of recent decades, for interreligious dialogue" (*TMA* 53). Even now, during this pneumatological year, it is fitting to pause and consider in what sense and in what ways the Holy Spirit is present in humanity's religious quest and in the various experiences and traditions that express it.

It must first be kept in mind that the Holy Spirit inspires every quest of the human spirit for truth and goodness, and in the last analysis, for God. The various religions arose precisely from this primordial human openness to God. At their origins we often find founders who, with the help of God's Spirit, achieved a deeper religious experience. Handed on to others, this experience took form in the doctrines, rites and precepts of the various religious.

In every authentic religious experience, the most characteristic expression is prayer. Because of the human spirit's constitutive openness to God's action of urging it to self-transcendence, we can hold that "every authentic prayer is called forth by the Holy Spirit, who is mysteriously present in the heart of every person."[1] We experienced an eloquent manifestation of this truth in Assisi at the World Day of Prayer for Peace on October 27, 1986, and on other similar occasions of great spiritual intensity.

---

1. *Address to the Members of the Roman Curia,* Dec. 22, 1986, n. 11; *L'Osservatore Romano,* English edition, Jan. 5, 1987, p. 7.

The Holy Spirit is not only present in other religions through authentic expressions of prayer. "The Spirit's presence and activity affect not only individuals but also society and history, peoples, cultures and religions" (*RM* 28). Normally, "it will be in the sincere practice of what is good in their own religious traditions and by following the dictates of their own conscience that the members of other religions respond positively to God's invitation and receive salvation in Jesus Christ, even while they do not recognize or acknowledge him as their Savior (cf. *AG* 3, 9, 11)."[2]

Indeed, as the Second Vatican Council teaches, "since Christ died for all men (cf. Rom 8:32), and since the ultimate vocation of man is in fact one and divine, we ought to believe that the Holy Spirit, in a manner known only to God, offers to every man the possibility of being associated with this paschal mystery" (*GS* 22). This possibility is achieved through sincere, inward adherence to the Truth, generous self-giving to one's neighbor and the search for the Absolute inspired by the Spirit of God. A ray of the divine Wisdom is also shown through the fulfillment of the precepts and practices that conform to the moral law and to authentic religious sense. Precisely by virtue of the Spirit's presence and action, the good elements found in the various religions mysteriously prepare hearts to receive the full revelation of God in Christ.

For the reasons mentioned here, the attitude of the Church and of individual Christians toward other religions is marked by sincere respect, profound sympathy, and when possible and appropriate, cordial collaboration. This does not mean forgetting that Jesus Christ is the one Mediator and Savior of the

---

2. Pontifical Council for Interreligious Dialogue and Congregation for the Evangelization of Peoples, Instruction *Dialogue and Proclamation,* May 19, 1991, n. 29; *L'Osservatore Romano,* English edition, July 1, 1991, p. 3.

human race. Nor does it mean lessening our missionary efforts, to which we are bound in obedience to the risen Lord's command: "Go, therefore, and make disciples of all nations, baptizing them in the name of the Father, and of the Son, and of the Holy Spirit" (Mt 28:19). The attitude of respect and dialogue is instead the proper recognition of the "seeds of the Word" and the "groanings of the Spirit." In this sense, far from opposing the proclamation of the Gospel, our attitude prepares it, as we await the times appointed by the Lord's mercy. "By dialogue we let God be present in our midst; for as we open ourselves in dialogue to one another, we also open ourselves to God."[3]

In view of the third millennium, may the Spirit of truth and love guide us on the paths of the proclamation of Jesus Christ and of the dialogue of peace and brotherhood with the followers of all religions!

General audience of September 9, 1998

---

3. *Address to Members of Other Religions,* Madras, Feb. 5, 1986, n. 4; *L'Osservatore Romano,* English edition, Feb. 10, 1986, p. 14.

The Spirit Is Active
Wherever the Truth Is Sought

Repeating a statement in the book of Wisdom (1:7), the Second Vatican Ecumenical Council teaches us that "the Spirit of the Lord," who bestows his gifts upon the People of God on pilgrimage through history, *"replet orbem terrarum,"* fills the whole universe (cf. *GS* 11). He ceaselessly guides people to the fullness of truth and love which God the Father revealed in Jesus Christ. This profound awareness of the Holy Spirit's presence and action has always illumined the Church's consciousness, guaranteeing that whatever is genuinely human finds an echo in the hearts of Christ's disciples (cf. *GS* 1). Already in the first half of the second century, the philosopher St. Justin could write: "Everything that has always been affirmed in an excellent way and has been discovered by those who study philosophy or make laws has been accomplished by seeking or contemplating a part of the Word" (*Apologia II,* 10, 1–3).

The opening of the human spirit to truth and goodness always takes place in the perspective of the "true light that enlightens every man" (Jn 1:9). This light is Christ the Lord himself, who has enlightened man's steps from the very beginning and has entered his "heart." With the Incarnation, in the fullness of time, the Light appeared in this world in its full brilliance, shining in the sight of man as the splendor of the truth (cf. Jn 14:6).

Already foretold in the Old Testament, the gradual manifestation of the fullness of truth, which is Jesus Christ, takes place down the centuries by the work of the Holy Spirit. This particular action of the "Spirit of truth" (cf. Jn 14:17; 15:26; 16:13) concerns not only believers, but also in a mysterious way all men and women who, though not knowing the Gospel through no fault of their own, sincerely seek the truth and try to live an upright life (cf. *LG* 16). In the footsteps of the Fathers of the Church, St. Thomas Aquinas can maintain that no spirit can be "so darkened as not to participate in some way in the divine light. In fact, every known truth from any source is totally due to this 'light which shines in the darkness,' since every truth, no matter who utters it, comes from the Holy Spirit" (*Comm. on John,* 1, 5, *lect.* 3, n. 103).

For this reason, the Church supports every authentic quest of the human mind and sincerely esteems the patrimony of wisdom built up and transmitted by the various cultures. It expresses the inexhaustible creativity of the human spirit, directed toward the fullness of truth by the Spirit of God. The word of truth preached by the Church encounters the wisdom expressed in cultures and elaborated by philosophies. This encounter calls on the latter to be open to and to find their fulfillment in the revelation that comes from God. As the Second Vatican Council stresses, this encounter enriches the Church, enabling her to penetrate the truth ever more deeply, to express it in the languages of the different cultural traditions, and to present it — unchanged in its substance — in the form most suited to the changing times (cf. *GS* 44). Trust in the presence and action of the Holy Spirit, even in the travail of the culture of our time, can serve as a starting point, at the dawn of the

third millennium, for a new encounter between
Christ and human thought.

In view of the Great Jubilee of the Year 2000, it is necessary to look more closely at the Council's teaching on this ever
fresh and fruitful encounter between revealed truth, preserved
and transmitted by the Church, and the many different forms of
human thought and culture. Unfortunately, Paul VI's observation in the Apostolic Exhortation *Evangelii Nuntiandi* that "the
division between the Gospel and culture is without a doubt the
tragedy of our time" (n. 20) is still valid.

To prevent this division, which has serious consequences
for consciences and behavior, it is necessary to reawaken in
Christ's disciples that vision of faith that can discover the
"seeds of truth" scattered by the Holy Spirit among our contemporaries. This can also contribute to their purification and maturation through the patient art of dialogue, whose particular goal
is to present Christ's face in all its splendor.

It is especially necessary to keep well in mind the great
principle formulated by the last Council, which I wanted to
recall in the Encyclical *Dives in Misericordia:* "While the various currents of human thought both in the past and at the
present have tended and still tend to separate theocentrism and
anthropocentrism, and even to set them in opposition to each
other, the Church, following Christ, seeks to link them up in
human history, in a deep and organic way" (n. 1).

This principle proves fruitful not only for philosophy and
humanistic culture, but also for the areas of scientific research
and art. In fact, "whoever labors to penetrate the secrets of
reality with a humble and steady mind, even though he is
unaware of the fact, is nevertheless being led by the hand of
God, who holds all things in existence and gives them their
identity" (*GS* 36). On the other hand, the true artist has the gift
of perceiving and expressing the luminous and infinite horizon
in which the existence of man and the world is immersed. If he

is faithful to the inspiration that dwells within him and transcends him, he acquires a hidden connaturality with the beauty with which the Holy Spirit clothes creation.

May the Holy Spirit, the Light that enlightens minds and the divine "artist of the world" (S. Bulgakov, *Il Paraclito,* Bologna: 1971, p. 311), guide the Church and contemporary humanity on the paths of a new and surprising encounter with the splendor of the Truth!

General audience of September 16, 1998

In the Spirit We Read the "Signs of the Times"

In the Apostolic Letter *Tertio Millennio Adveniente,* I urged the whole Church, with regard to the year dedicated to the Holy Spirit, to "gain a renewed appreciation of the Spirit as the One who builds the kingdom of God within the course of history and prepares its full manifestation in Jesus Christ, stirring people's hearts and quickening in our world the seeds of the full salvation which will come at the end of time" (n. 45). With the eyes of faith we can see history, especially after the coming of Jesus Christ, as totally enveloped and penetrated by the presence of God's Spirit. It is easy to understand why, today more than ever, the Church feels called to discern the signs of this presence in human history, with which she — in imitation of her Lord — "cherishes a feeling of deep solidarity" (*GS* 1).

So that the Church may fulfill this "responsibility she carries at all times" (cf. *GS* 4), she is invited to rediscover in an ever deeper and more vital way that Jesus Christ, the crucified and risen Lord, is "the key, the center and the purpose of all human history" (*GS* 10). He is "the goal of human history, the focal point of the longings of history and of civilization, the center of the human race, the joy of every heart and the answer to all its yearnings" (*GS* 45). At the same time, the Church recognizes that only the Holy Spirit, by impressing on the hearts of believers the living image of the Son of God made man, can enable them to search history and to discern in it the signs of God's presence and action.

The Apostle Paul writes: "What person knows a man's thoughts except the spirit of the man which is in him? So also no one comprehends the thoughts of God except the Spirit of God. Now we have received not the spirit of the world, but the Spirit which is from God, that we might understand the gifts bestowed on us by God" (1 Cor 2:11–12). Sustained by this unceasing gift of the Spirit, the Church experiences with deep gratitude that "faith throws a new light on everything, manifests God's design for man's total vocation, and thus directs the mind to solutions which are fully human" (*GS* 11).

Using an expression taken from the language of Jesus himself, the Second Vatican Council describes the significant clues to the presence and action of God's Spirit in history as the "signs of the times" (*GS* 4). Today, Jesus' admonition to his contemporaries rings clear and salutary for us as well: "You know how to interpret the appearance of the sky, but you cannot interpret the signs of the times. An evil and adulterous generation seeks for a sign, but no sign shall be given to it except the sign of Jonah" (Mt 16:3–4). In the eyes of Christian faith, the invitation to discern the signs of the times corresponds to the eschatological newness introduced into history by the coming of the Logos among us (cf. Jn 1:14).

In fact, Jesus invites us to discern the words and deeds which bear witness to the imminent coming of the Father's kingdom. He indicates and concentrates all the signs in the enigmatic "sign of Jonah." By doing so, he overturns the worldly logic aimed at seeking signs that would confirm the human desire for self-affirmation and power. As the Apostle Paul emphasizes: "Jews demand signs and Greeks seek wisdom, but we preach Christ crucified, a stumbling block to Jews and folly to Gentiles" (1 Cor 1:22–23).

As the firstborn among many brethren (cf. Rom 8:29), Christ was the first to overcome in himself the diabolic "temptation" to use worldly means to achieve the coming of God's kingdom. This happened from the time of the messianic testing in the desert to the sarcastic challenge flung at him as he hung upon the cross: "If you are the Son of God, come down from the cross" (Mt 27:40). In the crucified Jesus a kind of transformation and concentration of the signs occurs: he himself is the "sign of God," especially in the mystery of his death and resurrection. To discern the signs of his presence in history, it is necessary to free oneself from every worldly pretense and to welcome the Spirit who "searches everything, even the depths of God" (1 Cor 2:10).

If we were to ask when the kingdom of God will be fulfilled, Jesus would reply as he did to the apostles that it is not for us to "know times *(chrónoi)* or seasons *(kairoí)* which the Father has fixed by his own authority *(exousia)*." Jesus asks us, too, to welcome the power of the Spirit, in order to be his witnesses "in Jerusalem and in all Judea and Samaria and to the end of the earth" (Acts 1:7–8).

The providential ordering of the signs of the times was at first hidden in the secret of the Father's plan (cf. Rom 16:25; Eph 3:9), then broke into history and made its advance in the paradoxical sign of the crucified and risen Son (cf. 1 Pt 1:19–21). It was welcomed and interpreted by Christ's disciples in the light and power of the Spirit, in watchful and diligent expectation of the definitive coming that will bring history to fulfillment beyond itself, in the heart of the Father.

By the Father's design, time is thus extended as an invitation "to know the love of Christ which surpasses all knowledge," to "be filled with all the fullness of God" (Eph 3:18–19). The secret of this path is the Holy Spirit, who guides us "into all the truth" (Jn 16:13). With a heart trustfully open to this vision of hope, I implore from the Lord an abundance of the Spirit's gifts for the whole Church, "so that the 'springtime' of the Second Vatican Council can find in the new millennium its 'summertime,' that is, its full development" (*Address at the Ordinary Public Consistory,* February 21, 1998, n. 4; *L'Osservatore Romano,* English edition, February 25, 1998, p. 2).

General audience of September 23, 1998

Confirmation Perfects Baptismal Grace

In this second year of preparation for the Jubilee of the Year 2000, a renewed appreciation of the Holy Spirit's presence focuses our attention especially on the sacrament of Confirmation (cf. *TMA* 45). As the *Catechism of the Catholic Church* teaches, "It perfects baptismal grace; it...gives the Holy Spirit in order to root us more deeply in the divine filiation, incorporate us more firmly into Christ, strengthen our bond with the Church, associate us more closely with her mission, and help us bear witness to the Christian faith in words accompanied by deeds" (n. 1316). The sacrament of Confirmation closely associates the Christian with the anointing of Christ, whom "God anointed with the Holy Spirit" (Acts 10:38). This anointing is recalled in the very name "Christian," which derives from that of "Christ," the Greek translation of the Hebrew term "messiah," whose precise meaning is "anointed." Christ is the Messiah, the Anointed One of God.

Through the seal of the Spirit conferred by Confirmation, the Christian attains his full identity and becomes aware of his mission in the Church and the world. "Before this grace had been conferred on you," St. Cyril of Jerusalem writes, "you were not sufficiently worthy of this name, but were on the way to becoming Christians" (*Mystagogical Catecheses,* III, 4: *PG* 33, 1092).

To understand all the riches of grace contained in the sacrament of Confirmation, which forms an organic whole with Baptism and the Eucharist as the "sacraments of Christian initiation," it is necessary to grasp its meaning in the light of salvation history. In the Old Testament, the prophets proclaimed that the Spirit of God would rest upon the promised Messiah (cf. Is 11:2), and at the same time, would be communicated to all the messianic people (cf. Ez 36:25–27; Jl 3:1–2). In the "fullness of time" Jesus was conceived in the Virgin Mary's womb through the power of the Holy Spirit (cf. Lk 1:35). With the Spirit's descent upon Jesus at the time of his baptism in the River Jordan, he was revealed as the promised Messiah, the Son of God (cf. Mt 3:13–17; Jn 1:33–34). All his life was spent in total communion with the Holy Spirit, whom he gives "not by measure" (Jn 3:34) as the eschatological fulfillment of his mission, as he had promised (cf. Lk 12:12; Jn 3:5–8; 7:37–39; 16:7–15; Acts 1:8). Jesus communicates the Spirit by "breathing" on the apostles on the day of the resurrection (cf. Jn 20:22), and later by the solemn, amazing outpouring on the day of Pentecost (cf. Acts 2:1–4). Thus the apostles, filled with the Holy Spirit, began to "proclaim the mighty works of God" (cf. Acts 2:11). Those who believed in their preaching and were baptized also received "the gift of the Holy Spirit" (Acts 2:38).

The distinction between Confirmation and Baptism is clearly suggested in the Acts of the Apostles when Samaria was being evangelized. Philip, one of the seven deacons, preached the faith and baptized. Then the Apostles Peter and John arrived and laid their hands on the newly baptized so that they would receive the Holy Spirit (8:5–17). Similarly in Ephesus, the Apostle Paul laid his hands on a group of newly baptized and "the Holy Spirit came on them" (19:6).

The sacrament of Confirmation "in a certain way perpetuates the grace of Pentecost in the Church" (*CCC* 1288). Baptism, which Christian tradition calls "the gateway to life in the

Spirit" (*CCC* 1213), gives us a rebirth "of water and the Spirit" (cf. Jn 3:5), enabling us to share sacramentally in Christ's death and resurrection (cf. Rom 6:1–11). Confirmation in turn makes us share fully in the outpouring of the Holy Spirit by the risen Lord. The unbreakable bond between the paschal mystery of Jesus Christ and the outpouring of the Holy Spirit at Pentecost is expressed in the close connection between the sacraments of Baptism and Confirmation. This close bond can also be seen in the fact that in the early centuries Confirmation generally comprised "one single celebration with Baptism, forming with it a 'double sacrament,' according to the expression of St. Cyprian" (*CCC* 1290). This practice has been preserved to the present day in the East, while in the West, for many reasons, Confirmation came to be celebrated later, and there is normally an interval between the two sacraments.

Since apostolic times the full communication of the gift of the Holy Spirit to the baptized has been effectively signified by the laying on of hands. An anointing with perfumed oil, called "chrism," was added very early, the better to express the gift of the Holy Spirit. Indeed, through Confirmation, Christians consecrated by the anointing in Baptism share in the fullness of the Spirit with whom Jesus is filled, so that their whole life will spread the "aroma of Christ" (2 Cor 2:15).

Differences in the rite of Confirmation evolved down the centuries in the East and West, according to the different spiritual sensitivities of the two traditions and in response to various pastoral needs. These differences express the richness of the sacrament and its full meaning in Christian life. In the East, this sacrament is called "Chrismation," anointing with "chrism" or "myron." In the West, the term "Confirmation" suggests the ratification of Baptism as a strengthening of grace through the seal of the Holy Spirit. In the East, since the two sacraments are joined, Chrismation is conferred by the same priest who administers Baptism, although he performs the anointing with chrism consecrated by the bishop (cf. *CCC* 1312). In the Latin rite, the ordinary minister of Confirmation is the bishop, who, for grave reasons, may grant this faculty to priests delegated to administer it (cf. *CCC* 1313).

Thus "the practice of the Eastern Churches gives greater emphasis to the unity of Christian initiation. That of the Latin Church more clearly expresses the communion of the new Christian with the bishop as guarantor and servant of the unity, catholicity and apostolicity of his Church, and hence the connection with the apostolic origins of Christ's Church" (*CCC* 1292).

From what we have said, not only can we see the importance of Confirmation as an organic part of the sacraments of Christian initiation as a whole, but also its irreplaceable effectiveness for the full maturation of Christian life. A decisive task of pastoral ministry, to be intensified as part of the preparation for the Jubilee, consists in very carefully training the baptized who are preparing to receive Confirmation, and in introducing them to the fascinating depths of the mystery it signifies and brings about. At the same time, confirmands must be helped to rediscover with joyful wonder the saving power of this gift of the Holy Spirit.

General audience of September 30, 1998

Confirmation Seals Us
with the Gift of the Spirit

In the preceding catechesis we reflected on the sacrament of Confirmation as the fulfillment of baptismal grace. We will now examine the salvific value and spiritual effect expressed by the sign of anointing, which indicates the "seal of the gift of the Holy Spirit."[1]

Through this anointing, the confirmand fully receives the gift of the Holy Spirit, which he had already received in Baptism in an initial and fundamental way. As the *Catechism of the Catholic Church* explains, "a seal is a symbol of a person (cf. Gn 38:18; Song 8:6), a sign of personal authority (cf. Gn 41:42), or ownership of an object (cf. Dt 32:34)..." (n. 1295). Jesus himself says that "God the Father set his seal" on him (Jn 6:27). So we Christians, having been incorporated into the Body of Christ our Lord by faith and Baptism, are marked by the seal of the Spirit when we receive this anointing. The Apostle Paul explicitly teaches this in speaking to the Chris-

---

1. Cf. Paul VI, Apostolic Constitution *Divinae Consortium Naturae,* August 15, 1971; *L'Osservatore Romano,* English edition, September 23, 1971, p. 4.

tians of Corinth: "It is God who establishes us with you in Christ and has commissioned us; he has put his seal upon us and given us his Spirit in our hearts as a guarantee" (2 Cor 1:21–22; cf. Eph 1:13–14; 4:30).

The seal of the Holy Spirit, therefore, signifies and brings about the disciple's total belonging to Jesus Christ, his being always at the latter's service in the Church. At the same time it implies the promise of divine protection in the trials he will have to endure to witness to his faith in the world. Jesus himself foretold this, shortly before his passion: "They will deliver you up to councils, and you will be beaten in synagogues, and you will stand before governors and kings for my sake, to bear testimony before them.... When they bring you to trial and deliver you up, do not be anxious beforehand about what you are to say, but say whatever is given you in that hour, for it is not you who speak, but the Holy Spirit" (Mk 13:9, 11ff.). A similar promise recurs in the Book of Revelation, in a vision that embraces the Church's entire history and sheds light on the dramatic situation that the disciples of Christ are called to face in union with their crucified and risen Lord. They are presented in the evocative image of those whose foreheads have been marked with God's seal (cf. Rev 7:2–4).

By bringing baptismal grace to fulfillment, Confirmation unites us more firmly to Jesus Christ and to his Body, the Church. This sacrament also increases the gifts of the Holy Spirit in us, to give us "a special strength of the Holy Spirit to spread and defend the faith by word and action as true witnesses of Christ, to confess the name of Christ boldly, and never to be ashamed of the cross" (*CCC* 1303; cf. Council of Florence, *DS* 1319; *LG* 11–12).

St. Ambrose exhorts the confirmed in these vibrant words: "Recall that you have received the spiritual seal, the Spirit of wisdom and understanding, the Spirit of counsel and fortitude, the Spirit of knowledge and piety, the Spirit of the fear of God.

Guard what you have received. God the Father has marked you with his sign; Christ the Lord has confirmed you and has placed the Spirit in your hearts as a pledge" (*The Mysteries,* 7, 42; *PL* 16, 402–403).

The gift of the Spirit obliges us to bear witness to Jesus Christ and to God the Father, and ensures that we have the ability and the courage to do so. The Acts of the Apostles tells us clearly that the Spirit was poured out upon the apostles, so that they would become "witnesses" (1:8; cf. Jn 15:26–27).

St. Thomas Aquinas wonderfully summarizes the Church's tradition, saying that through Confirmation all the necessary help is communicated to the baptized so that they can profess publicly and in every circumstance the faith received in Baptism. "The fullness of the Holy Spirit," he explains, "is given *ad robur spirituale* (for spiritual strength) which is appropriate to adulthood" (*Summa Theol.,* III, 72, 2). This maturity is obviously not to be measured by human criteria, but from within the mysterious relationship of each individual to Christ.

This teaching, rooted in Sacred Scripture and developed by sacred Tradition, is expressed in the teaching of the Council of Trent. It says that the sacrament of Confirmation is imprinted on the soul like an "indelible spiritual mark": the "character" (cf. *DS* 1609), which is precisely the sign Jesus Christ imprints on the Christian with the seal of his Spirit.

This specific gift conferred by the sacrament of Confirmation enables the faithful to exercise their "prophetic office" of bearing witness to the faith. "The confirmed person," St. Thomas explains, "receives the power to profess faith in Christ publicly and as it were officially *(quasi ex officio)"* (cf. *Summa Theol.,* III, 72, 5, *ad* 2; *CCC* 1305). Furthermore, in explaining the sacred and organic nature of the priestly community, the Second Vatican Council stresses that the faithful "are more perfectly bound to the Church by the sacrament of Confirmation, and the Holy Spirit endows them with special strength so that they are more strictly obliged to spread and defend the faith, both by word and by deed, as true witnesses of Christ" (*LG* 11). The baptized who receive the sacrament of Confirmation with full and mature awareness solemnly declare before the Church, with the support of God's grace, their readiness to let themselves be grasped by the Spirit of God in an ever new and ever deeper way, to become witnesses to Christ the Lord.

Thanks to the Spirit who penetrates and fills their hearts, this readiness spurs them even to martyrdom, as we are shown by the uninterrupted series of Christian witnesses who, from the dawn of Christianity to our century, have not been afraid to sacrifice their earthly lives for love of Jesus Christ. "Martyrdom is the supreme witness given to the truth of the faith: it means bearing witness even unto death. The martyr bears witness to Christ who died and rose, to whom he is united by charity" (*CCC* 2473).

On the threshold of the third millennium, let us invoke the gift of the Paraclete to revive the effectiveness of the grace of the spiritual seal imprinted on us in the sacrament of Confirmation. Animated by the Spirit, our lives will spread the "aroma of Christ" (2 Cor 2:15) to the very ends of the earth.

General audience of October 14, 1998

The Spirit Bestows the Gift of Transcendent Life

The Holy Spirit is "the Lord, the giver of life." With these words of the Nicene-Constantinopolitan Creed, the Church continues to profess her faith in the Holy Spirit, whom St. Paul proclaims as the "Spirit of life" (Rom 8:2). In the history of salvation, life always appears as linked to God's Spirit. At the dawn of creation, through the divine breath, like a "breath of life," "man became a living being" (Gn 2:7). In the history of the Chosen People, the Spirit of the Lord repeatedly intervened to save and guide Israel through the patriarchs, judges, kings and prophets. Ezekiel vividly portrays the situation of the people brought low by the exile experience as an immense valley filled with bones to which God communicates new life (cf. 37:1–14): "And the spirit came into them and they lived and stood upon their feet" (37:10).

In Jesus' history in particular, the Holy Spirit discloses his life-giving power: the fruit of Mary's womb comes to life "through the power of the Holy Spirit" (Mt 1:18; cf. Lk 1:35). Jesus' whole mission is enlivened and guided by the Holy Spirit. In a special way the resurrection bears the seal of the "Spirit of him who raised Jesus from the dead" (Rom 8:11).

The Holy Spirit, equal to the Father and the Son, is the principal agent of that "Gospel of life," which the Church never tires of proclaiming and bearing witness to in the world. The Gospel of life, as I explained in the Encyclical Letter *Evangelium Vitae,* is not simply a reflection on human life, nor merely a commandment aimed at raising awareness. It is "something concrete and personal, for it consists in the proclamation of the very person of Jesus" (n. 29). He makes himself known as "the way and the truth and the life" (Jn 14:6). And to Martha, Lazarus' sister, he says: "I am the resurrection and the life" (Jn 11:25).

"He who follows me," he proclaims further, "will have the light of life" (Jn 8:12). The life that Jesus Christ gives us is a living water that satisfies man's deepest aspirations and brings him, as a son, into full communion with God. This living and life-giving water is the Holy Spirit. In his conversation with the Samaritan woman, Jesus foretold this divine gift: "If you knew the gift of God and who it is that is saying to you, 'Give me a drink,' you would have asked him and he would have given you living water.... Everyone who drinks of this water will thirst again, but whoever drinks of the water that I shall give him will never thirst: the water that I shall give him will become in him a spring of water welling up to eternal life" (Jn 4:10, 13–14). Later, on the feast of Tabernacles, Jesus foretold his death and resurrection, loudly exclaiming as if to be heard by people of all places and times: "If anyone thirsts, let him come to me and drink. He who believes in me, as the Scripture has said, 'Out of his heart shall flow rivers of living water.'" The Evangelist John notes that "He said this about the Spirit, which those who believed in him were to receive" (7:37–39).

In obtaining the gift of the Spirit for us by the sacrifice of his own life, Jesus fulfills the mission he received from the Father: "I came that they may have life and have it abundantly" (Jn 10:10). The Holy Spirit renews our hearts (cf. Ez 36:25–27;

Jer 31:31–34) and conforms them to Christ's. Thus the Christian can "appreciate and achieve the deepest and most authentic meaning of life: namely, that of being a gift which is fully realized in the giving of self" (*EV* 49). This is the new law, "the law of the Spirit of life in Christ Jesus" (Rom 8:2). Its essential expression, in imitation of the Lord who laid down his life for his friends (cf. Jn 15:13), is the loving gift of self: "We know that we have passed out of death into life, because we love the brethren" (1 Jn 3:14).

The life of Christians, who through faith and the sacraments are inwardly united with Jesus Christ, is "life in the Spirit." Indeed, the Holy Spirit, poured out in our hearts (cf. Gal 4:6), becomes in us and for us "a spring of water welling up to eternal life" (Jn 4:14). We must, therefore, let ourselves be docilely guided by God's Spirit, to become ever more fully what we already are through grace: sons of God in Christ (cf. Rom 8:14–16). "If we live by the Spirit," St. Paul urges us again, "let us also walk by the Spirit" (Gal 5:25).

This principle is the foundation of Christian spirituality, which consists in accepting all the life that the Spirit gives us. This concept of spirituality protects us from the misunderstandings that sometimes obscure its true nature. Christian spirituality does not consist in an effort to *perfect oneself,* as if man could further his overall personal growth and achieve salvation by his own strength. The human heart, wounded by sin, is healed only by the grace of the Holy Spirit. Man can live as a true son of God only if sustained by this grace. Nor does Christian spirituality consist in becoming "immaterial," disembodied as it were, without responsible involvement in human affairs. Indeed, the Holy Spirit's presence in us, far from urging us to seek an alienating "escape," penetrates and moves our entire being: intellect, will, emotions and bodily nature, so that our "new nature" (Eph 4:24) will imbue space and time with the newness of the Gospel.

On the threshold of the third millennium, the Church is preparing to receive the ever new gift of that Spirit, the giver of life, which flows from the pierced side of Jesus Christ, in order to proclaim the Gospel of life with deep joy to all. We ask the Holy Spirit to enable the Church of our time to echo faithfully the words of the apostles:

> That which was from the beginning, which we have heard, which we have seen with our eyes, which we have looked upon and touched with our hands, concerning the word of life — the life was made manifest and we saw it and testify to it, and proclaim to you the eternal life which was with the Father and was made manifest to us — that which we have seen and heard we proclaim also to you, so that you may have fellowship with us, and our fellowship is with the Father and with his Son, Jesus Christ (1 Jn 1:1–3).

General audience of October 21, 1998

Life in the Spirit
Transcends Even Death

"God so loved the world that he gave his only Son, so that whoever believes in him should not perish but have eternal life" (Jn 3:16). In these words from the Gospel of John, the gift of "eternal life" represents the ultimate purpose of the Father's loving plan. This gift gives us access through grace to the ineffable communion of love of the Father, the Son and the Holy Spirit: "This is eternal life, that they know you, the only true God, and Jesus Christ, whom you have sent" (Jn 17:3).

Through the Holy Spirit, Jesus in his paschal mystery communicates to us in its fullness the "eternal life" that flows from the Father. By receiving it we share in the risen Jesus' definitive victory over death. "Death and life," we proclaim in the liturgy, "have contended in that combat stupendous: the Prince of life, who died, reigns immortal" *(Sequence for Easter Sunday)*. In this decisive event of salvation, Jesus gives human beings "eternal life" in the Holy Spirit.

In the "fullness of time" Christ thus fulfills, beyond all expectation, that promise of "eternal life" which the Father has inscribed in the creation of man in his image and likeness since the beginning of the world (cf. Gn 1:26). As we sing in Psalm

104, man experiences that life in the cosmos and his own life in particular have their beginning in the "breath" communicated by the Spirit of the Lord: "When you hide your face, they are dismayed; when you take away their breath, they die and return to their dust. When you send forth your Spirit, they are created, and you renew the face of the earth" (vv. 29–30).

Communion with God, the gift of his Spirit, more and more becomes for the Chosen People the pledge of a life that is not limited to earthly existence, but mysteriously transcends and prolongs it forever. In the harsh period of the Babylonian exile, the Lord rekindled his people's hope, proclaiming a new and definitive covenant that would be sealed with an abundant out-pouring of the Spirit (cf. Ez 36:24–28): "Behold, I will open your graves and raise you from your graves, O my people, and I will bring you home into the land of Israel. And you shall know that I am the Lord, when I open your graves and raise you from your graves, O my people. I will put my Spirit within you and you shall live" (Ez 37:12–14). With these words God an-nounced the messianic renewal of Israel after the sufferings of the exile. The symbols used are well suited to suggesting the faith journey that Israel was slowly making, to the point of intuiting the truth of the resurrection of the flesh that the Spirit will accomplish at the end of time.

This truth became firmly established in the period shortly before the coming of Jesus Christ (cf. Dn 12:2; 2 Mc 7:9–14, 23, 36; 12:43– 45), who vigorously confirmed it and rebuked those who denied it: "Is not this why you are wrong, that you know neither the Scriptures nor the power of God?" (Mk 12:24). According to Jesus, belief in the resurrection is based on belief in God, who "is not God of the dead, but of the living" (Mk 12:27).

Moreover, Jesus linked belief in the resurrection to his own person: "I am the resurrection and the life" (Jn 11:25). In him, through the mystery of his death and resurrection, the divine promise of the gift of "eternal life" is fulfilled. This life implies total victory over death: "The hour is coming when all who are in the tombs will hear the voice [of the Son] and come forth, those who have done good, to the resurrection of life..." (Jn 5:28–29). "For this is the will of my Father, that everyone who sees the Son and believes in him should have eternal life, and I will raise him up at the last day" (Jn 6:40).

Christ's promise will thus be mysteriously fulfilled at the end of time, when he returns in glory "to judge the living and the dead" (2 Tim 4:1; cf. Acts 10:42; 1 Pt 4:5). Then our mortal bodies will live again through the power of the Holy Spirit, who has been given to us as "the pledge of our inheritance, the first payment against the full redemption" (Eph 1:14; cf. 2 Cor 1:21–22).

However, there is no need to think that life after death begins only with the final resurrection. The latter is preceded by the special state in which every human being finds himself after physical death. There is an intermediate stage in which, as the body decomposes, "a spiritual element survives and subsists after death, an element endowed with consciousness and will, so that the 'human self' subsists," although lacking the complement of its body.[1]

Believers also have the certitude that their life-giving relationship with Christ cannot be destroyed by death but continues in the hereafter. Christ said: "He who believes in me, even though he die, will live" (Jn 11:25). The Church has always professed this belief and has especially expressed it in the prayer of praise she offers to God in communion with all the saints, and in her prayer for the dead who are not fully purified. On the other hand, the Church insists on respect for the mortal remains of every human being because of the dignity of the person to whom they belonged, and because of the honor that is

---

1. Sacred Congregation for the Doctrine of the Faith, *Letter on Certain Questions Concerning Eschatology,* May 17, 1979: *AAS* 71 (1979), 941.

odies of those who became temples of the Holy
~~~gh Baptism. Particular evidence of this is the fu-
~~~gy and the veneration given to the relics of the saints,
which has developed from the earliest centuries. The latter's
bones, St. Paulinus of Nola says, "never lose the presence of
the Holy Spirit, whence a living grace comes to the sacred
tombs" (*Carmen,* XXI, 632–633).

Thus we see the Holy Spirit as the Spirit of life not only in
every stage of our earthly existence, but equally so in that state
which, after death, precedes the full life that the Lord has
promised even for our mortal bodies. All the more so, thanks to
the Spirit, we will make in Christ our final "journey" to the
Father. St. Basil the Great notes: "If anyone reflects carefully,
he will understand that, even as we await the Lord's appearing
from heaven, the Holy Spirit will not be absent, as some believe; no, he will also be present on the day of the Lord's
revelation, when he will judge the world in justice as its blessed
and only sovereign" (*On the Holy Spirit,* XVI, 40).

General audience of October 28, 1998

Our Bodies Will Share in the Resurrection

"Our citizenship," the Apostle Paul teaches, "is in heaven, and from it we await a Savior, the Lord Jesus Christ, who will change our lowly body to be like his glorious body, by the power which enables him even to subject all things to himself" (Phil 3:20–21). Just as the Holy Spirit transformed the body of Jesus Christ when the Father raised him from the dead, so the same Spirit will clothe our bodies with Christ's glory. St. Paul writes: "If the Spirit of him who raised Jesus from the dead dwells in you, he who raised Christ Jesus from the dead will give life to your mortal bodies also through his Spirit who dwells in you" (Rom 8:11).

From the start, Christian faith in the resurrection of the flesh has encountered misunderstanding and opposition. The Apostle experienced this firsthand when he was proclaiming the Gospel in the middle of the Areopagus in Athens: "When they heard of the resurrection of the dead, some mocked, but others said, 'We will hear you again about this'" (Acts 17:32). This difficulty has been raised in our time as well. On the one hand, even those who believe in some form of survival after death react skeptically to the truth of faith that clarifies this

141

ultimate question of human existence in the light of Jesus Christ's resurrection. On the other, many have noted the fascination with a belief like reincarnation, which is rooted in the religious soil of certain Eastern cultures (cf. *TMA* 9).

Christian revelation is not satisfied with a vague sense of survival, although it appreciates the intimation of immortality expressed in the teaching of some great God-seekers. We can also agree that the idea of reincarnation arose from an intense desire for immortality and from the perception that human life is the "test" in view of an ultimate end, as well as from the need for complete purification in order to attain communion with God. However, reincarnation does not ensure the unique, individual identity of each human creature as the object of God's personal love, nor the integrity of human existence as "incarnate spirit."

The witness of the New Testament emphasizes first of all the realism of the resurrection, corporal as well, of Jesus Christ. The apostles explicitly attest to this when referring to their experience of the risen Lord's appearances: "God raised him on the third day and made him manifest...to us who were chosen by God as witnesses, who ate and drank with him after he rose from the dead" (Acts 10:40–41). The fourth Gospel also stresses this realism when, for example, it recounts the episode in which Jesus invites the Apostle Thomas to put his finger in the mark of the nails and his hand in the Lord's pierced side (cf. Jn 20:24–29). In the appearance at the shore of the Sea of Tiberias, the risen Jesus "took the bread and gave it to them, and so with the fish" (Jn 21:13).

The realism of these appearances testifies that Jesus rose with his body and lives with this body at the Father's side. However, it is a glorious body, no longer subject to the laws of space and time, transformed in the glory of the Father. In the risen Christ we see revealed that eschatological state which all those who accept his redemption are one day called to reach, preceded by the Blessed Virgin who, "when the course of her earthly life was finished, was taken up body and soul into heavenly glory" (Pius XII, Apos. Const. *Munificentissimus Deus,* Nov. 1, 1950, *DS* 3903; cf. *LG* 59).

Referring to the account of creation in Genesis and interpreting Jesus' resurrection as the "new creation," the Apostle Paul can thus say: "The first man Adam became a living being; the last Adam became a life-giving spirit" (1 Cor 15:45). In a mysterious but real way, all who believe in Christ share in his glorified reality through the outpouring of the Holy Spirit.

Thus, in Christ "all will rise again with the bodies which they now bear" (Fourth Lateran Council, *DS* 801), but this body of ours will be changed into a glorious body (cf. Phil 3:21), into a "spiritual body" (1 Cor 15:44). Some asked Paul: "How are the dead raised? With what kind of body do they come?" He answered them in the First Letter to the Corinthians, using the image of the seed that dies in order to open into new life:

> What you sow does not come to life unless it dies. And what you sow is not the body which is to be, but a bare kernel, perhaps of wheat or of some other grain.... So it is with the resurrection of the dead. What is sown is perishable; what is raised is imperishable. It is sown in dishonor; it is raised in glory. It is sown in weakness; it is raised in power. It is sown in a physical body; it is raised in a spiritual body.... For this perishable nature must put on the imperishable, and this mortal nature must put on immortality (15:36–37, 42–44, 53).

Certainly, as the *Catechism of the Catholic Church* explains, "how" this will come about "exceeds our imagination and understanding; it is accessible only to faith. Yet our participation in the Eucharist already gives us a foretaste of Christ's transfiguration of our bodies" (n. 1000).

Through the Eucharist Jesus gives us, under the appearances of bread and wine, his flesh which is enlivened by the Holy Spirit and gives life to our flesh, so that we can share in his resurrection and state of glory with all our being, spirit and body. In this regard St. Irenaeus of Lyons teaches: "Just as bread that comes from the earth, after God's blessing has been invoked upon it, is no longer ordinary bread, but Eucharist, formed of two things, the one earthly and the other heavenly, so too our bodies, which partake of the Eucharist, are no longer corruptible, but possess the hope of resurrection" (*Adv. Haer.,* IV, 18, 4–5).

What we have said thus far, synthesizing the teaching of Sacred Scripture and the Church's Tradition, explains why "the Christian Creed...culminates in the proclamation of the resurrection of the dead on the last day and in life everlasting" (*CCC* 988). By the Incarnation the Word of God has taken on human flesh (cf. Jn 1:14), enabling it to share, through his death and resurrection, in his own glory as the Father's Only-begotten Son. Through the gifts of the Spirit, the Father instills in all man's being and, in a certain way, in the universe itself, a yearning for this destiny. As St. Paul says: "The creation waits with eager longing for the revealing of the sons of God ...because the creation itself will be set free from its bondage to decay and obtain the glorious liberty of the children of God" (Rom 8:19–21).

General audience of November 4, 1998

The Holy Spirit Is the Source of Hope

The Holy Spirit, poured out "without measure" by Jesus Christ, crucified and risen, is "the One who builds the kingdom of God within the course of history and prepares its full manifestation in Jesus Christ...which will come at the end of time" (*TMA* 45). In this eschatological perspective, believers are called to a renewed appreciation of the theological virtue of hope. This virtue "on the one hand encourages the Christian not to lose sight of the final goal which gives meaning and value to life, and on the other, offers solid and profound reasons for a daily commitment to transform reality in order to make it correspond to God's plan" (*TMA* 46).

St. Paul underlines the intimate and deep bond that exists between the gift of the Holy Spirit and the virtue of hope. In the Letter to the Romans, he says: "Hope does not disappoint us, because God's love has been poured into our hearts through the Holy Spirit who has been given to us" (5:5). Yes, the very gift of the Holy Spirit, filling our hearts with God's love and making us children of the Father in Jesus Christ (cf. Gal 4:6), instills in us the hope that nothing "will be able to separate us from the love of God in Christ Jesus our Lord" (Rom 8:39). For this reason, the God revealed in the "fullness of time" in Jesus

Christ is truly "the God of Hope," who fills believers with joy and peace, so that "by the power of the Holy Spirit [they] may abound in hope" (Rom 15:13). Thus Christians are called to be witnesses in the world to this joyful experience, and to "always be prepared to make a defense to anyone who calls [them] to account for the hope" that is in them (1 Pt 3:15).

Christian hope brings to fulfillment the hope inspired by God in the people of Israel, and finds its own origin and model in Abraham, who "believed against hope that he should become the father of many nations" (Rom 4:18). Ratified in the covenant made by the Lord with his people through Moses, the preaching of the prophets down the centuries constantly rekindled the hope of Israel. Lastly, it was centered on the promise of the eschatological outpouring of God's Spirit on the Messiah and on all his people (cf. Is 11:2; Ez 36:27; Jl 3:1–2).

This promise was fulfilled in Jesus. He is not only the witness to the hope that is open to anyone who becomes his disciple, but in his person and in his work of salvation, he himself is "our hope" (1 Tim 1:1), since he proclaims and brings about God's kingdom. The Beatitudes are the *Magna Carta* of this kingdom (cf. Mt 5:3–12). "The *Beatitudes* raise our hope toward heaven as the new Promised Land; they trace the path that leads through the trials that await the disciples of Jesus" (*CCC* 1820).

Made Christ and Lord through the paschal mystery (cf. Acts 2:36), Jesus becomes "a life-giving spirit" (1 Cor 15:45). Baptized in him with water and the Spirit (cf. Jn 3:5), believers are "born anew to a living hope" (1 Pt 1:3). Henceforth, the gift of salvation, through the Holy Spirit, is the pledge and seal (cf. 2 Cor 1:21–22; Eph 1:13–14) of the full communion with God to which Christ leads us. One reads in the Letter to Titus that the Holy Spirit was "poured out upon us richly, through Jesus Christ our Savior, so that we might be justified by his grace and become heirs in hope of eternal life" (Ti 3:6–7).

Also according to the Fathers of the Church, the Holy Spirit is "the gift which lavishes perfect hope upon us" (St. Hilary of Poitiers, *The Trinity*, II, 1). St. Paul says that it is the Spirit "bearing witness with our spirit that we are children of God and if children, then heirs, heirs of God and fellow heirs with Christ" (Rom 8:16–17). Christian life grows and matures to its fullness from that "already" of salvation, which is the life of God's children in Christ, in which the Holy Spirit makes us share. From the experience of this gift, it longs with trusting perseverance for the "not yet" and the "yet more," which God has promised us and will give us at the end of time. As St. Paul maintains, if one is really a son, then one is also heir to all that belongs to the Father with Christ, "firstborn among many brethren" (Rom 8:29). "All that the Father has is mine," says Jesus (Jn 16:15). For this reason, in communicating his Spirit to us, he makes us share in the inheritance of the Father and gives us the pledge and first fruits. This divine reality is the inexhaustible source of Christian hope.

The Church's teaching sees hope as one of the three theological virtues, poured out by God into the heart of believers through the Holy Spirit. It is that virtue "by which we desire the kingdom of heaven and eternal life as our happiness, placing our trust in Christ's promises and relying not on our own strength, but on the help of the grace of the Holy Spirit" (*CCC* 1817).

To the gift of hope "special attention should be given...especially in our day. Today many people, including quite a few Christians, are floundering in the illusion and myth of an unlimited capacity for self-redemption and self-fulfillment, and the temptation to pessimism from the experience of frequent disappointment and defeat" (*General Audience*, July 3, 1991; *L'Osservatore Romano*, English edition, July 8, 1991, p. 11). Many dangers seem to loom over the future of humanity; many uncertainties weigh on man's personal destiny. He frequently feels incapable of dealing with them. In addition, the crisis of the meaning of life and the enigma of pain and death keep knocking relentlessly at the door of our contemporaries' hearts.

The message of hope that comes from Jesus Christ brightens this horizon darkened by uncertainty and pessimism. Hope sustains and protects us in the good fight of faith (cf. Rom 12:12). It is nourished by prayer and most especially by the Our Father, "the summary of everything that hope leads us to desire" (*CCC* 1820).

Today it is not enough to reawaken hope in individual consciences; it is necessary *to cross the threshold of hope together.* Hope essentially has — as we will have the opportunity to examine — a community as well as a social dimension. What the Apostle says in the proper and direct sense for the Church can in a broader sense be applied to the vocation of all humanity: "There is one body and one Spirit, just as you were called to the one hope that belongs to your call" (Eph 4:4).

General audience of November 11, 1998

Signs of Hope at the
End of This Century

A deeper understanding of the Holy Spirit's action in the Church and in the world encourages us to pay attention to the "signs of hope present in the last part of this century, even though they often remain hidden from our eyes" (*TMA* 46). It is true that our century is marked by very serious crimes against humanity, and is darkened by ideologies that have encouraged neither the liberating encounter with the truth of Jesus Christ nor integral human development. But it is also true that God's Spirit, who "fills the world" (Wis 1:7; cf. *GS* 11), has not ceased to scatter abundant seeds of truth, love and life in the hearts of the men and women of our time. These seeds have produced fruits of progress, humanization and civilization, which are authentic signs of hope for humanity on its journey.

In the Apostolic Letter *Tertio Millennio Adveniente,* among these signs I first mentioned "scientific, technological and especially medical progress in the service of human life" (n. 46). Without doubt, human life in our world, at the social and personal level, has known and continues to experience remarkable improvement, thanks to extraordinary scientific developments.

When it respects authentic and integral human advancement, technological progress must also be accepted with gratitude, even if — as is obvious — science and technology are not enough to satisfy man's deepest longings. Among today's technological developments showing particular promise for humanity's future, I would like to mention those that have occurred in the medical field. In fact, when they improve man's overall life by lawful means, they eloquently reflect the creative and saving plan of God, who wanted man in Christ to have the fullness of life. Nor can we forget the enormous progress in the area of communications. If the *mass media* are handled in such a way that they are under full democratic control and are used to convey authentic values, humanity will be able to enjoy many benefits and will feel it is one great family.

Another sign of hope is represented by a "greater awareness of our responsibility for the environment" (*TMA* 46). In part as a reaction to the indiscriminate exploitation of natural resources that has often accompanied industrial development, human beings are today rediscovering the meaning and value of the environment as a hospitable dwelling *(oîkos),* where they are called to live their life. The threats that hang over humanity's future because of the lack of respect for the balance of the ecosystem are spurring men of culture and science, as well as the competent authorities, to study and implement various measures and projects. They aim not only at repairing the damage caused thus far, but especially at mapping out a social development that is in harmony with respect for and appreciation of the natural environment.

This keen sense of responsibility for the environment must also encourage Christians to rediscover the deep meaning of the creative plan revealed by the Bible. God wanted to entrust man and woman with the task of filling the earth and having dominion over it in his name, as his representative (cf. Gn 1:28), extending and in a certain way bringing to completion his own creative work.

Among the signs of hope in our time, we must also recall the "efforts to restore peace and justice wherever they have been violated, a desire for reconciliation and solidarity among different peoples, particularly the complex relationship between the North and the South of the world" (*TMA* 46). In the twentieth century, we have witnessed the terrible tragedy of two world wars. Today there are further wars and tensions, resulting in great suffering for peoples and nations throughout the world. Never as in the twentieth century have such enormous masses of people experienced and continued to experience conditions of life unworthy of man — due in part to pernicious mechanisms of exploitation.

For this reason too, the human conscience, urged by the mysterious action of the Spirit, has grown in its resolve to make peace and justice indispensable priorities. Today conscience sees the persistence of unjust conditions, underdevelopment and the violation of human rights as an intolerable crime. Moreover, war is rightly rejected as a way to resolve conflicts. There is a growing understanding that only the paths of dialogue and reconciliation can heal the wounds caused by history in the life of nations. They alone can lead to a positive resolution of the problems that still arise in international relations.

The contemporary world is definitely being structured into a system of interdependence at the economic, cultural and political levels. It is no longer possible to reason solely on the basis of the interests, however legitimate, of individual peoples and nations. A truly universal awareness must be achieved.

For this reason my venerable Predecessor Pope Paul VI wanted prophetically to focus humanity's sights on the goal of a "civilization of love," in which it would be possible to achieve the ideal of one human family, while respecting the identity of each of its members, and foster a mutual exchange of gifts.

On the way toward this "civilization of love," believers, docile to the action of the Holy Spirit, are called to make their irreplaceable contribution, radiating in history the light of Christ, the Word of God made flesh. As the Council recalls, "He himself revealed to us that 'God is love' (1 Jn 4:8), and at the same time taught us that the new command of love was the basic law of human perfection and hence of the world's transformation. To those, therefore, who believe in divine love, he gives assurance that the way of love lies open to men, and that the effort to establish a universal brotherhood is not a hopeless one" (*GS* 38).

General audience of November 18, 1998

The Spirit Leads the
Church on the Path of Renewal

In the previous catechesis we reflected on the "signs of hope" present in our world. Today we would like to continue our reflection, examining some of the "signs of hope" present in the Church, so that Christian communities can ever better understand and appreciate them. They stem from the action of the Holy Spirit who, down the centuries, "By the power of the Gospel...makes the Church keep the freshness of youth. Uninterruptedly he renews it and leads it to perfect union with its Spouse" (*LG* 4).

Among the ecclesial events that have left a deep mark on the twentieth century, the most important is the Second Vatican Ecumenical Council. Through it the Church took from her treasury "what is new and what is old" (cf. Mt 13:52) and experienced in a certain way the grace of a renewed Pentecost.[1] If we look closely, the signs of hope which enliven the Church's mission today are closely connected with the abundant out-

---

1. Cf. "Address of John XXIII at the Close of the Council's First Session," in *Discorsi, Messaggi, Colloqui,* vol. V, (1962/1963), 29.

. ouring of the Holy Spirit, which the Church experienced in the preparation, celebration and application of the Second Vatican Council.

Listening to what "the Spirit is saying to the Church and to the Churches" (*TMA* 23; cf. Rev 2:7 ff.) is expressed in acceptance of the *charisms* which he distributes in abundance. Their rediscovery and appreciation has developed a more intense communion between the various vocations of the People of God, such as a renewed, joyful enthusiasm for evangelization.

Today especially, the Holy Spirit is spurring the Church to promote the *vocation and mission of the lay faithful.* Their participation and coresponsibility in the life of the Christian community and the many forms of their apostolate and service in society give us reason, at the dawn of the third millennium, to await with hope a *mature and fruitful "epiphany" of the laity.* A similar expectation concerns the role that *woman* is called to assume. As in civil society, so in the Church, the *"feminine genius"* is becoming more and more apparent. It must be increasingly promoted in ways appropriate to the vocation of woman according to God's plan. Moreover, we cannot forget that one of the gifts the Spirit has generously bestowed in our time is the flourishing of *ecclesial movements.* From the beginning of my pontificate I have continued to point to them as a cause of hope for the Church and for society. They "are a sign of the freedom of forms in which the one Church is expressed, and they represent a sound newness, which still waits to be adequately understood in all its positive effectiveness, for the kingdom of God at work in the present moment of history" (*Insegnamenti,* VII/2 [1984], p. 696).

Our century has also seen the seed of the *ecumenical movement* blossom and grow. In this movement the Holy Spirit has led the members of the various ecclesial communities to seek the ways of dialogue in order to reestablish full unity. In particular, thanks to the Second Vatican Council, the search for unity and ecumenical concern have unquestionably become "a necessary dimension of the whole life of the Church," and a priority commitment to which the Catholic Church "wants to contribute in every possible way" (*Insegnamenti,* VIII/1 [1985], pp. 1991, 1999). The dialogue of *truth,* preceded and accompanied by the dialogue of *charity,* is gradually achieving remarkable results. There is also a stronger awareness that the real soul of the movement to restore Christian unity is spiritual ecumenism, that is, conversion of heart, prayer and holiness of life (cf. *UR* 8).

Lastly, among the many other signs of hope, I would like to mention "the increased interest in dialogue with other religions and with contemporary culture" (*TMA* 46). As to the former, one need only recall the prophetic significance that the Second Vatican Council's Declaration *Nostra Aetate,* on the Church's relations with non-Christian religions, has gradually assumed. Many experiences of meeting and dialogue at various levels have taken place and are taking place in every part of the world between representatives of the different religions. I am pleased to mention in particular the great progress that has been made in the dialogue with the Jews, our "elder brothers."

An important sign of hope for humanity is that the religions are trustingly engaged in dialogue, and feel the urgent need to join forces to encourage progress and to contribute to the moral commitment of nations. Faith in the constant action of the Spirit gives us hope that also by this path of mutual concern and esteem it will be possible for everyone to be open to Christ, the true Light that "enlightens every man" (Jn 1:9).

As for the dialogue with culture, the attitude expressed by the Second Vatican Council is showing its providential effectiveness: "Just as it is in the world's interest to acknowledge the Church as an historical reality and to recognize her good influence, so the Church herself knows how richly she has profited by the history and development of humanity" (*GS* 44). Contacts made in this area have already overcome unwarranted prejudices. The new attention paid by the various cultural currents of our time to religious experience and to Christianity in particular, spurs us to persevere on the path we have chosen toward a fresh meeting between the Gospel and culture.

In these many signs of hope, we cannot fail to recognize the action of God's Spirit. However, in full dependence upon and in communion with him, I also like to see in them the role of Mary, "as though fashioned by the Holy Spirit and formed as a new creature" (*LG* 56). Mary intercedes for the Church as a mother and leads her on the path of holiness and docility to the Paraclete. At the dawn of the new millennium, we can joyfully discern that "Marian profile" of the Church (cf. *Insegnamenti,* X/3 [1987], p. 1483), which epitomizes the deepest meaning of conciliar renewal.

General audience of November 25, 1998

We Await
New Heavens and a New Earth

The Holy Spirit is the source of the "hope that does not disappoint" (Rom 5:5). In this light, after examining some of the "signs of hope" present in our time, today we reflect on the meaning of Christian hope in this season of waiting and preparation for the coming of the kingdom of God in Christ at the end of time. In this regard, as I emphasized in my Apostolic Letter *Tertio Millennio Adveniente,* we must remember that "the basic attitude of hope, on the one hand, encourages the Christian not to lose sight of the final goal that gives meaning and value to life, and on the other, offers solid and profound reasons for a daily commitment to transform reality in order to make it correspond to God's plan" (n. 46).

Hope in the definitive coming of God's kingdom and the commitment to transform the world in the light of the Gospel have, in reality, one and the same source in the eschatological gift of the Holy Spirit. "The pledge of our inheritance, the first payment against the full redemption" (Eph 1:14), he awakens a longing for full and definitive life with Christ. At the same time he imbues us with the strength to spread the leaven of God's kingdom throughout the earth.

This anticipates, in a way, the coming of God's kingdom among men through Christ's resurrection. In him, the incarnate Word who died and rose for us, heaven descended to earth, and earth, in his glorified humanity, ascended to heaven. The risen Jesus is present among his people and in the heart of human history. Through the Holy Spirit, he fills those who open themselves to him in faith and love; indeed, he gradually transfigures them, making them share in his own glorified life. They now live and act in the world with their gaze always focused on the final goal: "If then you have been raised with Christ," St. Paul urges, "seek the things that are above, where Christ is seated at the right hand of God" (Col 3:1–4). Believers are therefore called to witness in the world to Christ's resurrection, and at the same time, to build a new society.

The sacramental sign par excellence of the ultimate realities, already anticipated and made present in the Church, is the *Eucharist*. In the Eucharist the Spirit, invoked in the *epiclesis,* "transubstantiates" the sensible reality of the bread and wine into the new reality of Christ's body and blood. In the Eucharist the risen Lord is truly present, and in him, humanity and the universe receive the seal of the new creation. In the Eucharist we have a taste of the definitive realities, and the world starts to become what it will be at the Lord's final coming.

The Eucharist, the summit of Christian life, not only shapes the personal life of the Christian but also the life of the ecclesial community, and in some way, that of all society. The People of God receive from the Eucharist that divine energy which prompts them to live deeply the communion of love signified and brought about by participation in the one table. This also results in a desire to share material goods in a spirit of brotherhood, using them to build the kingdom of God (Acts 2:42–45). In this way the Church becomes "bread broken" for the world: for the people among whom she lives and especially for the most needy. The celebration of the Eucharist is the source of the various works of charity and mutual aid, of missionary activity and the different forms of Christian witness, which help the world to understand the Church's vocation according to God's plan.

In addition, the Eucharist keeps alive the call not to be conformed to this world's mentality, and to live in expectation of Christ "until he comes." Thus, the Eucharist teaches the People of God how to purify and perfect their human activities by immersing them in the paschal mystery of the cross and resurrection.

This is how we understand the true meaning of Christian hope. In turning our gaze toward the "new heavens and new earth" in which righteousness dwells (cf. 2 Pt 3:13), "the expectation of a new earth must not weaken but rather stimulate our concern for cultivating this one. For here grows the body of a new human family, a body which even now is able to give some kind of foreshadowing of the new age" (*GS* 39). The message of hope offered by the Christian community, in particular, should be kneaded into the cultural, social, economic and political involvement of the lay faithful as leaven of the resurrection.

If it is true that earthly progress must be distinguished from the growth of God's kingdom (cf. *GS* 39), it is also true that in God's kingdom, brought to completion at the end of time, "charity and its works will remain (cf. 1 Cor 13:8; Col 3:14)" (*GS* 39). This means that everything accomplished in the love of Christ anticipates the final resurrection and the coming of the kingdom of God.

Thus, Christian spirituality appears in its true light: it is not a spirituality of flight from or rejection of the world, nor can it be reduced to mere temporal activity. Imbued by the Spirit with the life poured out by the Redeemer, it is a spirituality of the transfiguration of the world and of hope in the coming of God's kingdom. As a result, Christians can discover that when the achievements of thought and art, of science and technology, are lived in a Gospel spirit, they witness to the spreading of God's Spirit in all earthly realities. Thus, the voice of the Spirit and the Bride who cry out: "Come!... Come, Lord Jesus" (Rev 22:17–20) can be strongly heard, not only in prayer but also in our daily effort to prepare God's kingdom in history. It is the stupendous conclusion of revelation and, we can say, the Christian seal on history.

General audience of December 2, 1998

Mary's Motherhood Is Linked to the Spirit

To conclude our reflection on the Holy Spirit in this year dedicated to him on our journey to the Great Jubilee, we lift our eyes to Mary. Her consent given at the annunciation 2000 years ago represents the starting point of humanity's new history. The Son of God became incarnate and began to dwell among us when Mary said to the angel: "Behold, I am the handmaid of the Lord; let it be to me according to your word" (Lk 1:38).

Mary's cooperation with the Holy Spirit, shown in the annunciation and the visitation, was expressed in an attitude of continual docility to the Paraclete's inspirations. Conscious of the mystery of her divine Son, Mary let herself be guided by the Spirit to act in a way appropriate to her mission as mother. As a true woman of prayer, the Virgin asked the Holy Spirit to complete the work begun at conception, so that her child would grow "in wisdom and stature and favor with God and man" (Lk 2:52). Thus, Mary is presented as a model for parents by showing the need to call upon the Holy Spirit to find the right way in the difficult task of education.

The story of Jesus' presentation in the temple coincides with an important intervention of the Holy Spirit. Mary and Joseph went to the temple to "present" (cf. Lk 2:22), that is, to offer Jesus according to the law of Moses, which prescribed the redemption of the firstborn son and the purification of the mother. Experiencing the profound meaning of this rite as an expression of sincere offering, they were enlightened by the words Simeon spoke under the special impulse of the Holy Spirit.

Luke's account explicitly stresses the influence of the Holy Spirit on the life of this elderly man. The Spirit had promised him that he would not die without having seen the Messiah. And so, "inspired by the Spirit he came into the temple" (2:27), just as Mary and Joseph were bringing the child there. The Holy Spirit arranged the meeting. He inspired in the elderly Simeon a canticle celebrating the future of the child who came as "a light for revelation to the Gentiles" and "for glory to your people Israel" (Lk 2:32). Mary and Joseph marveled at these words that widened Jesus' mission to include all peoples.

Again, it was the Spirit who led Simeon to make a sorrowful prophecy: Jesus will be "a sign of contradiction," and "a sword will pierce [Mary's] soul" (Lk 2:34–35). With these words the Holy Spirit prepared Mary for the great trial that awaited her and gave to the rite of presenting her child the value of a sacrifice offered for love. When Mary took her son from Simeon's arms, she understood that she was receiving him in order to offer him. Her motherhood would be involved in Jesus' destiny, and any opposition to him would touch her heart as well.

Mary's presence at the cross is the sign that the mother followed to the end the sorrowful way the Holy Spirit had marked out through the mouth of Simeon. In the words Jesus spoke on Calvary to his Mother and to the beloved disciple, we see another feature of the Holy Spirit's action: he ensures that the sacrifice is fruitful. Jesus' words themselves reveal a

"Marian" aspect of this fruitfulness: "Woman, behold your son" (Jn 19:26). In these words the Holy Spirit does not explicitly appear. But since the event of the cross, like Christ's entire life, takes place in the Holy Spirit (cf. *DViv* 40–41), it is precisely in the same Spirit that the Savior asks his Mother to consent to her Son's sacrifice in order to become the mother of a multitude of children. He ensures that this supreme offering of Jesus' Mother will have immense fruit: a new motherhood destined to spread to all men and women.

From the cross the Savior wished to pour out upon humanity rivers of living water (cf. Jn 7:38), that is, the abundance of the Holy Spirit. But he wanted this outpouring of grace to be linked to a mother's face, *his* Mother's. Mary now appears as the new Eve, mother of the living, or the Daughter of Zion, mother of all peoples. The gift of a universal mother was included in the Messiah's redeeming mission. After the two statements: "Woman, behold your son!" and "Behold, your mother!" the evangelist writes: "After this, Jesus, knowing that all was now finished..." (Jn 19:26–28). From this scene we can sense the harmony of God's plan regarding Mary's role in the saving action of the Holy Spirit. In the mystery of the Incarnation, her cooperation with the Spirit played an essential role; in the mystery of the birth and development of God's children, Mary's maternal assistance also accompanies the work of the Holy Spirit.

In the light of Christ's statement on Calvary, Mary's presence in the community as it waited for Pentecost acquired its full value. St. Luke, who called attention to Mary's role in Jesus' birth, wanted to stress her significant presence at the Church's birth. The community was composed not only of the apostles and disciples, but also of women; the only one Luke names is "Mary, the Mother of Jesus" (Acts 1:14).

The Bible offers us no further information about Mary after the drama on Calvary. But it is very important to know that she shared in the life of the early community and in its fervent, unanimous prayer. Without doubt, she was present at the outpouring of the Spirit on the day of Pentecost. The Spirit who already dwelt in Mary, working marvels of grace in her, came down again into her heart, communicating the gifts and charisms necessary for the exercise of her spiritual motherhood.

Mary continues to exercise in the Church the motherhood entrusted to her by Christ. In this maternal mission, the humble servant of the Lord does not compete with the role of the Holy Spirit; on the contrary, she is called by the same Spirit to cooperate in a maternal way with him. He continually revives the Church's memory of Jesus' words to the beloved disciple: "Behold, your mother!" and invites believers to love Mary as Christ loved her. As the bond with Mary grows deeper, so the action of the Spirit in the life of the Church becomes more fruitful.

General audience of December 9, 1998

GOD THE FATHER

On Pilgrimage to the Father's House

"I came from the Father and have come into the world; again, I am leaving the world and going to the Father" (Jn 16:28). With these words of Jesus, today we begin a new cycle of catecheses focused on the figure of God the Father, thus following the thematic guide offered by *Tertio Millennio Adveniente* in preparation for the Great Jubilee of the Year 2000.

In the first year's cycle, we reflected on Jesus Christ the one Savior. Indeed, as a celebration of the Son of God's entry into human history, the Jubilee has a strong Christological tone. We meditated on the meaning of time, which reached its focal point in the Redeemer's birth 2000 years ago. While this event inaugurated the Christian era, it also opened a new phase of renewal of humanity and the universe, in expectation of Christ's last coming.

Then, in the catecheses of the second year of preparation for the Jubilee, our attention was turned to the Holy Spirit, whom Jesus sent from the Father. We reflected on him in the work of creation and in history, as Person-Love and Person-Gift. We emphasized his power, which draws out of chaos a cosmos rich in order and beauty. Divine life is communicated in him, and with him history becomes the way to salvation.

We now want to spend the third year of preparation for the now imminent Jubilee as a pilgrimage to the Father's house. Thus we set out on the journey, which starting from the Father, leads creatures back to the Father, in accordance with the loving plan fully revealed in Christ. The journey to the Jubilee must become a great act of praise to the Father (cf. *TMA* 49), so that in him the whole Trinity may be glorified.

The words of the Gospel that show us Jesus as the Son and Revealer of the Father will be the starting point for our reflection. His teaching, his ministry, his style of life, everything in him refers to the Father (cf. Jn 5:19, 36; 8:28; 14:10; 17:6). The Father is the center of Jesus' life, and Jesus in turn is the only way that gives us access to him. "No one comes to the Father, but by me" (Jn 14:6). Jesus is the meeting point of human beings with the Father, who is made visible in him: "He who has seen me has seen the Father; how can you say, 'Show us the Father?' Do you not believe that I am in the Father and the Father in me?" (Jn 14:9–10).

The most expressive manifestation of Jesus' relationship with the Father is his condition after the resurrection, the summit of his mission and the foundation of new and eternal life for those who believe in him. But the union between the Son and the Father, like that between the Son and believers, comes through the mystery of the "lifting up" of Jesus, according to a characteristic expression of John's Gospel. With the term "lifting up," the evangelist indicates both the crucifixion and the glorification of Christ. Both are reflected on the believer: "So must the Son of Man be lifted up, that whoever believes in him may have eternal life. For God so loved the world that he gave his only Son, that whoever believes in him should not perish but have eternal life" (Jn 3:14–16). This "eternal life" is no less than the participation of believers in the very life of the risen Jesus. It consists in their insertion into the movement of love uniting the Father and the Son, who are one (cf. Jn 10:30; 17:21–22).

The deep communion in which the Father, the Son and believers meet includes the Holy Spirit. For he is the eternal bond that unites the Father and the Son and involves human beings in this ineffable mystery of love. Given to them as the "Consoler," the Spirit "dwells" in the disciples of Christ (cf. Jn 14:16–17), making the Trinity present.

According to the Evangelist John, Jesus said to his disciples, precisely when he was promising to send the Paraclete: "In that day you will know that I am in my Father, and you in me, and I in you" (14:20). The Holy Spirit introduces man into the mystery of the Trinitarian life. "The Spirit of truth" (Jn 15:26; 16:13), he acts deep within believers, making the Truth that is Christ shine in their minds.

St. Paul also stresses our orientation to the Father through the Spirit of Christ who dwells in us. For the Apostle this is a true sonship, which enables us to call God the Father by the same familiar name that Jesus used: *Abba* (cf. Rom 8:15).

All creation is involved in this new dimension of our relationship with God, and "waits with eager longing for the revealing of the sons of God" (Rom 8:19). Creation has also "been groaning in travail together until now" (Rom 8:22), in expectation of the total redemption that will reestablish and perfect the harmony of the cosmos in Christ. In describing this mystery, which unites human beings and all creation with the Father, the Apostle expresses the role of Christ and the action of the Spirit. Through Christ, "the image of the invisible God" (Col 1:15), all things were created. He is "the beginning, the firstborn from the dead" (Col 1:18). In him "all things are united, things in heaven and things on earth" (cf. Eph 1:10), and it is his task to deliver them to the Father (cf. 1 Cor 15:24), so that God may be "everything to everyone" (1 Cor 15:28). This journey of humanity and the world to the Father is sustained by the power of the Holy Spirit, who helps us in our weakness and "intercedes for us with sighs too deep for words" (Rom 8:26).

Thus, the New Testament introduces us very clearly into this movement that flows from the Father and back to the Father. Let us consider it with special attention in this final year of preparation for the Great Jubilee.

General audience of December 16, 1998

God Gradually Reveals His Fatherhood

"You have made us for yourself, O Lord, and our heart is restless until it rests in you" (*Conf.,* 1, 1). This famous statement, which introduces the *Confessions* of St. Augustine, vividly expresses the irrepressible need that prompts man to seek the face of God. The various religious traditions testify to this experience. "From ancient times down to the present, there is found among various peoples a certain perception of that hidden power which hovers over the course of things and over the events of human history; at times, some indeed have come to the recognition of a Supreme Being, or even of a Father" (*NA* 2).

In fact, many prayers of the world's religious literature express the conviction that the Supreme Being can be perceived and called upon as father, who is reached through experience of the affectionate care received from one's earthly father. It is precisely this relationship that in certain currents of contemporary atheism has given rise to the suspicion that the very idea of God is a projection of the father figure, but this suspicion is groundless.

It is true, however, that on the basis of his experience, man is sometimes tempted to imagine the divinity with anthropomorphic features that too closely reflect the human world. The search for God thus continues "gropingly," as Paul said in his discourse to the Athenians (cf. Acts 17:27). It is therefore necessary to bear in mind this chiaroscuro aspect of religious experience by recognizing that only the full revelation in which God manifests himself can dispel these shadows and ambiguities and make the light shine brightly.

After the example of Paul, who in his discourse to the Athenians cites a verse by the poet Aratus about man's divine origins (cf. Acts 17:28), the Church looks with respect on attempts made by the different religions to discern the face of God, distinguishing in their beliefs what is acceptable from what is incompatible with Christian revelation. In this sense, the perception of God as universal Father of the world and of mankind must be considered a positive religious insight. However, the idea of a divinity ruled by his own willfulness and caprice is unacceptable. Among the ancient Greeks, for example, the Good as a supreme and divine being was also called father, but the god Zeus displayed his fatherhood in anger and malice as much as in kindness. We read in the *Odyssey:* "Father Zeus, you are the most deadly of gods: you take no pity on men after begetting them and abandoning them to misfortune and oppressive sorrows" (XX, 201–203).

However, the need for a God who is above capricious willfulness was also found among the ancient Greeks, as evidenced, for example, by the poet Cleanthes' "Hymn to Zeus." The idea of a divine father, prepared to make the generous gift of life and providing for its necessities, but who at the same time is severe and punishing — and not always for an obvious reason — is linked in ancient societies to the institution of patriarchy, and transfers the way it is most commonly conceived to the religious level.

In Israel the recognition of God's fatherhood was gradual and was continually endangered by the temptation to idolatry, which

the prophets vigorously denounced: "They say to a tree, '
my father,' and to a stone, 'You gave me birth'" (Jer 2:27). In fact,
for biblical religious experience the perception of God as
Father is linked less to his creative work than to his saving
interventions in history, by which he established a special covenant relationship with Israel. God often lamented that this
fatherly love had not received a suitable response: "The Lord
has spoken: 'Sons have I reared and brought up, but they have
rebelled against me'" (Is 1:2).

To Israel, God's fatherhood seems more solid than human
fatherhood: "For my father and my mother have forsaken me,
but the Lord will take me up" (Ps 27:10). The Psalmist, who
had this painful experience of abandonment and found in God a
father more caring than his earthly parent, shows us how he
reached this goal: "Of you my heart speaks, you my glance
seeks; your presence, O Lord, I seek" (Ps 27:8). To seek the
face of God is a necessary journey, to be taken with sincerity of
heart and constant commitment. Only the hearts of the righteous
can rejoice in seeking the face of the Lord (cf. Ps 105:3 f.), and so
it is on them that the fatherly face of God can shine (cf. Ps
119:135; cf. also 31:17; 67:2; 80:4; 8:20). By observing the
divine law, one also fully enjoys the protection of the God of
the covenant. The blessing with which God rewards his people
through the priestly mediation of Aaron insists precisely on this
luminous revealing of God's face: "The Lord make his face
shine upon you and be gracious to you. The Lord lift up his
countenance upon you and give you peace" (Num 6:25 f.).

From the time Jesus came into the world, the search for the
face of God the Father has taken on an even more significant
aspect. Jesus based his teaching on his own experience as Son,
and confirmed the conception of God as Father already outlined
in the Old Testament. In fact, he constantly stressed it, lived it
in an intimate and ineffable way, and offered it as a plan of life
for anyone wishing to be saved.

Above all, Jesus stands in an absolutely unique relationship to the divine fatherhood, revealing himself as "Son" and offering himself as the one way to reach the Father. To Philip, who asked "show us the Father and we shall be satisfied" (Jn 14:8), he replied that knowing him means knowing the Father, because the Father works through him (cf. Jn 14:8–11). Therefore, those who want to meet the Father must believe in the Son. Through him God does not merely assure us of his providential fatherly care, but communicates his own life, making us "sons in the Son." This is what the Apostle John emphasizes with a deep sense of gratitude: "See what love the Father has given us, that we should be called children of God, and so we are" (1 Jn 3:1).

General audience of January 13, 1999

God Shows Himself a Father to Israel

As we said in our last catechesis, the people of Israel experienced God as father. Like all other peoples, they sensed in him the fatherly feelings drawn from the universal experience of an earthly father. Above all, they discerned in God an especially paternal attitude, based on direct knowledge of his special saving action (cf. *CCC* 238).

From the first point of view, that of universal human experience, Israel recognized the divine fatherhood through wonder at the creation and renewal of life. The miracle of a child being formed in his mother's womb cannot be explained without God's intervention, as the Psalmist recalls: "For you formed my inward parts, you knit me together in my mother's womb" (Ps 139:13). Israel could also see God as Father by analogy with other figures who had a public and especially religious function and were considered fathers, such as priests (cf. Jgs 17:10; 18:19; Gn 45:8) or prophets (cf. 2 Kgs 2:12). Moreover, it is easy to understand how the respect for fathers required by Israelite society led Jews to see God as a demanding father. In fact, Mosaic law is very severe with children who do not respect their parents, to the point of prescribing the death penalty for anyone who strikes or merely curses his father or mother (Ex 21:15, 17).

But beyond this representation suggested by human experience, a more specific image of the divine fatherhood developed
in Israel on the basis of God's saving intervention. By saving
them from slavery in Egypt, God called Israel to enter into a
covenant relationship with him and even to consider itself his
firstborn. God thereby shows he is a father in a unique way, as is
clear from his words to Moses, "You shall say to Pharaoh, 'Thus
says the Lord, Israel is my firstborn son'" (Ex 4:22). In their
hour of desperation, this people-son will be able to call upon the
heavenly Father by the same privileged title, so that he will once
again renew the miracle of the Exodus: "Have mercy, O Lord,
upon the people called by your name, upon Israel, whom you
have likened to a firstborn son" (Sir 36:11). By virtue of this
situation, Israel is bound to observe a law that distinguishes it
from other peoples, to whom it must bear witness of the divine
fatherhood that it enjoys in a special way. Deuteronomy stresses
this in the context of the commitments stemming from the
covenant: "You are the sons of the Lord your God.... For you are
a people holy to the Lord your God, and the Lord has chosen
you to be a people for his own possession, out of all the peoples
that are on the face of the earth" (Dt 14:1f.).

By not observing God's law, Israel acted in opposition to
its filial status, earning reproofs from the heavenly Father:
"You were unmindful of the Rock that begot you and you
forgot the God who gave you birth" (Dt 32:18). This filial
status includes all the members of the people of Israel, but it
was applied in a unique way to the descendant and successor of
David, according to Nathan's well-known prophecy in which
God says: "I will be his father, and he shall be my son" (2 Sam
7:14; 1 Chr 17:13). On the basis of this prophecy, the messianic
tradition affirms a divine sonship for the Messiah: "You are my
son; today I have begotten you" (Ps 2:7; cf. 110:3).

The divine fatherhood in Israel's regard is marked by an
intense, constant and compassionate love. Despite the people's

infidelities and the consequent threats of punishment, God shows himself incapable of forsaking his love. He expresses it in terms of deep tenderness, even when he is forced to lament his children's lack of response: "It was I who taught Ephraim to walk, who took them up in my arms, but they did not know that I healed them. I led them with cords of compassion, with bands of love; I fostered them like one who raises an infant to his cheeks, and I bent down to them and fed them.... How can I give you up, O Ephraim! How can I hand you over, O Israel?... My heart recoils within me; my compassion grows warm and tender" (Hos 11:3f; Jer 31:20).

Even the reproof becomes the expression of a privileged love, as the Book of Proverbs explains: "My son, do not despise the Lord's discipline or be weary of his reproof, for the Lord reproves him whom he loves, as a father the son in whom he delights" (3:11–12).

Such a divine fatherhood, which at the same time is so "human" in its forms of expression, includes all the features that are usually attributed to a mother's love. Although rare, the Old Testament images in which God is compared to a mother are extremely significant. We read, for example, "Zion said, 'The Lord has forsaken me, my Lord has forgotten me.' 'Can a woman forget her suckling child, that she should have no compassion on the son of her womb?' Even if these forget, yet I will not forget you" (Is 49:14–15). And again: "As one whom his mother comforts, so I will comfort you" (Is 66:13).

Thus, God's attitude to Israel also appears with maternal features, which express tenderness and understanding (cf. *CCC* 239). This love, which God lavishes on his people in such abundance, prompts the elderly Tobit to proclaim: "Acknowledge him before the nations, O sons of Israel; for he has scattered us among them. Make his greatness known there and exalt him in the presence of all the living, because he is our Lord and God; he is our Father forever" (Tob 13:3–4).

A Unique Relationship with the Father

"Blessed be the God and Father of our Lord Jesus Christ" (Eph 1:3). Paul's words are a good introduction to the newness of our knowledge of the Father as it unfolds in the New Testament. Here God appears in his Trinitarian reality. His fatherhood is no longer limited to showing his relationship with creatures, but expresses the fundamental relationship that characterizes his inner life; it is no longer a generic feature of God, but the property of the First Person in God. In his Trinitarian mystery, God is a Father in his very being; he is always a Father, since from all eternity he generates the Word who is consubstantial with him and united to him in the Holy Spirit, "who proceeds from the Father and the Son." In his redemptive Incarnation, the Word unites himself with us, precisely in order to bring us into this filial life that he possesses from all eternity. The Evangelist John says: "To all who received him, who believed in his name, he gave power to become children of God" (1:12).

Jesus' experience is the basis for this specific revelation of the Father. It is clear from his words and attitudes that he experiences his relationship with the Father in a wholly unique way. In the Gospels we can see how Jesus distinguished "his sonship from that of his disciples by never saying 'Our Father,' except to command them: 'You, then, pray like this: "Our Father,"' and he emphasized this distinction, saying, 'my Father and your Father'" (*CCC* 443).

Even as a boy he answered Mary and Joseph, who had been looking for him anxiously: "Did you not know that I must be in my Father's house?" (Lk 2:48 f.). To the Jews who had been persecuting him because he had worked a miraculous cure on the Sabbath, he replied: "My Father is working still, and I am working" (Jn 5:17). On the cross Jesus prayed to the Father to forgive his executioners and to receive his spirit (Lk 23:34, 46). The distinction between the way Jesus perceives God's father-hood in relation to himself and in relation to all other human beings is rooted in his consciousness. He emphasized it in the words he addressed to Mary Magdalen after the resurrection: "Do not hold me, for I have not yet ascended to the Father, but go to my brethren and say to them, 'I am ascending to my Father and your Father, to my God and your God'" (Jn 20:17).

Jesus' relationship with the Father is unique. He knew that through him the Father reveals his glory, even when men may doubt it and need to be convinced by him. We see all this in the episode of the raising of Lazarus: "So they took away the stone. Jesus lifted up his eyes and said, 'Father, I thank you that you have heard me. I know that you hear me always, but I have said this on account of the people standing by, that they may believe that you sent me'" (Jn 11:41f.). Because of this unique under-standing, Jesus can present himself as the One who reveals the Father with a knowledge that is the fruit of an intimate and mysterious reciprocity, as he emphasizes in his joyful hymn: "All things have been delivered to me by me Father, and no one knows the Son except the Father, and no one knows the Father except the Son, and anyone to whom the Son chooses to reveal him" (Mt 11:27; cf. *CCC* 240). For his part the Father expresses the Son's unique relationship with him by calling him his "beloved" Son, as he did at the baptism in the Jordan (cf. Mk 1:11) and at the Transfiguration (cf. Mk 9:7). Jesus is also depicted as the son in a special sense in the parable of the wicked tenants, who first mistreat the two servants and then the "beloved son" of the vineyard owner, sent to collect some of the fruit of the vineyard (Mk 12:1–11, especially v. 6).

The Gospel of Mark has preserved for us the Aramaic word *"Abba"* (cf. 14:36), with which Jesus, during his painful hour in Gethsemane, called on God, praying to him to let the cup of the passion pass him by. In the same episode Matthew's Gospel has given us the translation "my Father" (cf. 26:39, also v. 42), while Luke simply has "Father" (22:42). The Aramaic word, which we can translate into contemporary language as "dad" or "daddy," expresses the affectionate tenderness of a child. Jesus used it in an original way to address God, and in the full maturity of his life that was about to end on the cross, to indicate the close relationship that even at that critical moment bound him to his Father. "Abba" indicates the extraordinary closeness that exists between Jesus and God the Father, an intimacy unprecedented in the biblical or non-biblical religious context. Through the death and resurrection of Jesus, the only Son of this Father, we too, as St. Paul said, are raised to the dignity of sons and have received the Holy Spirit who prompts us to cry "Abba! Father!" (cf. Rom 8:15; Gal 4:6). This simple, childish expression, in daily use in Jesus' time and among all peoples, thus acquired a highly significant doctrinal meaning to express the unique divine Fatherhood in relation to Jesus and his disciples.

Although he felt united with the Father in such an intimate way, Jesus admitted that he did not know the hour of the final and decisive coming of the kingdom. "But of that day and hour no one knows, not even the angels of heaven, nor the Son, but the Father only" (Mt 24:36). This indicates the "emptying of himself" proper to the Incarnation, which concealed the eschatological end of the world from his human nature. In this way Jesus disappoints human calculations, in order to invite us to be watchful and to trust in the Father's providential intervention. On the other hand, from the standpoint of the Gospels, the intimacy and absoluteness of his being "Son" is in no way prejudiced by this lack of knowledge. On the contrary, precisely because he is so united with us, he becomes crucial for us before the Father: "Every one who acknowledges me before men, I also will acknowledge before my Father who is in heaven, but whoever denies me before men, I also will deny before my Father who is in heaven" (Mt 10:32 f.).

Acknowledging Jesus before men is indispensable for being acknowledged by him before the Father. In other words, our filial relationship with the heavenly Father depends on our courageous fidelity to Jesus, his beloved Son.

General audience of March 3, 1999

Revelation of the Trinitarian Mystery

As we saw in our last catechesis, Jesus enjoys a very special relationship with "his" Father through his words and actions. John's Gospel stresses that Jesus communicates to men the fruit of this intimate and extraordinary union: "The Father and I are one" (10:30). And again: "All that the Father has is mine" (16:15). There is a reciprocity between the Father and the Son in what they know of each other (cf. 10:15), in what they are (cf. 14:10), in what they do (cf. 5:19; 10:38), and in what they possess: "Everything of mine is yours, and everything of yours is mine" (17:10). It is a reciprocal exchange which finds full expression in the glory Jesus receives from the Father in the supreme mystery of his death and resurrection, after he himself had given it to the Father during his earthly life: "Father, the hour has come; glorify your Son that the Son may glorify you.... I glorified you on earth...and now Father, glorify me in your own presence..." (17:1, 4 f.).

This essential union with the Father not only accompanies Jesus' activity, but defines his whole being. "The Incarnation of God's Son reveals that God is the eternal Father and that the Son is consubstantial with the Father, which means that, in the Father and with the Father, the Son is one and the same God" (*CCC* 262). The Evangelist John stresses that the religious leaders of the people reacted precisely to this divine claim, for they could not tolerate him calling God his Father and, therefore, making himself equal to God (5:18; cf. 10:33; 19:7).

In virtue of this consonance in being and acting, Jesus reveals the Father in words and deeds: "No one has ever seen God: the only Son, who is in the bosom of the Father, he has made him known" (Jn 1:18). As we are told in the synoptic Gospels (cf. Mk 1:11; Mt 3:17; Lk 3:22), the fact that Christ is the "beloved" one is proclaimed at his baptism. The Evangelist John refers this back to its Trinitarian root, that is, to the mysterious existence of the Word "with" the Father (1:1), who generates him from all eternity.

Starting with the Son, New Testament reflection and the theology based on it have plumbed the mystery of God's "fatherhood." The Father is the absolute principle in Trinitarian life, the one who has no origin and from whom the divine life flows. The unity of the three Persons is a sharing in the one divine essence, but in the dynamism of reciprocal relations that have their source and foundation in the Father. "It is the Father who generates, the Son who is begotten, and the Holy Spirit who proceeds" (Fourth Lateran Council: *DS* 804).

The Apostle John offers us a key to this mystery that infinitely surpasses our understanding, when in his First Letter he proclaims: *"God is love"* (4:8). This summit of revelation indicates that God is *agape,* that is, the gratuitous and total gift of self which Christ proved to us, especially by his death on the cross. The Father's infinite love for the world is revealed in Christ's sacrifice (cf. Jn 3:16; Rom 5:8). The capacity to love infinitely, to give oneself without reserve or measure, belongs to God. By virtue of his being Love, even before his free creation of the world, he is Father in the divine life itself: a loving Father who generates the beloved Son and gives rise with him to the Holy Spirit, the Person-Love, the reciprocal bond of communion.

On this basis the Christian faith understands the equality of the three Divine Persons: the Son and the Spirit are equal to the Father, not as autonomous principles, as though they were three gods, but because they receive the whole divine life from the Father and are distinct from him and from one another only in the diversity of their relations (cf. *CCC* 254).

A great mystery, a mystery of love, an ineffable mystery, before which words must give way to the silence of wonder and worship. A divine mystery that challenges and involves us, because a share in the Trinitarian life was given to us through grace, through the redemptive Incarnation of the Word and the gift of the Holy Spirit: "Anyone who loves me will be true to my word and my Father will love him; we will come to him and make our dwelling place with him" (Jn 14:23).

For us believers, the reciprocity between the Father and the Son thus becomes a principle of new life that enables us to participate in the very fullness of the divine life: "Whoever confesses that Jesus is the Son of God, God abides in him and he in God" (1 Jn 4:15). The dynamism of Trinitarian life is lived by creatures in such a way that everything is directed *to* the Father, *through* Jesus Christ, *in the* Holy Spirit. The *Catechism of the Catholic Church* stresses this: "The whole Christian life is a communion with each of the divine persons, without in any way separating them. Everyone who glorifies the Father does so through the Son in the Holy Spirit" (n. 259).

The Son has become "the firstborn among many brethren" (Rom 8:29); through his death the Father communicated new life to us (1 Pt 1:3; cf. also Rom 8:32; Eph 1:3), so that we might call upon him in the Holy Spirit with the same term that Jesus used: *Abba* (Rom 8:15; Gal 4:6). St. Paul explains this mystery further, saying that "the Father...has qualified us to share in the inheritance of the saints in light. He has delivered us from the dominion of darkness and transferred us to the kingdom of his beloved Son" (Col 1:12–13). This is how the

Book of Revelation describes the eschatological destiny of whoever fights and conquers the power of evil with Christ: "He who conquers, I will grant him to sit with me on my throne, as I myself conquered and sat down with my Father on his throne" (Rev 3:21). Christ's promise opens to us the wondrous prospect of sharing in his heavenly intimacy with the Father.

General audience of March 10, 1999

Eternal Life Means Knowing the Father

At the dramatic moment when he was preparing to face death, Jesus ended his great farewell discourse (cf. Jn 13ff.) with a wonderful prayer to the Father. It can be considered a spiritual testament in which Jesus returns to the Father's hands the mandate he had received: to make his love known to the world, through the gift of eternal life (cf. Jn 17:2). The life he offers is significantly explained as a gift of knowledge. "This is eternal life, that they know you, the only true God, and Jesus Christ whom you have sent" (Jn 17:3).

In the biblical language of the Old and New Testaments, knowledge is not only intellectual, but usually implies a whole human person including his capacity to love. This knowledge leads to an "encounter" with God, as part of that process which the Eastern theological tradition likes to call "divinization," which takes place through the interior, transforming action of God's Spirit (cf. St. Gregory of Nyssa, *Oratio catechetica,* 37: *PG* 45, 98B). We already touched on these topics in the catechesis for the year of the Holy Spirit. Returning now to the words of Jesus just quoted, we want to reflect on what it means to have a living knowledge of God the Father.

God can be known as father at various levels, depending on the perspective from which we look at him and the aspect of the mystery considered. There is a natural knowledge of God that is based on creation; this leads us to recognize him as the origin and transcendent cause of the world and of man, and in this sense to perceive his fatherhood. This knowledge is deepened in the progressive light of revelation, that is, on the basis of God's words and his interventions in salvation history (cf. *CCC* 287).

In the Old Testament, knowing God as father means returning to the origins of the people of the covenant: "Is he not your father, who created you, who made you and established you?" (Dt 32:6). The reference to God as father guarantees and maintains the unity of those who belong to the same family: "Have we not all the one Father? Has not the one God created us?" (Mal 2:10). God is recognized as father even when he rebukes the son for his own good: "For the Lord reproves him whom he loves, as a father the son in whom he delights" (Prv 3:12). Obviously, a father can always be called upon in times of discouragement: "I called out: O Lord, you are my father, you are my champion and my savior; do not abandon me in time of trouble, in the midst of storms and dangers" (Sir 51:10).

In all these forms, the values experienced in human fatherhood are applied preeminently to God. We immediately realize that it is impossible to know the full meaning of this fatherhood except to the extent that God himself reveals it.

In the events of salvation history there is a gradual revelation of the Father's initiative: by his interior action he opens the hearts of believers to accepting the incarnate Son. By knowing Jesus, they will also be able to know him, the Father. This is what Jesus himself teaches in reply to Thomas: "If you had known me, you would have known my Father" (Jn 14:7; cf. vv. 7–10).

Thus, it is necessary to believe in Jesus and to see him, the light of the world, in order not to remain in the darkness of ignorance (cf. Jn 12:44–46), and to know that his teaching

comes from God (cf. Jn 7:17 f.). On this condition it is possible
to know the Father and to become capable of worshiping him
"in spirit and truth" (Jn 4:23). This living knowledge is inseparable from love. It is communicated by Jesus, as he said in his
priestly prayer: "O righteous Father...I made known to them
your name and I will make it known, that the love with which
you have loved me may be in them" (Jn 17:25–26).

"When we pray to the Father, we are *in communion with
him* and with his Son, Jesus Christ. Then we know and recognize
him with an ever new sense of wonder" (*CCC* 2781). Knowing
the Father, then, means finding in him the source of our being
and our unity as members of one family, but it also means being
immersed in a "supernatural" life, the very life of God.

The message of the Son, therefore, remains the royal road
for knowing the Father and making him known; in fact, as the
expressive words of St. Irenaeus recall, "knowledge of the
Father is the Son" (*Adv. Haer.,* IV 6, 7: *PG* 7, 990B). This
possibility is offered to Israel but also to the Gentiles, as Paul
emphasizes: "Is God the God of Jews only? Is he not the God of
Gentiles also? Yes, of Gentiles also since God is one, and he
will justify the circumcised on the ground of their faith and the
uncircumcised through their faith" (Rom 3:29f.). God is one
and he is the Father of all, who is eager to offer everyone the
salvation brought by the Son: this is what John's Gospel calls
the gift of eternal life. This gift must be accepted and communicated on the surge of that gratitude which led Paul to say: "We
are bound to give thanks to God always for you, brethren
beloved by the Lord, because God chose you from the beginning to be saved through sanctification by the Spirit and belief
in the truth" (2 Thes 2:13).

General audience of March 17, 1999

The Father's Love Is Generous and Providential

Continuing our meditation on God the Father, today we would like to reflect on his generous and providential love. "The witness of Scripture is unanimous that the solicitude of divine providence is *concrete* and *immediate;* God cares for all, from the least things to the great events of the world and its history" (*CCC* 303). We can begin with a text from the Book of Wisdom, in which divine Providence is seen guiding a boat in the middle of the sea: "It is your providence, O Father, that steers its course, because you have given it a path in the sea and a safe way through the waves, showing that you can save from every danger, so that even if a man lacks skill, he may put to sea" (14:3–4).

In a psalm we find another image of the sea, plowed by ships and teeming with animals large and small, which recalls the nourishment that God provides for all living things: "These all look to you, to give them their food in due season. When you give to them, they gather it up; when you open your hand, they are filled with good things" (104:27–28).

The image of the ship in the middle of the sea well describes our situation before our providential Father. As Jesus

says, he "makes his sun rise on the evil and on the good, and
sends rain on the just and on the unjust" (Mt 5:45). However, in
the light of this message of the Father's providential love, we
naturally wonder how suffering can be explained. It is necessary to recognize that the problem of suffering is an enigma that
perplexes human reason. Divine revelation helps us understand
that it is not willed by God, since it entered the world because
of human sin (cf. Gn 3:16–19). "Almighty God...because he is
supremely good, would never allow any evil whatsoever to
exist in his works if he were not so all-powerful and good as to
cause good to emerge from evil itself" (St. Augustine, *Enchiridion on Faith, Hope and Charity,* 11, 3: *PL* 40, 236). In
this regard, the reassuring words that Joseph spoke to his brothers, who had sold him and later depended on his power, are
significant: "It was not you who sent me here but God.... As for
you, you meant evil against me, but God meant it for good, to
bring it about that many people should be kept alive, as they are
today" (Gn 45:8; 50:20).

God's plans do not coincide with those of man; they are
infinitely better, but often incomprehensible to the human
mind. The Book of Proverbs says: "A man's steps are ordered
by the Lord; how then can man understand his way?" (20:24).
In the New Testament, Paul will announce this consoling principle: "In everything, God works for good with those who love
him" (Rom 8:28).

What should be our attitude to God's providential and
farsighted action? We certainly should not wait passively for
what he sends us, but cooperate with him in bringing to
completion the work he has begun in us. We must be eager to
seek first the things of heaven. These must come first, as Jesus
said: "Seek first his kingdom and his righteousness" (Mt 6:33).
Other matters must not be the object of excessive concern,
because our heavenly Father knows our needs; this is what
Jesus teaches us when he asks his disciples for "childlike aban-

donment to the providence of our heavenly Father who takes care of his children's smallest needs" (*CCC* 305): "Do not seek what you are to eat and what you are to drink, nor be anxious of mind. For all the nations of the world seek these things, and your Father knows that you need them" (Lk 12:29 f.).

We are called to cooperate with God in an attitude of great trust. Jesus teaches us to ask the heavenly Father for our daily bread (cf. Mt 6:11; Lk 11:3). If we receive it with gratitude, we will also spontaneously remember that nothing belongs to us, and that we must be ready to give: "Give to everyone who begs from you, and of him who takes away your goods do not ask them again" (Lk 6:30).

The certainty that God loves us makes us trust in his fatherly providence even in life's most difficult moments. St. Teresa of Jesus admirably expresses this complete trust in God, the providential Father, even in the midst of adversity: "Let nothing trouble you; let nothing frighten you. Everything passes; God never changes. Patience obtains all. Whoever has God wants for nothing. God alone is enough" (*Poems,* 30).

Scripture offers us an eloquent example of total trust in God when it tells how Abraham reached the decision to sacrifice his son Isaac. In reality, God did not want the death of the son, but the faith of the father. And Abraham demonstrated it completely, for when Isaac asked him where the lamb was for the burnt offering, he dared to answer: "God will provide" (Gn 22:8). Then he immediately experienced the benevolent Providence of God, who saved the young boy and rewarded Abraham's faith, filling him with blessings.

Such texts must be interpreted, then, in light of revelation as a whole, which reaches its fullness in Jesus Christ. He teaches us to place great confidence in God even in the most difficult moments: nailed to the cross, Jesus abandoned himself totally to the Father: "Father, into your hands I commit my spirit" (Lk 23:46). With this attitude he raised to a sublime level what Job had summed up in his famous words: "The Lord gave and the Lord has taken away; blessed be the name of the Lord" (Jb 1:21). Even what is humanly a misfortune can be part of that great plan of infinite love in which the Father provides for our salvation.

General audience of March 24, 1999

The Demanding Love of God the Father

God the Father's love for us cannot leave us indifferent but seeks to be reciprocated with a constant commitment to love. This commitment takes on an ever deeper meaning the closer we draw to Jesus, who fully lives in communion with the Father, making himself a model for us.

In the cultural context of the Old Testament, paternal authority was absolute and was used as a term of comparison to describe the authority of God the Creator, who may not be contested. We read: "Woe to him who says to a father, 'What are you begetting?' or to a woman, 'With what are you in travail?' Thus says the Lord, the Holy One of Israel and his Maker: 'Will you question me about my children, or command me concerning the work of my hands?'" (Is 45:10 f.). A father also has the task of guiding his son and severely reprimanding him, if necessary. The Book of Proverbs recalls that this is also true of God: "The Lord reproves him whom he loves, as a father the son in whom he delights" (3:12; cf. Ps 103:13). The prophet Malachi, for his part, attests to God's compassionate affection for his children (3:17), but his is always a demanding love: "Remember the law of my servant Moses, the statutes and ordinances that I commanded him at Horeb for all Israel" (4:4).

The law that God gives his people is not a burden imposed by a tyrannical master, but the expression of fatherly love that shows the right path for human conduct and the condition for inheriting the divine promises. This is the sense of the injunction: "You shall keep the commandments of the Lord your God, by walking in his ways and by fearing him. For the Lord your God is bringing you into a good land" (Dt 8:5–7). Inasmuch as it ratifies the covenant between God and the children of Israel, the law is dictated by love. But to transgress it is not without consequences, bringing painful results that are, nevertheless, always governed by the logic of love, because they compel man to take salutary note of a constitutive dimension of his being. "It is in discovering the greatness of God's love that our heart is shaken by the horror and weight of sin and begins to fear offending God by sin and being separated from him" (*CCC* 1432).

If he separates himself from the Creator, man necessarily falls under the power of evil, death and nothingness. Obedience to God, on the contrary, is the source of life and blessing. The Book of Deuteronomy stresses this: "See, I have set before you this day life and good, death and evil. If you obey the commandments of the Lord your God that I command you this day, by loving the Lord your God, by walking in his ways and by keeping his statutes and his ordinances, then you shall live and multiply, and the Lord your God will bless you in the land that you are entering to take possession of " (30:15 f.).

Jesus did not abolish the law in regard to its fundamental values, but perfected it, as he himself said in the Sermon on the Mount: "Think not that I have come to abolish the law and the prophets; I have come not to abolish them, but to fulfill them" (Mt 5:17). Jesus identified the heart of the law with the precept of love and developed its radical demands. Broadening the Old Testament precept, he commanded us to love friends and enemies and explained this extension of the precept by referring to God's fatherhood: "So that you may be sons of the Father who is in heaven, for he makes his sun rise on the evil and on the good and sends rain on the just and on the unjust" (Mt 5:43–45; cf. *CCC* 2784).

A qualitative leap occurred with Jesus: he summed up the law and the prophets in a single norm, as simple in its formulation as difficult in its practice: "Whatever you wish that others would do to you, do so to them" (Mt 7:12). This is also presented as the way to be perfect as our heavenly Father (cf. Mt 5:48). Whoever acts in this way bears witness before men so that they may give glory to the heavenly Father (cf. Mt 5:16) and is ready to receive the kingdom he has prepared for the just, in accordance with Christ's words at the last judgment: "Come, O blessed of my Father, inherit the kingdom prepared for you from the foundation of the world" (Mt 25:34).

While he proclaimed the Father's love, Jesus never failed to recall that it is a demanding love. This feature of God's face can be seen in all of Jesus' life. His "food" is precisely to do the will of the One who sent him (cf. Jn 4:34). Precisely because he is not seeking his own will, but the will of the Father who sent him into the world, his judgment is just (cf. Jn 5:30). Therefore, the Father bears witness to him (cf. Jn 5:37) as do the Scriptures (cf. Jn 5:39). Above all, the works he does in the Father's name guarantee that he has been sent by him (cf. Jn 5:36; 10:25, 37–38). The greatest of these is the offering of his own life, as the Father commanded him; this gift of self is even the reason why the Father loves him (cf. Jn 10:17–18) and is the sign that he loves the Father (cf. Jn 14:31). If the law of Deuteronomy was already a path and guarantee of life, the law of the New Testament is so in an unprecedented and paradoxical way, expressed in the commandment to love one's brothers and sisters to the point of giving one's life for them (cf. Jn 15:12–13).

The ultimate reason for the "new commandment" of love, as St. John Chrysostom recalls, is found in God's love: "You cannot call the God of all kindness your Father if you preserve a cruel and inhuman heart, for in this case you no longer have in you the marks of the heavenly Father's kindness" (*Hom. in illud "Augusta est porta": PG* 51, 44B). In this perspective there is continuity and transcendence: the law is transformed and deepened as the law of love, the only one worthy of the fatherly face of God.

General audience of April 7, 1999

The Christian Response
to Modern Atheism

Man's religious orientation stems from his nature as a creature, which spurs him to long for God who created him in his own image and likeness (cf. Gn 1:26). The Second Vatican Council taught: "The root reason for human dignity lies in man's call to communion with God. From the very circumstance of his origin, man is already invited to converse with God. For man would not exist were he not created by God's love and constantly preserved by it, and he cannot live fully according to truth unless he freely acknowledges that love and devotes himself to his Creator" (*GS* 19).

The way that leads human beings to knowledge of God the Father is Jesus Christ, the Word made flesh, who comes to us in the power of the Holy Spirit. As I emphasized in our previous catecheses, this knowledge is authentic and complete if it is not reduced to a mere intellectual achievement, but vitally involves the whole human person. The latter must give a response of faith and love to the Father, in the awareness that before knowing him, he already knew and loved us (cf. Gal 4:9; 1 Cor 13:12; 1 Jn 4:19).

Unfortunately, this intimate and vital relationship with God, weakened by the sin of our first parents from the beginning of history, is lived by man in a fragile and contradictory way, beset by doubt and often broken by sin. The contemporary era has known especially devastating forms of "theoretical" and "practical" atheism (cf. *Fides et Ratio,* 46–47). *Secularism* proves especially ruinous with its indifference to ultimate questions and to faith; it expresses a model of man lacking all reference to the transcendent. "Practical" atheism is thus a bitter and concrete reality. While it is true that it primarily appears in economically and technologically more advanced civilizations, its effects also extend to those situations and cultures that are in the process of development.

We must be guided by the Word of God in order to interpret this situation in the contemporary world and to answer the serious questions it raises. Starting with Sacred Scripture, we immediately note that there is no mention of "theoretical" atheism, while there is a concern to reject "practical" atheism. The Psalmist calls foolish anyone who says in his heart: "There is no God" and behaves accordingly: "They are corrupt, they do abominable deeds, there is none that does good" (Ps 14:1). Another psalm condemns the wicked man who "boasts, 'He will not avenge it'; all their thoughts are, 'There is no God'" (Ps 10:4).

Rather than atheism, the Bible speaks of *wickedness and idolatry.* Whoever prefers to the true God a series of human products, falsely considered divine, living and active, is wicked and idolatrous. Lengthy prophetic reproaches are devoted to the impotence of idols and likewise of those who make them. With dialectical vehemence, the emptiness and worthlessness of man-made idols is countered with the power of God, the Creator and Wonderworker (cf. Is 44:9–20; Jer 10:1–16).

This doctrine is most fully developed in the Book of Wisdom (cf. 13–15), which presents the way, later recalled by St. Paul (cf. Rom 1:18–23), to the knowledge of God based on created things. Being an "atheist," then, means not knowing the true nature of created reality but absolutizing it, and therefore "idolizing" it, instead of considering it a mark of the Creator and the path that leads to him.

Atheism can even become a kind of intolerant ideology, as history shows. The last two centuries have known currents of theoretical atheism that denied God in order to assert the absolute autonomy of man, nature or science. This is what the *Catechism of the Catholic Church* emphasizes: "Atheism is often based on a false conception of human autonomy, exaggerated to the point of refusing any dependence on God" (n. 2126).

This systematic atheism has been widespread for decades, giving the illusion that by eliminating God, man would be freer, both psychologically and socially. The principal objections raised, especially about God the Father, are based on the idea that religion has a compensatory value for people. Having repressed the image of the earthly father, adults are said to project onto God the need for a greater father, from whom they must free themselves because he hinders the growth process of human beings.

What is the Church's attitude to these forms of atheism and their ideological justifications? The Church does not scorn serious study of the psychological and sociological elements of the religious phenomenon, but firmly rejects the interpretation of religiosity as a projection of the human psyche or the result of sociological conditioning. In fact, authentic religious experience is not an expression of immaturity, but a mature and noble attitude of acceptance of God, which in turn gives meaning to life and implies a responsibility to work for a better world.

The Council recognized that, by not always showing the true face of God, believers may have contributed to the rise of atheism (cf. *GS* 19; *CCC* 2125). In this regard, bearing witness to the real face of God gives the most convincing response to atheism. This obviously does not exclude, but rather demands, a correct presentation of the rational reasons that lead to the recognition of God. Unfortunately, these reasons are often obscured by the influence of sin and of many cultural circumstances. The Gospel message, confirmed by the witness of a sensible charity (cf. *GS* 21), is thus the most effective way for people to understand something of God's goodness and gradually to recognize his merciful face.

General audience of April 14, 1999

Dialogue Is Part of the Church's Saving Mission

"One God and Father of us all, who is above all and through all and in all" (Eph 4:6). In light of these words from the Apostle Paul's letter, today we wish to reflect on how to witness to God the Father in dialogue with the followers of all religions. In our reflection we have two reference points: the Second Vatican Council's Declaration *Nostra Aetate (On the Relation of the Church to Non-Christian Religions)* and the goal of the now imminent Great Jubilee.

The Declaration *Nostra Aetate* laid the foundations for a new style of dialogue in the Church's relationship with the various religions. For its part, the Great Jubilee of the Year 2000 is a privileged opportunity to witness to this style. In *Tertio Millennio Adveniente* (cf. nn. 52–53), I invited people, precisely in this year dedicated to God the Father, to take a closer look at the dialogue with the great religions, which includes meetings in places of significance to them.

In Sacred Scripture the theme of the one God in relation to the universality of the peoples seeking salvation is gradually developed until it culminates in the full revelation in Christ.

The God of Israel, expressed by the sacred Tetragrammaton, is the God of the patriarchs, the God who appeared to Moses in the burning bush (cf. Ex 3) to free Israel and make it the people of the covenant. The Book of Joshua tells how they chose the Lord at Shechem, where a great multitude of people opted for God, who had shown himself benevolent and provident, and forsook all other gods (cf. ch. 24).

In the religious awareness of the Old Testament, this choice increasingly took the form of a rigorous and universalistic monotheism. If the Lord God of Israel is not one god among many but the only true God, it follows that all the nations "to the ends of the earth" (Is 49:6) must be saved by him. The universal salvific will transforms human history into a great pilgrimage of peoples toward one destination, Jerusalem, but without loss of any of their ethnic-cultural differences (cf. Rev 7:9). The prophet Isaiah vividly expresses this outlook in the image of a road connecting Egypt to Assyria, stressing that the divine blessing will join Israel, Egypt and Assyria (cf. 19:23– 25). While fully preserving their own identity, all peoples are called to turn more and more to the one God who revealed himself to Israel.

This "universalistic" inspiration in the Old Testament is further developed in the New Testament, which reveals to us that God "desires all men to be saved and to come to the knowledge of the truth" (1 Tim 2:4). The conviction that God is really preparing all people for salvation is the basis of Christian dialogue with the followers of other religious beliefs. The Council described the Church's attitude to non-Christian religions in this way:

> The Catholic Church rejects nothing that is true and holy in these religions. She regards with sincere reverence those ways of conduct and of life, those precepts and teachings which, though differing in many aspects from

the ones she holds and sets forth, nonetheless often reflect a ray of that Truth which enlightens all men. Indeed, she proclaims and ever must proclaim Christ "the way, the truth, and the life" (Jn 14:6), in whom men may find the fullness of religious life, in whom God has reconciled all things to himself (cf. 2 Cor 5:18–19) (*NA* 2).

In years past, some considered *dialogue* with the followers of other religions to be opposed to *proclamation,* a primary duty of the Church's mission. In fact, interreligious dialogue is an integral part of the Church's evangelizing mission (cf. *CCC* 856). As I have often stressed, it is fundamental for the Church; it is an expression of her saving mission, and it is a dialogue of salvation (cf. *Insegnamenti,* VII/1 [1984], pp. 595–599). Thus, interreligious dialogue does not mean abandoning proclamation, but answering a divine call so that exchange and sharing may lead to a mutual witness of one's own religious viewpoint, deeper knowledge of one another's convictions, and agreement on certain fundamental values.

Reference to the common "fatherhood" of God will, therefore, not prove vaguely universalistic, but will be lived by Christians with full knowledge of that saving dialogue which comes through the mediation of Jesus and the action of his Spirit. Thus, for example, while taking from religions such as Islam the powerful affirmation of the personal Absolute who transcends the cosmos and man, on our part we can offer the witness of God in his inner Trinitarian life, explaining that the Trinity of Persons does not diminish but characterizes the divine unity itself.

Therefore, in religious journeys that lead to a monistic conception of ultimate reality as an undifferentiated "Self" into which everything is resolved, Christianity also discerns the call to respect the deepest meaning of the divine mystery, beyond every human word and concept. Yet it does not hesitate to affirm God's personal transcendence, while proclaiming his universal and loving fatherhood, which is fully revealed in the mystery of his crucified and risen Son.

May the Great Jubilee be a valuable opportunity for the followers of all religions to grow in knowledge, esteem and love for one another through a dialogue that will be an encounter of salvation for all!

General audience of April 21, 1999

Jews and Christians
Share Much Together

The interreligious dialogue which the Apostolic Letter *Tertio Millennio Adveniente* encourages as a characteristic feature of this year dedicated to God the Father (cf. nn. 52–53) first of all concerns Jews, our "elder brothers," as I called them on the occasion of my memorable meeting with the Jewish community of Rome on April 13, 1986 (*L'Osservatore Romano,* English edition, April 21, 1986, p. 6). Reflecting on the spiritual patrimony we share, the Second Vatican Council, especially in the Declaration *Nostra Aetate,* gave a new direction to our relationship with the Jewish religion. We must reflect ever more deeply on that teaching, and the Jubilee of the Year 2000 can be a magnificent occasion to possibly meet in places of significance for the great monotheistic religions (cf. *TMA* 53).

We know that from the beginnings of the Church down to our century, relations with our Jewish brothers and sisters have, unfortunately, been difficult. However, throughout this long and tormented history, there have been occasions of peaceful and constructive dialogue. We should recall in this regard that the first theological work entitled "Dialogue" was significantly dedicated by the philosopher and martyr Justin to his encounter with Trypho the Jew in the second century. Also of note is the vivid dialogical dimension strongly present in contemporary neo-Jewish literature, which has deeply influenced the philosophical and theological thought of the twentieth century.

This dialogical attitude between Christians and Jews not only expresses the general value of interreligious dialogue, but also the long journey they share leading from the Old to the New Testament. There is a long period of salvation history that Christians and Jews can view together. "The Jewish faith, unlike other non-Christian religions, is already a response to God's revelation in the Old Covenant" (*CCC* 839). This history is illumined by an immense group of holy people whose lives testify to the possession, in faith, of what they hope for. Indeed, the Letter to the Hebrews emphasizes this response of faith throughout the history of salvation (cf. Heb 11).

Today, the courageous witness of faith should also mark the collaboration of Christians and Jews in proclaiming and realizing God's saving plan for all humanity. If his plan is interpreted in a different way regarding the acceptance of Christ, this obviously involves a crucial difference, which is at the very origin of Christianity itself, but does not change the fact that there are many elements in common.

It is still our duty to work together in promoting a human condition that more closely conforms to God's plan. The Great Jubilee of the Year 2000, which refers precisely to the Jewish tradition of jubilee years, points to the urgent need for this common effort to restore peace and social justice. Recognizing God's dominion over all creation, especially the earth (cf. Lv 25), all believers are called to translate their faith into a practical commitment to protecting the sacredness of human life in all its forms, and to defending the dignity of every brother and sister.

In meditating on the mystery of Israel and its "irrevocable calling" (cf. *Insegnamenti,* IX/1, 1986, p. 1028), Christians also explore the mystery of their own roots. In the biblical sources they share with their Jewish brothers and sisters, they find the indispensable elements for living and deepening their own faith.

For example, this can be seen in the liturgy. Like Jesus, whom Luke shows us as he opens the book of the prophet Isaiah in the synagogue of Nazareth (cf. Lk 4:16 ff.), the Church draws from the liturgical wealth of the Jewish people. She arranges the Liturgy of the Hours, the liturgy of the Word and even the structure of her Eucharistic prayers according to the models of the Jewish tradition. A few great feasts, such as Easter and Pentecost, recall the Jewish liturgical year and are excellent occasions for remembering in prayer the people God chose and loves (cf. Rom 11:2). Today dialogue means that Christians should be more aware of these elements that bring us closer together. Just as we take note of the "covenant never revoked by God" (cf. *Insegnamenti,* III/2, 1980, pp. 1272–1276), so we should consider the intrinsic value of the Old Testament (cf. *DV* 3), even if this only acquires its full meaning in light of the New Testament and contains promises that are fulfilled in Jesus. Did not Jesus' interpretation of the Hebrew Scriptures make the hearts of the disciples "burn within" them on the road to Emmaus (Lk 24:32), enabling them to recognize the risen Christ as he broke the bread?

Not only the shared history of Christians and Jews, but especially their dialogue must look to the future (cf. *CCC* 840), becoming as it were a *"Memoria futuri."*[1] The memory of these sorrowful and tragic events of the past can open the way to a renewed sense of brotherhood, the fruit of God's grace, and to working so that the seeds infected with anti-Judaism and anti-Semitism will never again take root in human hearts.

---

1. *We Remember: A Reflection on the "Shoah," L'Osservatore Romano,* English edition, March 18, 1998, p. 6.

Israel, a people who build their faith on the promise God made to Abraham: "You shall be the father of a multitude of nations" (Gn 17:4; Rom 4:17), shows Jerusalem to the world as the symbolic place of the eschatological pilgrimage of peoples united in their praise of the Most High. I hope that at the dawn of the third millennium, sincere dialogue between Christians and Jews will help create a new civilization founded on the one, holy and merciful God, fostering a humanity reconciled in love.

General audience of April 28, 1999

Muslims and Christians Adore the One God

Continuing our discussion of interreligious dialogue, today we will reflect on dialogue with Muslims, who "together with us...adore the one, merciful God" (*LG* 16; cf. *CCC* 841). The Church has a high regard for them, convinced that their faith in the transcendent God contributes to building a new human family based on the highest aspirations of the human heart.

Like Jews and Christians, Muslims see the figure of Abraham as a model of unconditional submission to the decrees of God (cf. *NA* 3). Following Abraham's example, the faithful strive to give God his rightful place in their lives as the origin, teacher, guide and ultimate destiny of all beings.[1] This human docility and openness to God's will is translated into an attitude of prayer that expresses the existential condition of every person before the Creator. Along the path marked out by Abraham in his submission to the divine will, we find his descendant, the Blessed Virgin Mary, Mother of Jesus, who is also devoutly invoked by Muslims, especially in popular piety.

---

1. Pontifical Council for Interreligious Dialogue, *Message to Muslims for the End of Ramadan,* 1417/1997.

We Christians joyfully recognize the religious values we have in common with Islam. Today I would like to repeat what I said to young Muslims some years ago in Casablanca: "We believe in the same God, the one God, the living God, the God who created the world and brings his creatures to their perfection" (*Insegnamenti,* VIII/2, 1985, p. 497). The patrimony of revealed texts in the Bible speaks unanimously of the oneness of God. Jesus himself reaffirmed it, making Israel's profession his own: "The Lord our God, the Lord is one" (Mk 12:29; cf. Dt 6:4–5). This oneness is also affirmed in the words of praise that spring from the heart of the Apostle Paul: "To the king of ages, immortal, invisible, the only God, be honor and glory forever and ever. Amen." (1 Tim 1:17).

We know that in light of the full revelation in Christ, this mysterious oneness cannot be reduced to a numerical unity. The Christian mystery leads us to contemplate in God's substantial unity the persons of the Father, the Son and the Holy Spirit: each possesses the divine substance whole and indivisible, but each is distinct from the other by virtue of their reciprocal relations.

Their relations in no way compromise the oneness of God, as the Fourth Lateran Council explains: "Each of the persons is that supreme reality, namely, the divine substance, essence or nature.... It does not generate, is not begotten and does not proceed" (*DS* 804). The Christian doctrine on the Trinity, confirmed by the Councils, explicitly rejects any form of "tritheism" or "polytheism." In this sense, that is, with reference to the one divine substance, there is significant correspondence between Christianity and Islam.

However, this correspondence must not let us forget the difference between the two religions. We know that the unity of God is expressed in the mystery of the three divine Persons. Indeed, since he is Love (cf. 1 Jn 4:8), God has always been a

Father who gives his whole self in begetting the Son, and both are united in a communion of love that is the Holy Spirit. This distinction and compenetration *(perichoresis)* of the three divine Persons is not something added to their unity but is its most profound and characteristic expression. On the other hand, we should not forget that the Trinitarian monotheism distinctive of Christianity is a mystery inaccessible to human reason, which is, nevertheless, called to accept the revelation of God's inmost nature (cf. *CCC* 237).

Interreligious dialogue, which leads to a deeper knowledge and esteem for others, is a great sign of hope.[2] The Christian and Muslim traditions both have a long history of study, philosophical and theological reflection, literature and science, which have left their mark on Eastern and Western cultures. The worship of the one God, Creator of all, encourages us to increase our knowledge of one another in the future.

In today's world, where God is tragically forgotten, Christians and Muslims are called in one spirit of love to defend and always promote human dignity, moral values and freedom. The common pilgrimage to eternity must be expressed in prayer, fasting and charity, but also in joint efforts for peace and justice, for human advancement, and for the protection of the environment. By walking together on the path of reconciliation and renouncing in humble submission to the divine will any form of violence as a means of resolving differences, the two religions will be able to offer a sign of hope, radiating in the world the wisdom and mercy of that one God who created and governs the human family.

General audience of May 5, 1999

---

2. Pontifical Council for Interreligious Dialogue, *Message to Muslims for the End of Ramadan,* 1418/1998.

Dialogue with the Great World Religions

The Acts of the Apostles relate St. Paul's discourse to the Athenians, which seems very timely for the areopagus of religious pluralism in our times. To present the God of Jesus Christ, Paul starts with the religious practices of his audience, expressing his appreciation: "Athenians, I see how extremely religious you are in every way. For as I went through the city and looked carefully at the objects of your worship, I found among them an altar with the inscription, 'To an unknown god.' What therefore you worship as unknown, this I proclaim to you" (Acts 17:22–23).

On my spiritual and pastoral pilgrimage around today's world, I have repeatedly expressed the Church's esteem for "whatever is true and holy" in the religions of the various peoples. I have added, following the Council, that Christian truth serves to encourage "the good things, spiritual and moral, as well as the socio-cultural values" found among them (*NA* 2). The universal fatherhood of God, revealed in Jesus Christ, spurs us also to dialogue with religions outside Abraham's stock. This dialogue offers a wealth of themes and challenges, when we think, for example, of Asian cultures deeply imbued with the religious spirit, or of African traditional religions, which are a source of wisdom and life for so many peoples.

At the root of the Church's encounter with world religions, there is a discernment of their specific features, that is, of the way they approach the mystery of God the Savior, the ultimate reality of human life. Every religion presents itself as a search for salvation and offers ways to attain it (cf. *CCC* 843). Dialogue presupposes the certitude that man, created in God's image, is also the privileged "place" of his saving presence.

Prayer, as an adoring recognition of God, as gratitude for his gifts, as an invocation of his help, is a special form of encounter, especially with those religions which, although not having discovered the mystery of God's fatherhood, nevertheless "have, as it were, their arms stretched out toward heaven" (*EN* 53). However, dialogue is more difficult with certain contemporary forms of religious belief in which prayer often ends up as an enhancement of one's vital potential in exchange for salvation.

Christianity's dialogue with other religions takes various forms and operates at different levels, beginning with the *dialogue of life,* in which "people strive to live in an open and neighborly spirit, sharing their joys and sorrows, their human problems and preoccupations" (*DP* 42).

The *dialogue of action* has particular importance. Among these works we should mention education in peace and respect for the environment, solidarity with the world of suffering, the promotion of social justice, and the integral development of peoples. Christian charity, which knows no borders, gladly joins forces with the shared witness given by the members of other religions, rejoicing over the good they accomplish.

Then there is the *theological dialogue,* in which experts try to deepen their understanding of their respective religious heritages and to appreciate their spiritual values. Meetings between the specialists of different religions, however, cannot be limited to the search for a least common denominator. Their purpose is to lend courageous service to the truth by highlighting areas of convergence as well as fundamental differences, in a sincere effort to overcome prejudice and misunderstanding.

The *dialogue of religious experience* is also becoming more and more important. The practice of contemplation answers the great thirst for inner life of those who are spiritually searching, and helps all believers to enter more deeply into the mystery of God. Some practices derived from the great Eastern religions hold a certain attraction for people today. Christians must exercise spiritual discernment in their regard, so as not to lose sight of the conception of prayer as it has been explained by the Bible throughout salvation history (cf. Letter *Some Aspects of Christian Meditation*).

This necessary discernment does not hinder interreligious dialogue. In fact, for many years, meetings with the various monastic communities of other religions, marked by cordial friendship, are opening ways for the mutual sharing of other spiritual riches "with regard to prayer and contemplation, faith and ways of searching for God or the Absolute" (*DP* 42). Mysticism, however, can never be invoked to support religious relativism in the name of an experience that would lessen the value of God's revelation in history. As disciples of Christ, we feel the urgent need and the joy of witnessing to the fact that God manifested himself precisely in him, as John's Gospel tells us: "No one has ever seen God; the only Son, who is in the bosom of the Father, he has made him known" (1:18).

This witness must be given without any reservation, but also in the awareness that the action of Christ and his Spirit is already mysteriously present in all who live sincerely according to their religious convictions. With all genuinely religious people, the Church continues her pilgrimage through history toward the eternal contemplation of God in the splendor of his glory.

General audience of May 19, 1999

We Await a New Heaven and New Earth

In this final year of preparation for the Jubilee, the theme on which we are reflecting — humanity's journey to the Father — suggests that we meditate on the eschatological perspective, in other words, on the final end of human history. Especially in our time, everything proceeds at incredible speed, both because of scientific and technological discoveries and because of the media's influence. As a result, we spontaneously ask ourselves what is humanity's destiny and final goal. The Word of God offers us a precise answer to this question, and shows us the plan of salvation that the Father carries out in history through Christ by the work of the Spirit.

In the Old Testament, the fundamental reference point is the Exodus, with its focus on entering the Promised Land. The Exodus is not only a historical event, but also the revelation of God's saving work that will be gradually fulfilled, as the prophets endeavor to show by shedding light on the present and future of Israel.

During the exile, the prophets foretold a new Exodus, a return to the Promised Land. With this renewed gift of land, God would not only bring together his people scattered among the nations, but he would also transform the heart of each one, that is, his capacity to know, love and act: "I will give them one heart and put a new spirit within them; I will take the stony heart out of their flesh and give them a heart of flesh, that they may walk in my statutes and keep my ordinances and obey them, and they shall be my people, and I will be their God" (Ez 11:19–20; cf. 36:26–28).

Through their commitment to observing the norms established by the covenant, the people would be able to live in an environment similar to the one that came from God's hands at the moment of creation: "This land that was desolate has become like the garden of Eden, and the waste and desolate and ruined cities are now inhabited and fortified" (Ez 36:35). This would be a new covenant, expressed concretely in the observance of a law written upon their hearts (cf. Jer 31:31–34).

Then the horizon broadens and a new land is promised. The final goal is a New Jerusalem, where all afflictions will cease: "For behold, I create new heavens and a new earth.... I create Jerusalem as a joy and her people a delight. I will rejoice in Jerusalem and be glad in my people; no more shall be heard in it the sound of weeping and the cry of distress" (Is 65:17–19).

The Book of Revelation takes up this vision. John writes: "Then I saw a new heaven and a new earth; for the first heaven and the first earth had passed away, and the sea was no more. And I saw the holy city, New Jerusalem, coming down out of heaven from God, prepared as a bride adorned for her husband" (21:1f.).

The passage to this new creation requires a commitment to holiness, which the New Testament will clothe in absolute radicalism: "Since all these things are thus to be dissolved, what sort of persons ought you to be in lives of holiness and godliness, waiting for and hastening the coming of the day of God, because of which the heavens will be kindled and dissolved and the elements will melt with fire! But according to his promise we wait for new heavens and a new earth in which righteousness dwells" (2 Pt 3:11–13).

Christ's resurrection, ascension and the announcement of his second coming have opened new eschatological horizons. In the Last Supper discourse, Jesus says: "I go to prepare a place for you. And when I go and prepare a place for you, I will come again and will take you to myself, that where I am you may be also" (Jn 14:2–3). Therefore, St. Paul wrote: "For the Lord himself will descend from heaven with a cry of command, with the archangel's call and with the sound of the trumpet of God. And the dead in Christ will rise first; then we who are alive, who are left, shall be caught up together with them in the clouds to meet the Lord in the air, and so we shall always be with the Lord" (1 Thes 4:16–17).

We have not been told the date of this final event. We must wait patiently for the risen Jesus, who, when asked by the apostles themselves to restore the kingdom of Israel, answered by inviting them to preach and to bear witness: "It is not for you to know times or seasons which the Father has fixed by his own authority. But you shall receive power when the Holy Spirit has come upon you, and you shall be my witnesses in Jerusalem and in all Judea and Samaria and to the end of the earth" (Acts 1:7–8).

We should await the final event with serene hope, as we build in our time that kingdom which at the end Christ will hand over to the Father: "After that will come the end, when, after having destroyed every sovereignty, authority and power, he will hand over the kingdom to God the Father" (1 Cor 15:24). With Christ, victorious over the enemy powers, we too will share in the new creation, which will consist in a definitive return of all things to the One from whom all things come: "When finally all has been subjected to the Son, he will then subject himself to the One who made all things subject to him, so that God may be all in all" (1 Cor 15:28).

Therefore, we must be convinced that "our citizenship is in heaven, and from it we await as Savior the Lord Jesus Christ" (Phil 3:20). Here we have no lasting city (cf. Heb 13:14). Pilgrims in search of a permanent dwelling place, we must long, like our fathers in the faith, for a better country, "that is, a heavenly one" (Heb 11:16).

General audience of May 26, 1999

Believers in Christ
Need Not Fear Death

After reflecting on humanity's common destiny as it will be fulfilled at the end of time, today we want to turn our attention to another topic that directly concerns us: the meaning of death. It has become difficult to speak of death today, because prosperous societies are inclined to disregard this reality, the thought of which alone causes anxiety. Indeed, as the Council observed, "It is in the face of death that the riddle of human existence grows most acute" (*GS* 18). But about this reality the Word of God offers us, although gradually, a light to illumine and comfort us.

In the Old Testament, the first indications stem from the common experience of mortals who are not yet enlightened by the hope of a blessed life after death. It was generally believed that human life ended in "Sheol," a place of shadows incompatible with life in its fullness. In this regard, the words of the Book of Job are very significant: "Are not the days of my life few? Let me alone, that I may find a little comfort before I go whence I shall not return, to the land of gloom and chaos, where light is as darkness" (10:20–22).

God's revelation gradually surpassed this severe view of death, and human reflection was opened to new horizons that would receive their full light in the New Testament. First we can understand that if death is the relentless enemy of man and tries to overpower and dominate him, God could not have created it, because he cannot delight in the destruction of the living (cf. Wis 1:13). God's original plan was different, but it was impeded by the sin man committed under the devil's influence, as the Book of Wisdom explains: "For God created man for incorruption and made him in the image of his own eternity, but through the devil's envy death entered the world, and those who belong to his company experience it" (2:23–24). Jesus also refers to this idea (cf. Jn 8:44). St. Paul's teaching on the redemption achieved by Christ, the new Adam (cf. Rom 5:12, 17; 1 Cor 15:21), is based on it. By his death and resurrection, Jesus overcame sin and death, which is its consequence.

In light of what Jesus accomplished, we can understand God the Father's attitude toward the life and death of his creatures. The Psalmist had already sensed that God could not abandon his faithful servants in the tomb, nor permit his godly one to undergo corruption (cf. Ps 16:10). Isaiah pointed to a future in which God would destroy death forever, wiping away "tears from all faces" (25:8) and raising the dead to new life: "Your dead shall live; their bodies shall rise. O dwellers in the dust, awake and sing for joy! For your dew is a dew of night and on the land of the shades you will let it fall" (26:19). Over death, which levels all the living, is superimposed the image of the earth as a mother preparing to give birth to a new living being, and bringing into the world the righteous destined to live in God. Consequently, even if the righteous "in the sight of men were punished, their hope is full of immortality" (Wis 3:1, 4).

The seven brothers and their mother magnificently affirm the hope of resurrection in the Second Book of Maccabees at the time of their martyrdom. One of them says of his hands: "It was from heaven that I received these; for the sake of his laws I disdain them; from him I hope to receive them again" (7:11); another, "when he was near death, said, 'It is my choice to die at the hands of men with the God-given hope of being restored to life by him'" (7:14). Their mother heroically encouraged them to face death with this hope (cf. 7:29).

Already in the Old Testament the prophets warn people to await "the day of the Lord" with an upright heart, or it would become "darkness and not light" (cf. Am 5:18, 20). The full revelation of the New Testament emphasizes that everyone will be subject to judgment (cf. 1 Pt 4:5; Rom 14:10). But the righteous should not fear it, since as the elect they are destined to receive the promised inheritance; they will be set at the right hand of Christ, who will call them "blessed of my Father" (Mt 25:34; cf. 22:14; 24:22, 24).

The death that the believer experiences as a member of the Mystical Body discloses the way to the Father, who has shown us his love in the death of Christ, the victim of "expiation for our sins" (1 Jn 4:10; cf. Rom 5:7). In regard to death, the *Catechism of the Catholic Church* stresses: "For those who die in Christ's grace it is a participation in the death of the Lord, so that they can also share his resurrection" (n. 1006).

Jesus "loves us and has freed us from our sins by his blood and made us a kingdom, priests for his God and Father" (Rev 1:5–6). Of course, it is necessary to pass through death, but now with the certainty that we will meet the Father, when "this corruptible body puts on incorruptibility, this mortal body immortality" (1 Cor 15:54). Then it will be clearly seen that "death is swallowed up in victory," and we will be able to face it defiantly and fearlessly: "O death, where is your victory? O death, where is your sting?" (1 Cor 15:55).

It is precisely because of this Christian vision of death that St. Francis of Assisi could exclaim: "Praised be you, my Lord, for our sister bodily death" (*Fonti Francescanne,* n. 263). With

this comforting outlook, we can understand the beatitude proclaimed by the Book of Revelation as the fulfillment of the
Gospel Beatitudes: "Blessed are the dead who die in the Lord
henceforth. 'Blessed indeed,' says the Spirit, 'that they may rest
from their labors, for their deeds follow them!'" (Rev 14:13).

General audience of June 2, 1999

God's Judgment Is Rich in Mercy

"Gracious is the Lord and righteous; our God is merciful" (Ps 116:5). At first sight judgment and mercy would seem to be two irreconcilable realities, or at least, the second seems to be connected with the first only if it mitigates its own inexorable power. It is necessary instead to understand the logic of Sacred Scripture, which links them and indeed presents them in a way that one cannot exist without the other.

In the Old Testament the sense of divine justice was perceived gradually, beginning with the situation of one who has acted well and feels unjustly threatened. He then finds refuge and defense in God. This experience is expressed several times in the psalms that state, for example: "I know that the Lord maintains the cause of the afflicted and executes justice for the needy. Surely the righteous shall give thanks to your name; the upright shall dwell in your presence" (Ps 140:13–14).

Scripture conceives of intervention on behalf of the oppressed primarily as justice, that is, as God's fidelity to the saving promises made to Israel. God's justice is therefore one that stems from the gratuitous and merciful initiative by which he bound himself to his people in an eternal covenant. God is just because he saves, thus fulfilling his promises, while the judgment of sin and the wicked is only a secondary aspect of his mercy. The sinner who has sincerely repented can always trust in this merciful justice (cf. Ps 51:6, 16).

Regarding the difficulty of finding justice in human beings and their institutions, the Bible shows a growing awareness that justice will only be fully realized in the future, through the action of a mysterious figure who will gradually assume more precise "messianic" features: a king or a king's son (cf. Ps 72:1), a shoot that "will come forth from the stump of Jesse" (Is 11:1), a "righteous branch," a descendant of David (Jer 23:5).

The figure of the Messiah, foreshadowed in many passages, especially in the prophetic books, assumes in the perspective of salvation the functions of governance and judgment for the prosperity and growth of the community and its individual members. The judicial function will be exercised over the good and the wicked, who will appear together for judgment, where the triumph of the just will become fear and amazement for the wicked (cf. Wis 4:20 — 5:23; cf. also Dn 12:1–3). The effect of the judgment entrusted to the "Son of Man" in the apocalyptic vision of the book of Daniel will be the triumph of the holy people of the Most High over the downfall of earthly kingdoms (cf. Dn 7, especially vv.18, 27).

On the other hand, even those who can expect a favorable judgment are aware of their own limits. Thus there is a growing sense that it is impossible to be just without divine grace, as the Psalmist recalls: "O Lord...in your justice answer me. Enter not into judgment with your servant, for before you no living man is just" (Ps 143:1–2).

We find the same basic logic again in the New Testament, where divine judgment is linked to Christ's saving work. Jesus is the Son of Man to whom the Father has given the power to judge. He will pass judgment on all who will come forth from their tombs, separating those destined for the resurrection of life from those who will experience the resurrection of judgment (cf. Jn 5:26–30). However, as the Evangelist John stresses: "God sent the Son into the world, not to condemn the world, but that the world might be saved through him" (3:17). Only those who will have rejected the salvation offered by God in his boundless mercy will be condemned, because they will have condemned themselves.

St. Paul delves into the salvific meaning of this concept of "the justice of God," which is accomplished "through faith in Jesus Christ for all who believe" (Rom 3:22). The justice of God is closely connected with the gift of reconciliation; if we are reconciled with the Father through Christ, we too, through him, can become the justice of God (cf. 2 Cor 5:18–21).

Judgment and mercy can thus be understood as two dimensions of the same mystery of love: "For God has consigned all men to disobedience, that he may have mercy upon all" (Rom 11:32). Love, which is the basis of the divine attitude and must become a fundamental virtue for the believer, thus prompts us to have trust in the day of judgment, casting out all fear (cf. 1 Jn 4:18). In imitation of this divine judgment, human judgment must also be exercised according to a law of freedom, in which it is precisely mercy that must prevail: "Always speak and act as those destined for judgment under the law of freedom. Merciless is the judgment on the one who has not shown mercy, but mercy triumphs over judgment" (Jas 2:12–13).

God is the Father of mercy and of all consolation. For this reason in the fifth request of the prayer par excellence, the Our Father, "our petition begins with a 'confession' of our wretchedness and his mercy" (*CCC* 2839). In revealing the fullness of the Father's mercy to us, Jesus also taught us that we only have access to this Father, so just and merciful, through the experience of that mercy which must mark our relations with our neighbor. "This outpouring of mercy cannot penetrate our hearts as long as we have not forgiven those who have trespassed against us.... In refusing to forgive our brothers and sisters, our hearts are closed and their hardness makes them impervious to the Father's merciful love" (*CCC* 2840).

General audience of July 7, 1999

Heaven Is Fullness of Communion with God

When the form of this world has passed away, those who have welcomed God into their lives and have sincerely opened themselves to his love, at least at the moment of death, will enjoy that fullness of communion with God that is the goal of human life. As the *Catechism of the Catholic Church* teaches, "This perfect life with the Most Holy Trinity — this communion of life and love with the Trinity, with the Virgin Mary, the angels and all the blessed — is called 'heaven.' Heaven is the ultimate end and fulfillment of the deepest human longings, the state of supreme, definitive happiness" (n. 1024). Today we will try to understand the biblical meaning of "heaven," in order to have a better understanding of the reality to which this expression refers.

In biblical language "heaven," when it is joined to the "earth," indicates part of the universe. Scripture says about creation: "In the beginning God created the heavens and the earth" (Gn 1:1). Metaphorically speaking, heaven is understood as the dwelling place of God, who is thus distinguished from human beings (cf. Ps 104:2 f.; 115:16; Is 66:1). He sees and judges from the heights of heaven (cf. Ps 113:4–9) and comes down when he is called upon (cf. Ps 18:9, 10; 144:5). However, the biblical metaphor makes it clear that God does not identify himself with heaven, nor can he be contained in it (cf. 1 Kgs 8:27). This is true even though in some passages of the First Book of the Maccabees, "Heaven" is simply one of God's names (3:18, 19, 50, 60; 4:24, 55).

The depiction of heaven as the transcendent dwelling place of the living God is joined with that of the place to which believers, through grace, can also ascend, as we see in the Old Testament accounts of Enoch (cf. Gn 5:24) and Elijah (cf. 2 Kgs 2:11). Thus, heaven becomes an image of life in God. In this sense Jesus speaks of a "reward in heaven" (Mt 5:12) and urges people to "lay up for yourselves treasures in heaven" (Mt 6:20; cf. 19:21).

The New Testament amplifies the idea of heaven in relation to the mystery of Christ. To show that the Redeemer's sacrifice acquires perfect and definitive value, the Letter to the Hebrews says that Jesus "passed through the heavens" (4:14), and "entered, not into a sanctuary made with hands, a copy of the true one, but into heaven itself" (9:24). Since the Father loves believers in a special way, they are raised with Christ and made citizens of heaven. It is worthwhile listening to what the Apostle Paul tells us about this in a very powerful text: "God, who is rich in mercy, out of the great love with which he loved us, even when we were dead through our trespasses, made us alive together with Christ — by grace you have been saved — and raised us up with him and made us sit with him in the heavenly places in Christ Jesus, that in the coming ages he might show the immeasurable riches of his grace in kindness toward us in Christ Jesus" (Eph 2:4–7). Creatures experience the fatherhood of God, who is rich in mercy, through the love of God's crucified and risen Son, who sits in heaven at the right hand of the Father as Lord.

After the course of our earthly life, participation in complete intimacy with the Father thus comes through our insertion into Christ's paschal mystery. St. Paul emphasizes our meeting with Christ in heaven at the end of time with a vivid spatial image: "Then we who are alive, who are left, shall be caught up together with them in the clouds to meet the Lord in the air, and so we shall always be with the Lord. Therefore, comfort one another with these words" (1 Thes 4:17–18). In the context of revelation, we know that the "heaven" or "happiness" in which we will find ourselves is neither an abstraction nor a physical place in the clouds, but a living, personal relationship with the Holy Trinity. It is our meeting with the Father that takes place in the risen Christ through the communion of the Holy Spirit.

It is always necessary to maintain a certain restraint in describing these "ultimate realities," since their depiction is always unsatisfactory. Today, personal language is better suited to describing the state of happiness and peace we will enjoy in our definitive communion with God.

The *Catechism of the Catholic Church* sums up the Church's teaching on this truth: "By his death and resurrection, Jesus Christ has 'opened' heaven to us. The life of the blessed consists in the full and perfect possession of the fruits of the redemption accomplished by Christ. He makes partners in his heavenly glorification those who have believed in him and remained faithful to his will. Heaven is the blessed community of all who are perfectly incorporated into Christ" (n. 1026).

This final state, however, can be anticipated in some way today in sacramental life, whose center is the Eucharist and in the gift of self through fraternal charity. If we are able to enjoy properly the good things that the Lord showers upon us every day, we will already have begun to experience that joy and peace which one day will be completely ours. We know that on this earth everything is subject to limits, but the thought of the "ultimate" realities helps us to live better the "penultimate" realities. We know that as we pass through this world we are called to seek "the things that are above, where Christ is seated at the right hand of God" (Col 3:1), in order to be with him in the eschatological fulfillment, when the Spirit will fully reconcile with the Father "all things, whether on earth or in heaven" (Col 1:10).

General audience of July 21, 1999

Hell Is the State of
Those Who Reject God

God is our infinitely good and merciful Father. But man, called to respond to him freely, can unfortunately choose to reject his love and forgiveness once and for all, thus separating himself forever from joyful communion with him. Christian doctrine explains precisely this tragic situation when it speaks of eternal damnation or hell. It is not a punishment imposed externally by God, but a development of premises already set by people in this life. The very dimension of unhappiness that this obscure condition brings can, in a certain way, be sensed in the light of some of the terrible experiences we have suffered which, as is commonly said, make life "hell."

In a theological sense however, hell is something else: it is the ultimate consequence of sin itself, which turns against the person who committed it. It is the state of those who definitively reject the Father's mercy, even at the last moment of their life.

To describe this reality, Sacred Scripture uses a symbolic language that was gradually explained. In the Old Testament the condition of the dead had not yet been fully disclosed by revelation. Moreover, it was thought that the dead were amassed in Sheol, a land of darkness (cf. Ez 28:8; 31:14; Jb 10:21f.; 38:17; Ps 30:10; 88:7, 13), a pit from which one cannot reascend (cf. Jb 7:9), a place in which it is impossible to praise God (cf. Is 38:18; Ps 6:6).

The New Testament sheds new light on the condition of the dead, proclaiming above all that Christ by his resurrection conquered death and extended his liberating power to the kingdom of the dead.

Nevertheless, redemption remains an offer of salvation, which is up to people to accept freely. This is why they will all be judged "by what they [have done]" (Rev 20:13). By using images, the New Testament presents the place destined for evildoers as a fiery furnace, where people will "weep and gnash their teeth" (Mt 13:42; cf. 25:30, 41), or like Gehenna with its "unquenchable fire" (Mk 9:43). All this is narrated in the parable of the rich man, which explains that hell is a place of eternal suffering, with no possibility of return, nor of the alleviation of pain (cf. Lk 16:19–31).

The Book of Revelation also figuratively portrays in a "pool of fire" those who exclude themselves from the book of life, thus meeting with a "second death" (Rev 20:13f.). Therefore, whoever continues to be closed to the Gospel is preparing for "eternal destruction and exclusion from the presence of the Lord and from the glory of his might" (2 Thes 1:9).

The images of hell that Sacred Scripture presents to us must be correctly interpreted. They show the complete frustration and emptiness of life without God. Rather than a place, hell indicates the state of those who freely and definitively separate themselves from God, the source of all life and joy. This is how the *Catechism of the Catholic Church* summarizes the truths of faith on this subject: "To die in mortal sin without repenting and accepting God's merciful love means remaining separated from him for ever by our own free choice. This state of definitive self-exclusion from communion with God and the blessed is called 'hell'" (n. 1033).

"Eternal damnation," therefore, is not attributed to God's initiative, because in his merciful love he can only desire the salvation of the beings he created. In reality, it is the creature who closes himself to his love. Damnation consists precisely in definitive separation from God, freely chosen by the human person and confirmed with death, which seals his choice forever. God's judgment ratifies this state.

Christian faith teaches that in taking the risk of saying "yes" or "no," which marks the human creature's freedom, some have already said no. They are the spiritual creatures who rebelled against God's love and are called demons (cf. Fourth Lateran Council, *DS* 800–801). What happened to them is a warning to us: it is a continuous call to avoid the tragedy that leads to sin, and to conform our life to that of Jesus, who lived his life with a "yes" to God.

Eternal damnation remains a real possibility, but we are not granted, without special divine revelation, the knowledge of whether or which human beings are effectively involved in it. The thought of hell — and even less the improper use of biblical images — must not create anxiety or despair, but is a necessary and healthy reminder of freedom within the proclamation that the risen Jesus has conquered Satan, giving us the Spirit of God who makes us cry "Abba, Father!" (Rom 8:15; Gal 4:6).

This prospect, rich in hope, prevails in Christian proclamation. It is effectively reflected in the liturgical tradition of the Church, as the words of the Roman Canon attest: "Father, accept this offering from your whole family...save us from final damnation, and count us among those you have chosen."

General audience of July 28, 1999

Purgatory Is
a Necessary Purification

As we have seen in the previous two catecheses, on the basis of the definitive option for or against God, the human being finds he faces one of these alternatives: either to live with the Lord in eternal beatitude, or to remain far from his presence. For those who find themselves in a condition of being open to God, but still imperfectly, the journey toward full beatitude requires a purification, which the faith of the Church illustrates in the doctrine of purgatory (cf. *CCC* 1030–1032).

In Sacred Scripture, we can grasp certain elements that help us to understand the meaning of this doctrine, even if it is not formally described. They express the belief that we cannot approach God without undergoing some kind of purification. According to the Old Testament religious law, what is destined for God must be perfect. As a result, physical integrity is also specifically required for the realities that come into contact with God at the *sacrificial* level, such as sacrificial animals (cf. Lv 22:22), or at the *institutional* level, as in the case of priests or ministers of worship (cf. Lv 21:17–23). Total dedication to the God of the covenant, along the lines of the great teachings found in Deuteronomy (cf. 6:5), and which must correspond to

this physical integrity, is required of individuals a[nd]
a whole (cf. 1 Kgs 8:61). It is a matter of loving
one's being, with purity of heart and the witness ᴏꜰ ᴅᴇᴇᴅꜱ (cf.
1 Kgs 10:12 f.).

The need for integrity obviously becomes necessary after
death, for entering into perfect and complete communion with
God. Those who do not possess this integrity must undergo
purification. This is suggested by a text of St. Paul, in which the
Apostle speaks of the value of each person's work, which will
be revealed on the day of judgment. He says: "If the work
which any man has built on the foundation [which is Christ]
survives, he will receive a reward. If any man's work is burned
up, he will suffer loss, though he himself will be saved, but
only as through fire" (1 Cor 3:14–15).

At times, to reach a state of perfect integrity a person's
intercession or mediation is needed. For example, Moses obtained pardon for the people with a prayer in which he recalled
the saving work God did in the past, and prayed for God's
fidelity to the oath made to his ancestors (cf. Ex 32:30, 11–13).
The figure of the servant of the Lord, outlined in the Book of
Isaiah, is also portrayed by his role of intercession and expiation for many; at the end of his suffering he "will see the light"
and "will justify many," bearing their iniquities (cf. 52:13–
53, 12, especially vv. 53:11).

Psalm 51 can be considered, according to the perspective
of the Old Testament, as a synthesis of the process of reintegra-
tion: the sinner confesses and recognizes his guilt (v. 3), asking
insistently to be purified or "cleansed" (vv. 2, 9, 10, 17) so as to
proclaim the divine praise (v. 15).

In the New Testament, Christ is presented as the intercessor who assumes the functions of high priest on the day of
expiation (cf. Heb 5:7; 7:25). But in him the priesthood is
presented in a new and definitive form. He enters the heavenly shrine once and for all, to intercede with God on our behalf

(cf. Heb 9:23–26, especially v. 24). He is both priest and "victim of expiation" for the sins of the whole world (cf. 1 Jn 2:2).

As the great intercessor who atones for us, Jesus will fully reveal himself at the end of our life when he will express himself with the offer of mercy, but also with the inevitable judgment for those who refuse the Father's love and forgiveness. This offer of mercy does not exclude the duty to present ourselves to God, pure and whole, rich in that love which Paul calls a "[bond] of perfect harmony" (Col 3:14).

In following the Gospel exhortation to be perfect like the heavenly Father during our earthly life (cf. Mt 5:48), we are called to grow in love, to be sound and flawless before God the Father "at the coming of our Lord Jesus with all his saints" (1 Thes 3:12 f.). Moreover, we are invited to "cleanse ourselves from every defilement of body and spirit" (2 Cor 7:1; cf. 1 Jn 3:3), because the encounter with God requires absolute purity.

Every trace of attachment to evil must be eliminated, every imperfection of the soul corrected. Purification must be complete, and indeed this is precisely what is meant by the Church's teaching on *purgatory*. The term does not indicate a place, but a condition of existence. Those who, after death, exist in a state of purification, are already in the love of Christ who removes from them the remnants of imperfection.[1]

It is necessary to explain that the state of purification is not a prolongation of the earthly condition, almost as if after death one were given another possibility to change one's destiny. The Church's teaching in this regard is unequivocal and was reaffirmed by the Second Vatican Council, which teaches:

---

1. Cf. Ecumenical Council of Florence, *Decree for the Greeks: DS* 1304; Ecumenical Council of Trent, *Decree on Justification*: *DS* 1580; *Decree on Purgatory: DS* 1820.

Since, however, we know not the day nor the hour, on our Lord's advice we must be constantly vigilant so that, having finished the course of our earthly life (cf. Heb 9:27), we may merit to enter into the marriage feast with him and to be numbered among the blessed (cf. Mt 25:31–46), and that we may not be ordered to go into eternal fire (cf. Mt 25:41) like the wicked and slothful servant (cf. Mt 25:26), into the exterior darkness where "there will be the weeping and the gnashing of teeth" (Mt 22:13; 25:30) (*LG* 48).

One last important aspect that the Church's tradition has always pointed out should be reproposed today: the *dimension of "communio."* Those who find themselves in the state of purification are united both with the blessed who already enjoy the fullness of eternal life, and with us on this earth on our way toward the Father's house (cf. *CCC* 1032). Just as in their earthly life believers are united in the one Mystical Body, so after death those who live in a state of purification experience the same ecclesial solidarity which works through prayer, prayers for suffrage and love for their other brothers and sisters in the faith. Purification is lived in the essential bond created between those who live in this world and those who enjoy eternal beatitude.

General audience of August 4, 1999

Salvation Is
Humanity's Ultimate Destiny

After meditating on the eschatological goal of our existence, that is, eternal life, we now reflect on the journey that leads to it. To do this, we develop the perspective presented in the Apostolic Letter *Tertio Millennio Adveniente:* "The whole of the Christian life is like a great *pilgrimage to the house of the Father,* whose unconditional love for every human creature and in particular for the 'prodigal son' (cf. Lk 15:11–32), we discover anew each day. This pilgrimage takes place in the heart of each person, extends to the believing community and then reaches to the whole of humanity" (n. 49). In fact, what Christians will one day live to the full is already in some way anticipated today. Indeed, the Passover of the Lord inaugurates the life of the world to come.

The Old Testament prepared for the announcement of this truth through the complex theme of the Exodus. The journey of the chosen people to the Promised Land (cf. Ex 6:6) is like a magnificent icon of the Christian's journey toward the Father's house. Obviously there is a fundamental difference: while in the ancient Exodus liberation was oriented to the possession of land, a temporary gift like all human realities, the new "Exodus" consists in the journey toward the Father's house, with the definitive prospect of eternity that transcends human and cosmic history. The Promised Land of the Old Testament was lost *de facto* with the fall of the two kingdoms and the Babylonian Exile, after which the idea of returning developed like a new Exodus. However, this journey did not end in another geographical or political settlement, but opened itself to an "eschatological" vision that was henceforth a prelude to full revelation in Christ. The universalistic images, which in the Book of Isaiah describe the journey of peoples and history toward a New Jerusalem, the center of the world (cf. chs. 56–66), point in this direction.

The New Testament announces the fulfillment of this great expectation, holding up Christ as the Savior of the world: "When the time had fully come, God sent forth his Son, born of woman, born under the law, to redeem those who were under the law, so that we might receive adoption as sons" (Gal 4:4–5). In the light of this announcement, this life is already under the sign of salvation. It is fulfilled in the coming of Jesus of Nazareth, which culminates in the Passover but will have its full realization in the "parousia," the final coming of Christ.

According to the Apostle Paul, this journey of salvation which links the past to the present, directing it to the future, is the fruit of God's plan, totally focused on the mystery of Christ. This is the "mystery of his will, according to his purpose which he set forth in Christ as a plan for the fullness of time, to unite all things in him, things in heaven and things on earth" (Eph 1:9–10; cf. *CCC* 1042 f.).

In this divine plan, the present is the time of the "already and not yet." It is the time of salvation already accomplished and the journey toward its full actualization: "Until we all attain to the unity of the faith and of the knowledge of the Son of God, to mature manhood, to the measure of the stature of the fullness of Christ" (Eph 4:3).

Growth toward this perfection in Christ, and therefore growth toward the experience of the Trinitarian mystery, implies that the Passover will be fulfilled and fully celebrated only in the eschatological kingdom of God (cf. Lk 22:16). But the events of the Incarnation, the crucifixion and the resurrection already constitute the definitive revelation of God. The offer of redemption that this event implies is inscribed in the history of our human freedom, called to respond to the call of salvation. Christian life is a participation in the paschal mystery, like the way of the cross and the resurrection. It is a way of the cross, because our life is continually subject to the purification that leads to overcoming the old world marked by sin. It is a way of resurrection, because, in raising Christ, the Father conquered sin, so that for the believer the "justice of the cross" becomes the "justice of God," that is, the triumph of his truth and his love over the wickedness of the world.

In short, Christian life is growing toward the mystery of the eternal Passover. Therefore, it requires that we keep our gaze on the goal, the ultimate realities, but at the same time, that we strive for the "penultimate" realities: between these and the eschatological goal there is no opposition, but on the contrary a mutually fruitful relationship. Although the primacy of the eternal is always asserted, this does not prevent us from living historical realities righteously in the light of God (cf. *CCC* 1048 f.).

It is a matter of purifying every human activity and every earthly task, so that the mystery of the Lord's Passover will increasingly shine through them. As the Council reminded us, human activity, which is always marked by the sign of sin, is purified and raised to perfection by the paschal mystery, so that "After we have obeyed the Lord, and in his Spirit nurtured on earth the values of human dignity, brotherhood and freedom, and indeed all the good fruits of our nature and enterprise, we will find them again, but freed of stain, burnished and transfigured, when Christ hands over to the Father: 'a kingdom eternal and universal, a kingdom of truth and life, of holiness and grace, of justice, love and peace'" (*GS* 39). This eternal light illumines the life and the entire history of humanity on earth.

General audience of August 11, 1999

Fight Evil and Sin

Among the themes especially suggested to the People of God for their reflection in this third year of preparation for the Great Jubilee of the year 2000, we find conversion, which includes deliverance from evil (cf. *TMA* 50). This theme has a profound effect on our experience. Our entire personal and community history, in fact, is a struggle against evil. The petition contained in the Our Father: "Deliver us from evil" or from the "evil one," punctuates our prayer to overcome sin and be liberated from all connivance with evil. It reminds us of our daily struggle, but above all, of the secret for overcoming it: the strength of God, revealed and offered to us in Jesus (cf. *CCC* 2853).

Moral evil causes suffering which is presented, especially in the Old Testament, as a punishment connected with conduct that is contrary to God's law. Moreover, Sacred Scripture reveals that after sinning, one can ask God for mercy, that is, for his pardon for the fault and the end of the pain it has brought. A sincere return to God and deliverance from evil are two aspects of one process. Thus, for example, Jeremiah urges the people: "Return, O faithless sons, I will heal your faithlessness" (3:22). The Book of Lamentations underlines the prospect of returning to the Lord (cf. 5:21) and the experience of his mercy: "The steadfast love of the Lord never ceases; his mercies never come to an end; they are new every morning; great is your faithfulness" (3:22; cf. v. 32). Israel's whole history is read in the light of the dialectic: "sin, punishment, repentance — mercy" (cf., eg., Jgs 3:7–10); this is the nucleus central to the tradition of Deuteronomy. Indeed, the historical defeat of the kingdom and city of Jerusalem is interpreted as divine punishment for the lack of fidelity to the covenant.

In the Bible, the lamentations people raised to God when they fell prey to suffering are accompanied by recognition of the sin committed, and trust in his liberating intervention. The confession of sin is one of the elements through which this trust emerges. In this regard, certain psalms that forcefully express the confession of sin and the individual's repentance for it are very revealing (Ps 38:18; 41:4). The admission of guilt, effectively described in Psalm 51, is indispensable to start life anew. The confession of one's sin highlights God's justice as a reflection: "Against you, you only, have I sinned, and done what is evil in your sight, so that you are justified in your sentence and blameless in your judgment" (v. 4). In the psalms we continuously see the prayer for help and the trusting expectation of liberation for Israel (cf. Pss 88; 130). On the cross, Jesus himself prayed with the words of Psalm 22 to obtain the Father's loving intervention in his last hour.

In expressing these words to the Father, Jesus voiced that expectation of deliverance from evil which, in the biblical perspective, occurs through a person who accepts suffering together with its expiatory value: this is the case of the mysterious figure of the servant of the Lord in Isaiah (42:1–9; 49:1–6; 50:4–9; 52:13—53:12). Other figures also assume this role, like the prophet who suffers for and expiates the iniquities of Israel (cf. Ez 4:4–5), he whom they have pierced, on whom they will turn their eyes (cf. Zech 12:10–11; Jn 19:37; Rev 1:7), and the martyrs who accept their suffering in expiation for their people's sins (cf. 2 Mc 7:37–38). Jesus is the synthesis of all these figures and reinterprets them. It is only in and through him that we become aware of evil and call on the Father to deliver us from it.

In the prayer of the Our Father, the reference to evil becomes explicit; here, the term *poneròs* (Mt 6:13), which in itself is an adjectival form, can indicate a personification of evil. In the world, this is provoked by that spiritual being, called by biblical revelation the devil or Satan, who deliberately set himself against God (cf. *CCC* 2851f.). Human "evil" constituted by the evil one or instigated by him is also presented in our time in an attractive form that seduces minds and hearts so as to cause the very sense of evil and sin to be lost. It is a question of that "mystery of evil" of which St. Paul speaks (cf. 2 Thes 2:7). This is certainly linked to human freedom, "but deep within its human reality there are factors at work which place it beyond the merely human, in the border area where man's conscience, will and sensitivity are in contact with the dark forces which, according to St. Paul, are active in the world almost to the point of ruling it" (*Reconciliatio et Paenitentia,* 14). Unfortunately, human beings can become the protagonists of evil, that is, of "an evil and adulterous generation" (Mt 12:39).

We believe that Jesus conquered Satan once and for all, thereby removing our fear of him. To every generation the Church presents, as the Apostle Peter did in his discourse to Cornelius, the liberating image of Jesus of Nazareth who "went about doing good and healing all who were oppressed by the devil, for God was with him" (Acts 10:38).

If in Jesus, the devil was defeated, the Lord's victory must still be freely accepted by each of us, until evil is completely eliminated. The struggle against evil, therefore, requires determination and constant vigilance. Ultimate deliverance from it can only be seen in an eschatological perspective (cf. Rev 21:4). Over and above our efforts and even our failures, these comforting words of Christ endure: "In the world you have tribulation; but be of good cheer, I have overcome the world" (Jn 16:33).

General audience of August 18, 1999

Personal Sin has Repercussions on Society

As we continue our reflection on conversion, sustained by the certainty of the Father's love, today we will focus our attention on the meaning of sin, both personal and social. Let us first look at Jesus' attitude, since he came to deliver mankind from sin and from Satan's influence.

The New Testament strongly emphasizes Jesus' authority over demons, which he cast out "by the finger of God" (Lk 11:20). In the Gospel perspective, the deliverance of those possessed by demons (cf. Mk 5:1–20) acquires a broader meaning than mere physical healing, in that the physical ailment is seen in relation to an interior one. The disease from which Jesus sets people free is primarily that of sin. Jesus himself explains this when he heals the paralytic: "'That you may know that the Son of Man has authority on earth to forgive sins,' he said to the paralytic, 'I say to you, rise, take up your pallet and go home'" (Mk 2:10–11). Even before working cures, Jesus had already conquered sin by overcoming the "temptations" which the devil presented to him during the time he spent in the wilderness after John baptized him (cf. Mk 1:12–13; Mt 4:1–11; Lk 4:1–13).

To fight the sin that lurks in us and around us, we must follow in Jesus' footsteps and learn the sense of his constant "yes" to the Father's plan of love. This "yes" demands our total commitment, but we would not be able to say it without the help of that grace which Jesus himself obtained for us by his work of redemption.

Looking at the world today we have to admit that there is a marked decline in the consciousness of sin. Because of widespread religious indifference or the rejection of all that right reason and revelation tell us about God, many men and women lack a sense of God's covenant and of his commandments. All too often the human sense of responsibility is blurred by a claim to absolute freedom, which is considered threatened and compromised by God, the supreme legislator.

The current tragic situation, which seems to have forsaken certain fundamental moral values, is largely due to the loss of the sense of sin. This fact makes us aware of the great distance to be covered by the new evangelization. Consciences must recover the sense of God, of his mercy and of the gratuitousness of his gifts, in order to be able to recognize the gravity of sin, which sets man against his Creator. Personal freedom should be recognized and defended as a precious gift of God, resisting the tendency to lose it in the structures of social conditioning, or to remove it from its inalienable reference to the Creator.

It is also true that personal sin always has a social impact. While he offends God and harms himself, the sinner also becomes responsible for the bad example and negative influences linked to his behavior. Even when the sin is interior, it still causes a worsening of the human condition, and diminishes that contribution which every person is called to make to the spiritual progress of the human community.

Besides all this, the sins of individuals strengthen those forms of social sin, which are actually the fruit of an accumulation of many personal sins. Obviously the real responsibility lies with individuals, given that the social structure as such is not the subject of moral acts. As the Post-Synodal Apostolic Exhortation *Reconciliatio et Paenitentia* recalls: "Whenever the Church speaks of *situations* of sin, or when she condemns as *social sins* certain situations or the collective behavior of certain social groups, big or small, or even of whole nations and blocs of nations, she knows and she proclaims that such cases of *social sin* are the result of the accumulation and concentration of many *personal sins*.... The real responsibility, then, lies with individuals" (n. 16).

Nevertheless, it is an indisputable fact, as I have often pointed out, that the interdependence of social, economic and political systems creates multiple structures of sin in today's world. (cf. *Sollicitudo Rei Socialis,* 36; *CCC* 1869). Evil exerts a frightening power of attraction that causes many types of behavior to be judged "normal" and "inevitable." Evil then grows, having devastating effects on consciences, which become confused and even incapable of discernment. If one then thinks of the structures of sin that hinder the development of the peoples most disadvantaged from the economic and political standpoint (cf. *SRS* 37), one might almost surrender in the face of a moral evil which seems inevitable. So many people feel powerless and bewildered before an overwhelming situation from which there seems no escape. But the proclamation of Christ's victory over evil gives us the certainty that even the strongest structures of evil can be overcome and replaced by "structures of good" (cf. *SRS* 39).

The "new evangelization" faces this challenge. It must work to ensure that people recover the awareness that in Christ, evil can be conquered with good. People must be taught a sense of personal responsibility, closely connected with moral obligations and the consciousness of sin. The path of conversion entails the exclusion of all connivance with those structures of sin, which today in particular, influence people in life's various contexts.

The Jubilee offers individuals and communities a providential opportunity to walk in this direction by promoting an authentic "metanoia," that is, a change of mentality that will help create ever more just and human structures for the benefit of the common good.

General audience of August 25, 1999

Church Asks Pardon
for Her Members' Sins

"Blessed are you, O Lord, the God of our fathers.... For we have sinned and transgressed by departing from you, and we have done every kind of evil. Your commandments we have not heeded or observed" (Dn 3:26, 29–30). This is how the Jews prayed after the Exile (cf. also Bar 2:11–13), accepting responsibility for the sins committed by their fathers. The Church imitates their example and also asks forgiveness for the historical sins of her children.

In our century, the Second Vatican Council gave an important impetus to the Church's renewal, so that, as a community of the saved, she might become an ever more vivid image of Jesus' message to the world. Faithful to the teaching of the most recent Council, the Church is more and more aware that she can offer the world a consistent witness to the Lord only through the continual purification of her members. Therefore, "the Church, embracing in its bosom sinners, at the same time holy and always in need of being purified, always follows the way of penance and renewal" (*LG* 8).

Recognition of the community implications of sin spurs the Church to ask forgiveness for the "historical" sins of her children. She is prompted to do this by the valuable opportunity offered by the Great Jubilee of the Year 2000, which, following the teaching of the Second Vatican Council, intends to turn a new page of history by overcoming the obstacles that still divide human beings and Christians in particular. In my Apostolic Letter *Tertio Millennio Adveniente,* I therefore asked that at the end of this second millennium "the Church should become more fully conscious of the sinfulness of her children, recalling all those times in history when they departed from the spirit of Christ and his Gospel, and instead of offering to the world the witness of a life inspired by the values of faith, indulged in ways of thinking and acting which were truly forms of counter witness and scandal" (n. 33).

The recognition of historical sins presupposes taking a stand in relation to events as they really happened and which only a serene and complete historical reconstruction can reveal. On the other hand, the judging of historical events cannot prescind from a realistic study of the conditioning caused by individual cultural contexts, before attributing specific moral responsibilities to individuals. The Church is certainly not afraid of the truth that emerges from history and is ready to acknowledge mistakes wherever they have been identified, especially when they involve the respect that is owed to individuals and communities. She is inclined to mistrust generalizations that excuse or condemn various historical periods. She entrusts the investigation of the past to patient, honest, scholarly reconstruction, free from confessional or ideological prejudices, regarding both the accusations brought against her and the wrongs she has suffered.

When they have been established by serious historical research, the Church feels it her duty to acknowledge the sins of her members and to ask God and her brethren to forgive them. This request for pardon must not be understood as an expression of false humility or as a denial of her 2000-year history, which is certainly richly deserving in the areas of charity, culture and holiness. Instead, she responds to a necessary requirement of the truth, which, in addition to the positive aspects, recognizes the human limitations and weaknesses of the various generations of Christ's disciples.

The approach of the Jubilee calls attention to certain types of sin, past and present, for which we especially need to ask the Father's mercy. I am thinking first of all of the painful reality of the division among Christians. The wounds of the past, certainly not without sins on both sides, continue to scandalize the world. A second act of repentance concerns the acquiescence given to intolerance and even the use of violence in the service of truth (cf. *TMA* 35). Although many acted here in good faith, it was certainly not evangelical to think that the truth should be imposed by force. Then there is the lack of discernment by many Christians in situations where basic human rights were violated. The request for forgiveness applies to whatever should have been done or was passed over in silence because of weakness or bad judgment, to what was done or said hesitantly or inappropriately.

On this and other points "the consideration of mitigating factors does not exonerate the Church from the obligation to express profound regret for the weaknesses of so many of her sons and daughters who sullied her face, preventing her from fully mirroring the image of her crucified Lord, the supreme witness of patient love and of humble meekness" (*TMA* 35). Thus, the penitent attitude of the Church in our time, on the threshold of the third millennium, is not intended as a convenient historical revisionism, which at any rate would be as suspect as it is useless. Instead, it turns our gaze to the past and to the recognition of sins, so that they will serve as a lesson for a future of ever clearer witness.

General audience of September 1, 1999

Jesus Reveals the Father's Merciful Face

Continuing our reflection on the meaning of conversion, today we will also try to understand the meaning of the forgiveness of sins offered to us by Christ through the sacramental mediation of the Church. First, we want to consider the biblical message about God's forgiveness: a message that is amply developed in the Old Testament and reaches its fullness in the New. The Church has inserted this article of her faith into the Creed itself, where she professes the forgiveness of sins: *Credo in remissionem peccatorum.*

The Old Testament speaks to us in various ways about the forgiveness of sins. In this regard we find a variety of terms: sin is "forgiven," "blotted out" (Ex 32:32), "purged" (Is 6:7), "cast behind your back" (Is 38:17). For example, Psalm 103 says, "who forgives all your iniquity, who heals all your diseases" (v. 3). "He does not deal with us according to our sins, nor requite us according to our iniquities.... As a father pities his children, so the Lord pities those who fear him" (vv. 10, 13). God's willingness to forgive does not lessen man's responsibility and need to be converted. However, as the prophet Ezekiel stresses, if the wicked man turns away from his wrongful behavior, his sins will not be remembered and he will live (Ez 18, especially vv. 19–22).

In the New Testament, God's forgiveness is revealed through Jesus' words and deeds. In pardoning sins, Jesus shows the face of God the merciful Father. By opposing certain religious tendencies marked by hypocritical severity toward sinners, he shows on various occasions how great and profound is the Father's mercy toward all his children (cf. *CCC* 1443).

The high point of this revelation can be considered the sublime parable that is usually called "the prodigal son," but which should be called "the merciful father" (Lk 15:11–32). Here God's attitude is presented in terms that are truly overwhelming in comparison with human criteria and expectations. The father's conduct in the parable can be understood in all its originality, if we keep in mind that in the social context of Jesus' time it was normal for sons to work in their father's house, like the two sons of the vineyard owner, of whom he speaks in another parable (cf. Mt 21:28–31). This system continued until the father's death, and only then did the sons divide the property they had inherited. In our case, instead, the father agrees to give the younger son his share of the inheritance and divides his possessions between him and his elder son (cf. Lk 15:12).

The younger son's decision to be emancipated, squandering the goods he had received from his father and living a dissolute life (cf. Lk 15:13), is a shameless rejection of family communion. Leaving the father's house clearly expresses the meaning of sin as an act of ungrateful rebellion with its humanly painful consequences. Human reasonableness, in some way expressed in the elder brother's protest, would have recommended an appropriately severe punishment for the younger son's decision before he could fully rejoin the family.

But the father, catching sight of him while still a long way off, runs to meet him full of compassion (or better, "inwardly moved with pity," as the Greek text literally says: Lk 15:20), embraces him lovingly, and wants everyone to celebrate with him.

The father's mercy is even more apparent when he tenderly reprimands the elder brother for demanding his own rights (cf. Lk 15:29 f.) and invites him to the communal banquet of joy. Mere legalism is surpassed by the father's generous and gratuitous love, which exceeds human justice and calls both brothers to be seated again at the father's table. Forgiveness consists not only in taking back under the paternal roof the son who has left, but also in welcoming him with the joy of restored communion, bringing him from death to life. This is why "it was fitting to make merry and be glad" (Lk 15:32).

The merciful Father who embraces the prodigal son is the definitive icon of God revealed by Christ. First and foremost he is Father — God the Father who extends his arms in blessing and forgiveness, always waiting, never forcing any of his children. His hands support, clasp, give strength and at the same time, comfort, console and caress. They are the hands of both a father and a mother.

The merciful father in the parable possesses and transcends all the traits of fatherhood and motherhood. In throwing himself on his son's neck, he resembles a mother who caresses her son and surrounds him with her warmth. In the light of this revelation of the face and heart of God the Father, we can understand Jesus' saying, so disconcerting to human logic: "There will be more joy in heaven over one sinner who repents than over ninety-nine righteous persons who need no repentance" (Lk 15:7). And "There is joy before the angels of God over one sinner who repents" (Lk 15:10).

The mystery of "homecoming" wonderfully expresses the encounter between the Father and humanity, between mercy and misery, in a circle of love that touches not only the son who was lost, but is extended to all. The invitation to the banquet that the father extends to the elder son implies the heavenly Father's exhortation to all the members of the human family to be merciful as well. The experience of God's fatherhood implies the acceptance of "brotherhood," precisely because God is the Father of all, even of our erring brother.

In recounting this parable, Jesus does not only speak of the Father but also lets us glimpse his own sentiments. To the Pharisees and the scribes who accused him of receiving sinners and eating with them (cf. Lk 15:2), he shows his preference for the sinners and tax collectors who were approaching him with trust (cf. Lk 15:1), and thus reveals that he has been sent to manifest the Father's mercy. This is the mercy that shines brightly especially on Golgotha, in the sacrifice offered by Christ for the forgiveness of sins (cf. Mt 26:28).

General audience of September 8, 1999

Penance:
Encounter with the Merciful Father

The journey to the Father, proposed for special reflection during this year of preparation for the Great Jubilee, also implies a rediscovery of the sacrament of Penance in its profound meaning as an encounter with the One who forgives us through Christ in the Spirit (cf. *TMA* 50). There are various reasons why a serious reflection on this sacrament is urgently needed in the Church. It is called for especially by the message of the Father's love as the basis of Christian living and acting in the context of contemporary society, where the ethical vision of human life is often obscured. If many have lost their perspective on good and evil, it is because they have lost their sense of God, interpreting guilt only from a psychological or sociological viewpoint. Secondly, pastoral ministry must give a new impetus to a journey of faith growth that stresses the value of the spirit and practice of penance throughout the Christian life.

The biblical message presents this "penitential" dimension as an ongoing commitment to conversion. Doing works of penance presupposes a transformation of conscience that is the result of God's grace. In the New Testament especially, conversion is required as a fundamental choice of those to whom the kingdom of God is preached: "Repent and believe in the Gospel" (Mk 1:15; cf. Mt 4:17). Jesus began his ministry with these words, announcing the fulfillment of time and the imminence of the kingdom. "Repent" (in Greek, *metanoeite*) is a call to change one's way of thinking and acting.

This invitation to conversion forms the vital conclusion of the apostles' preaching after Pentecost. It fully explains the content of the message: it is no longer generically the "kingdom," but Jesus' very work as part of the divine plan foretold by the prophets. The proclamation of what occurred in Jesus Christ, who died, rose again and now lives in the Father's glory, is followed by the pressing invitation to "conversion," to which the forgiveness of sins is also connected. All of this can be clearly seen in Peter's address in Solomon's portico: "What God foretold by the mouth of all the prophets, that his Christ should suffer, he thus fulfilled. Repent, therefore, and turn again, that your sins may be blotted out" (Acts 3:18–19).

In the Old Testament God promises this forgiveness of sins in the context of the "New Covenant" (cf. Jer 31:31–34). God will write his law in their hearts. From this standpoint, conversion is a requirement of the definitive covenant with God as well as a permanent attitude of those who accept the content of the Gospel message and enter into the historical and eschatological dynamism of God's kingdom.

The sacrament of Reconciliation conveys and makes visible in a mysterious way these fundamental values proclaimed by the Word of God. It reinserts man into the saving context of the covenant and opens him again to the Trinitarian life, which is a dialogue of grace, a circuit of love, the gift and acceptance of the Holy Spirit.

A careful rereading of the *Ordo Paenitentiae (Rite of Penance)* will be a great help during the Jubilee for deepening our understanding of the essential elements of this sacrament. The maturity of ecclesial life depends in large part on its rediscovery. The sacrament of Reconciliation is not limited to the liturgical celebration, but leads to a penitential attitude of life as an ongoing dimension of the Christian experience. It is "a drawing near to the holiness of God, a rediscovery of one's true identity which has been upset and disturbed by sin, a liberation in the very depth of self and thus a regaining of lost joy, the joy of being saved, which the majority of people in our time are no longer capable of experiencing" (*RP* 31, III).

For the doctrinal meaning of this sacrament, I refer you to the Apostolic Exhortation *Reconciliatio et Paenitentia* (cf. nn. 28–34) and to the *Catechism of the Catholic Church* (cf. 1420–1484), as well as to the other statements of the Church's Magisterium. Here I would like to recall the importance of the necessary pastoral care for instilling a greater appreciation of this sacrament in the People of God, so that the message of reconciliation, the path of conversion and the very celebration of the sacrament can more deeply touch the hearts of the men and women of our day.

In particular, I wish to remind pastors that, to be good confessors, they themselves must be authentic penitents. Priests know that they have been entrusted with a power that comes from on high: the forgiveness imparted by them "is the effective sign of the intervention of the Father" (*RP* 31, III) which brings resurrection from spiritual death. Therefore, when carrying out such an essential dimension of their ministry with Gospel humility and simplicity, confessors should not neglect their own growth and renewal, so that they will never lack those human and spiritual qualities that are so necessary for their relationship to consciences.

But along with pastors, the entire Christian community must be involved in the pastoral renewal of reconciliation. This is required by the "ecclesial nature" of the sacrament itself. The ecclesial community is the embrace that welcomes the repentant and forgiven sinner, and even before, creates a suitable climate for the journey back to the Father. In a reconciled and reconciling community, sinners can find the way they had lost, and the help of their brethren. In the end, through the Christian community it is possible again to mark out a sound path of charity, which visibly expresses through good works the for-giveness refound, the evil redressed, the hope of being able once again to experience the Father's merciful embrace.

General audience of September 15, 1999

Reconciliation
with God and One Another

Continuing our reflection on the sacrament of Penance, today let us explore a dimension that is one of its essential features: reconciliation. This aspect of the sacrament serves as an antidote or remedy to the destructive nature of sin. By sinning, man not only distances himself from God, but also sows the seed of division in himself and in his relations with others. The process of returning to God, therefore, implies restoration of the unity jeopardized by sin.

Reconciliation is *the Father's gift:* he alone can achieve it. This is why it is primarily an appeal which comes from on high: "In Christ's name: be reconciled to God" (2 Cor 5:20). As Jesus explains in the parable of the prodigal son (cf. Lk 15:11–32), forgiving and reconciling people to himself is a celebration for him. In this as in other Gospel passages, the Father not only offers his forgiveness and reconciliation, but at the same time shows how these gifts are a source of joy for everyone.

In the New Testament there is a significant link between the divine fatherhood and the festive joy of a banquet. The kingdom of God is compared to a joyful feast at which the host is actually the Father (cf. Mt 8:11; 22:4; 26:29). The fulfillment of all salvation history is again expressed in the image of a banquet prepared by God the Father for the wedding feast of the Lamb (cf. Rev 19:6–9).

The reconciliation that comes from the Father is concentrated in Christ himself, the Lamb without blemish offered for our sins (1 Pt 1:19; Rev 5:6; 12:11). Jesus Christ is not only the Reconciler, but Reconciliation itself. As St. Paul teaches, our becoming new creatures, renewed by the Spirit, "is from God, who through Christ reconciled us to himself and gave us the ministry of reconciliation; that is, God was in Christ reconciling the world to himself, not counting their trespasses against them, and entrusting to us the message of reconciliation" (2 Cor 5:18–19).

It is precisely through the mystery of the cross that our Lord Jesus Christ overcomes the tragedy of the division between man and God. Indeed, with Easter the mystery of the Father's infinite mercy penetrates the darkest roots of human iniquity. There a movement of grace begins, which if accepted with free consent, leads us to taste the sweetness of full reconciliation. The abyss of Christ's pain and abandonment is thus turned into an inexhaustible source of compassionate and reconciling love. The Redeemer retraces a path leading back to the Father, making it possible to experience again the filial relationship that was lost, and to confer on human beings the necessary strength to preserve this deep communion with God.

Unfortunately, even in redeemed existence there is the possibility of sinning again, and this calls for constant vigilance. Furthermore, even after forgiveness, the "residue of sin" remains and must be removed and combated by a program of penance involving a greater commitment to doing good. This requires first the reparation of physical or moral wrongs done to groups or individuals. Conversion thus becomes a continual journey, in which the mystery of reconciliation made present in the sacrament is the point of arrival and departure.

The encounter with the forgiving Christ increases in our hearts that dynamism of Trinitarian love which the *Ordo Paenitentiae* describes in the following way: "In the sacrament of Penance the Father receives the repentant children who come back to him; Christ places the lost sheep on his shoulders and brings them back to the sheepfold, and the Holy Spirit resanctifies those who are the temple of God or dwells more fully in them. The expression of all this is the sharing in the Lord's table, begun again or made more ardent; such a return of children from afar brings great rejoicing at the banquet of God's Church" (n. 6; cf. also nn. 5, 19).

In the formula of absolution, the "Rite of Penance" expresses the relationship between forgiveness and peace, offered by God the Father in the death and resurrection of his Son and the mediation of "the ministry of the Church" (*OP* 46). While the sacrament signifies and brings about the gift of reconciliation, it also highlights the fact that reconciliation concerns our relationship not only with God the Father, but also with our brothers and sisters. These two aspects of reconciliation are closely correlated. Christ's reconciling work occurs in the Church. She cannot reconcile on her own but only as a living instrument of Christ's pardon, on the basis of the Lord's precise mandate (cf. Jn 20:23; Mt 18:18). This reconciliation in Christ is achieved in a preeminent way in the celebration of the sacrament of Penance. But the Church's whole inner being in its community dimension is characterized by a permanent disposition to reconciliation.

It is necessary to overcome a certain individualism in the way one thinks of reconciliation: the entire Church cooperates in the conversion of sinners through prayer, exhortation, fraternal correction and charitable support. Without reconciliation with our brothers and sisters, love would not take flesh in the individual. Just as sin damages the tissue of the Body of Christ, so reconciliation restores solidarity among the People of God.

Ancient penitential practice highlighted the community-ecclesial aspect of reconciliation, particularly at the final moment of absolution by the bishop with full readmission of the penitents into the community. The Church's teaching and the penitential discipline promulgated after the Second Vatican Council urge the faithful to rediscover and restore to honor this community-ecclesial dimension of reconciliation (cf. *LG* 11 and *Sacrosanctum Concilium,* 27), while maintaining the doctrine on the need for individual confession.

In the context of the Great Jubilee of the Year 2000, it will be important to offer effective and updated paths of reconciliation that will lead to rediscovering the community dimension not only of penance, but of the Father's entire plan of salvation for humanity. Thus, the teaching of the Constitution *Lumen Gentium* will be put into practice: "God, however, does not make men holy and save them merely as individuals, without bond or link between one another. Rather has it pleased him to bring men together as one people, a people which acknowledges him in truth and serves him in holiness" (n. 9).

General audience of September 22, 1999

Indulgences Are an Expression of God's Mercy

In close connection with the sacrament of Penance, our reflection today turns to a theme particularly related to the celebration of the Jubilee: I am referring to the gift of indulgences, which are offered in particular abundance during the Jubilee Year, as indicated in the Bull *Incarnationis Mysterium* and the attached decree of the Apostolic Penitentiary. This sensitive subject has suffered historical misunderstandings that have had a negative impact on communion between Christians. In the present ecumenical context, the Church is aware of the need for this ancient practice to be properly understood and accepted as a significant expression of God's mercy. Experience shows that indulgences are sometimes received with superficial attitudes that ultimately frustrate God's gift and cast a shadow on the very truths and values taught by the Church.

The starting point for understanding indulgences is the abundance of God's mercy revealed in the cross of Christ. The crucified Jesus is the great "indulgence" that the Father has offered humanity through the forgiveness of sins and the possibility of living as children (cf. Jn 1:12–13) in the Holy Spirit (cf. Gal 4:6; Rom 5:5; 8:15–16). However, in the logic of the covenant, which is the heart of the whole economy of salvation, this gift does not reach us without our acceptance and response.

In the light of this principle, it is not difficult to understand how reconciliation with God, although based on a free and abundant offer of mercy, at the same time implies an arduous process that involves the individual's personal effort and the Church's sacramental work. For the forgiveness of sins committed after Baptism, this process is centered on the sacrament of Penance, but it continues after the sacramental celebration. The person must be gradually "healed" of the negative effects which sin has caused in him (what the theological tradition calls the "punishments" and "remains" of sin).

At first sight, to speak of punishment after sacramental forgiveness might seem inconsistent. The Old Testament, however, shows us how normal it is to undergo reparative punishment after forgiveness. God, after describing himself as "a God merciful and gracious...forgiving iniquity and transgression and sin," adds: "yet not without punishing" (Ex 34:6–7). In the Second Book of Samuel, King David's humble confession after his grave sin obtains God's forgiveness (cf. 2 Sam 12:13), but not the prevention of the foretold chastisement (cf. 2 Sam 12:11; 16:21). God's fatherly love does not rule out punishment, even if the latter must always be understood as part of a merciful justice that reestablishes the violated order for the sake of man's own good (cf. Heb 12:4–11).

In this context temporal punishment expresses the condition of suffering of those who, although reconciled with God, are still marked by those "remains" of sin that do not leave them totally open to grace. Precisely for the sake of complete healing, the sinner is called to undertake a journey of conversion toward the fullness of love. In this process God's mercy comes to his aid in special ways. The temporal punishment itself serves as "medicine" to the extent that the person allows it to challenge him to undertake his own profound conversion. This is the meaning of the "satisfaction" required in the sacrament of Penance.

The meaning of indulgences must be seen against this background of man's total renewal by the grace of Christ the Redeemer through the Church's ministry. They began historically with the ancient Church's awareness of being able to express the mercy of God by mitigating the canonical penances imposed for the sacramental remission of sins. The mitigation was offset, however, by personal and community obligations as a substitute for the punishment's "medicinal" purpose.

We can now understand how an indulgence is "a remission before God of the temporal punishment due to sins whose guilt has already been forgiven, which the faithful Christian who is duly disposed gains under certain prescribed conditions through the action of the Church, which as the minister of redemption, dispenses and applies with authority the treasure of the satisfactions of Christ and the saints."[1]

The Church has a treasury that is "dispensed" as it were through indulgences. This "distribution" should not be understood as a sort of automatic transfer, as if we were speaking of "things." It is, instead, the expression of the Church's full confidence of being heard by the Father when — in view of Christ's merits, and by his gift, those of Our Lady and the saints — she asks him to mitigate or cancel the painful aspect of punishment by fostering its medicinal aspect through other channels of grace. In the unfathomable mystery of divine wisdom, this gift of intercession can also benefit the faithful departed, who receive its fruits in a way appropriate to their condition.

---

1. *Enchiridion Indulgentiarum, Normae de Indulgentiis* (Handbook of indulgences) (Vatican City: Libreria Editrice Vaticana, 1999), 21; cf. *CCC* 1471).

We can see, then, how indulgences, far from being a sort of "discount" on the duty of conversion, are instead an aid to its prompt, generous and radical fulfillment. This is required to such an extent that the spiritual condition for receiving a plenary indulgence is the exclusion "of all attachment to sin, even venial sin" (*EI,* p. 25). Therefore, it would be a mistake to think that we can receive this gift by simply performing certain outward acts. On the contrary, they are required as the expression and support of our progress in conversion. They particularly show our faith in God's mercy and in the marvelous reality of communion, which Christ has achieved by indissolubly uniting the Church to himself as his Body and Bride.

General audience of September 29, 1999

God's Essence Is a
Mystery of Infinite Love

Conversion, which we treated in the pervious catecheses, is aimed at fulfilling the commandment of love. In this year dedicated to God the Father, it is especially appropriate to emphasize the theological virtue of charity, as indicated in the Apostolic Letter *Tertio Millennio Adveniente* (cf. n. 50). The Apostle John urges us: "Beloved, let us love one another; for love is of God, and he who loves is born of God and knows God. He who does not love does not know God; for God is love" (1 Jn 4:7–8). While these sublime words reveal to us the very essence of God as a mystery of infinite charity, they also lay the basis for the Christian moral life, which is summed up in the commandment of love. The human person is called to relate to his brothers and sisters with a loving attitude inspired by God's own love. Conversion means being converted to love.

In the Old Testament the inner dynamics of this commandment can already be seen in the covenant relationship established by God with Israel: on the one hand, there is the initiative of God's love, and on the other, the response of love that he expects from Israel. This is how, for example, the divine initiative is presented in the Book of Deuteronomy: "It was not because you were more numerous than any other people that the Lord chose you, for you were the fewest of all peoples, but it is because the Lord loves you" (7:7–8). The basic commandment that directs Israel's entire religious life corresponds to this preferential, totally gratuitous love: "You shall love the Lord your God with all your heart and with all your soul and with all your might" (Dt 6:5).

The loving God is a God who is not remote, but intervenes in history. When he reveals his name to Moses, he does so to assure him of his loving assistance in the saving event of the Exodus, an assistance that will last forever (cf. Ex 3:15). Through the prophets' words, he would continually remind his people of this act of love. We read, for example, in Jeremiah: "Thus says the Lord: 'The people who survived the sword found grace in the wilderness; when Israel sought for rest, the Lord appeared to him from afar. I have loved you with an everlasting love; therefore I have continued my faithfulness to you'" (31:2–3).

This love takes on tones of immense tenderness (cf. Hos 11:8 f.; Jer 31:20) and normally uses the image of a father, but sometimes is also expressed in a spousal metaphor: "I will betroth you to me forever; I will betroth you to me in righteousness and in justice, in steadfast love and in mercy" (Hos 2:19; cf. vv. 18–25). Even after seeing his people's repeated unfaithfulness to the covenant, this God is still willing to offer his love, creating in man a new heart that enables him to accept the law he is given without reserve, as we read in the prophet Jeremiah: "I will put my law within them and I will write it upon their hearts" (Jer 31:33). Likewise in Ezekiel we read: "A new heart I will give you and a new spirit I will put within you, and I will take out of your flesh the heart of stone and give you a heart of flesh" (Ez 36:26).

In the New Testament this dynamic of love is centered on Jesus, the Father's beloved Son (cf. Jn 3:35; 5:20; 10:17), who reveals himself through him. Men and women share in this love by knowing the Son, that is, by accepting his teaching and his work of redemption. We can only come to the Father's love by imitating the Son in his keeping of the Father's commandments: "As the Father has loved me, so have I loved you; abide in my love. If you keep my commandments, you will abide in my love, just as I have kept my Father's commandments and abide in his love" (Jn 15:9–10). In this way we also come to share in the Son's knowledge of the Father: "No longer do I call you servants, for the servant does not know what his master is doing; but I have called you friends, for all that I have heard from my Father I have made known to you" (Jn 15:15).

Love enables us to enter fully into the filial life of Jesus, making us sons in the Son: "See what love the Father has given us, that we should be called children of God, and so we are. The reason why the world does not know us is that it did not know him" (1 Jn 3:1). Love transforms life and enlightens our knowledge of God to the point that it reaches that perfect knowledge of which St. Paul speaks: "Now I know in part; then I shall understand fully, even as I have been fully understood" (1 Cor 13:12).

It is necessary to stress the relationship between knowledge and love. The inner conversion which Christianity offers is a genuine experience of God, in the sense indicated by Jesus in his priestly prayer at the Last Supper: "This is eternal life, that they know you, the only true God, and Jesus Christ whom you have sent" (Jn 17:3). Knowledge of God, of course, also has an intellectual dimension (cf. Rom 1:19–20), but the living experience of the Father and the Son occurs through love, that is, in the last analysis, in the Holy Spirit, because "God's love has been poured into our hearts through the Holy Spirit" (Rom 5:5).

The Paraclete is the One through whom we experience God's fatherly love. Moreover, the most comforting effect of his presence in us is precisely the certainty that this eternal and boundless love with which God loved us first will never abandon us: "Who shall separate us from the love of Christ?... For I am sure that neither death, nor life, nor powers, nor height, nor depth, nor anything else in all creation, will be able to separate us from the love of God in Christ Jesus our Lord" (Rom 8:35, 38–39). The new heart, which loves and knows, beats in harmony with God who loves with an everlasting love.

General audience of October 6, 1999

Charity Is a Response
to God's Call to Love

In ancient Israel the fundamental commandment to love God was part of daily prayer: "The Lord our God is one Lord, and you shall love the Lord your God with all your heart and with all your soul and with all your might. And these words which I command you this day shall be upon your heart; and you shall teach them diligently to your children and shall talk of them when you sit in your house and when you walk by the way and when you lie down and when you rise" (Dt 6:4–7). The basis of this requirement to love God totally is the love that God himself has for us. He waits for a true response of love from the people he loves with the fondest love. He is a jealous God (cf. Ex 20:5) who cannot tolerate the idolatry that constantly tempts his people. "You shall have no other gods before me" (Dt 6:3).

Israel gradually understood that, in addition to this relationship of profound respect and exclusive worship, its attitude to the Lord had to be filial or even nuptial. The Song of Songs should be understood and interpreted in this sense, transfiguring the beauty of human love into the spousal dialogue between God and his people.

The Book of Deuteronomy recalls two essential characteristics of this love. The first is that man would never be capable of it, if God did not give him strength through "circumcision of the heart" (cf. 30:6), which frees it from every attachment to sin. The other is that this love, far from being reduced to sentiment, is concretely expressed by "walking in the ways" of God and by keeping "his commandments and his statutes and his ordinances" (30:16). This is the condition for "life and good," while turning the heart to other gods leads to "death and evil" (30:15).

The commandment in Deuteronomy remains unchanged in the teaching of Jesus, who describes it as "the great and first commandment," closely relating it to love of neighbor (cf. Mt 22:34–40). By expressing this commandment in the same terms as the Old Testament, Jesus shows that on this point revelation had already reached its apex. At the same time, the meaning of this commandment achieves its fullness precisely in Jesus' own person. In fact, it is in him that man's love for God reaches its greatest intensity. From now on, loving God with all our heart, with all our mind, and with all our strength means loving that God who revealed himself in Christ, and loving him by sharing in the very love of Christ "poured into our hearts through the Holy Spirit who has been given to us" (Rom 5:5).

Charity is the essence of the new "commandment" that Jesus taught. It is the soul of all the commandments, whose observance is further confirmed and indeed becomes a clear proof of one's love for God: "For this is the love of God, that we keep his commandments" (1 Jn 5:3). This love, which is also love for Jesus, is the condition for being loved by the Father: "He who has my commandments and keeps them, he it is who loves me; and he who loves me will be loved by my Father, and I will love him and manifest myself to him" (Jn 14:21).

Love for God, made possible by the gift of the Spirit, is therefore based on the mediation of Jesus, as he himself says in his priestly prayer: "I made known to them your name and I will make it known, that the love with which you have loved me may be in them and I in them" (Jn 17:26). This mediation becomes concrete especially in the gift he made of his life, a gift which, on the one hand, testifies to the greatest love and on the other, demands the observance of what Jesus commands: "Greater love has no man than this, that a man lay down his life for his friends. You are my friends if you do what I command you" (Jn 15:13–14). Christian charity draws from this source of love, which is Jesus, the Son of God offered for us. The ability to love as God loves is offered to every Christian as a fruit of the paschal mystery of his death and resurrection.

The Church has expressed this sublime reality by teaching that charity is a *theological virtue,* which means a virtue that refers directly to God and enables human creatures to enter the circuit of Trinitarian love. Indeed, God the Father loves us as he loves Christ, seeing his image in us. This image is painted in us, so to speak, by the Spirit, who, like an "iconographer," accomplishes it over time. Again, it is the Holy Spirit who draws the basic traits of the Christian response in our inmost depths. The dynamism of love for God thus flows from a sort of "connaturality" brought about by the Holy Spirit who "divinizes" us, in the language of the Eastern tradition.

Through the power of the Holy Spirit, charity shapes the moral activity of the Christian; it directs and strengthens all the other virtues, which build up the new man within us. As the *Catechism of the Catholic Church* says: "The practice of all the virtues is animated and inspired by charity, which 'binds everything together in perfect harmony' (Col 3:14); it is the *form of the virtues;* it articulates and orders them among themselves; it is the source and the goal of their Christian practice. Charity upholds and purifies our human ability to love, and raises it to the supernatural perfection of divine love" (n. 1827). As Christians, we are always called to love.

General audience of October 13, 1999

Love Is the Greatest
of All the Spirit's Gifts

"If anyone says, 'I love God,' and hates his brother, he is a liar; for he who does not love his brother whom he has seen, cannot love God whom he has not seen. And this commandment we have from him, that he who loves God should love his brother also" (1 Jn 4:20–21). The theological virtue of charity, which we spoke of in our last catechesis, is expressed in two dimensions: love of God and love of neighbor. In both these dimensions it is the fruit of the dynamism of Trinitarian life within us.

Indeed, love has its source in the Father; it is fully revealed in the Passover of the crucified and risen Son and is infused in us by the Holy Spirit. Through it God lets us share in his own love. If we truly love with the love of God, we will also love our brothers or sisters as God loves them. This is the great newness of Christianity: one cannot love God if one does not love one's brethren, creating a deep and lasting communion of love with them.

In this regard, the teaching of Sacred Scripture is unequivocal. The Israelites were already encouraged to love one another: "You shall not take vengeance or bear any grudge against the sons of your own people, but you shall love your neighbor as yourself" (Lv 19:18). At first this commandment seemed restricted to the Israelites, but it nonetheless gradually took on an ever broader sense to include the strangers who sojourned among them, in remembrance that Israel too was a stranger in the land of Egypt (cf. Lv 19:34; Dt 10:19).

In the New Testament this love becomes a command in a clearly universal sense: it presupposes a concept of neighbor that knows no bounds (cf. Lk 10:29–37), and is even extended to enemies (cf. Mt 5:43–47). It is important to note that love of neighbor is seen as an imitation and extension of the merciful goodness of the heavenly Father who provides for the needs of all without distinction (cf. Mt 5:45). However, it remains linked to love of God: indeed, the two commandments of love are the synthesis and epitome of the law and the prophets (cf. Mt 22:40). Only those who fulfill both these commandments are close to the kingdom of God, as Jesus himself stressed in answer to a scribe who had questioned him (cf. Mk 12:28–34).

Abiding by these guidelines which link love of neighbor with love of God and both of these to God's life in us, we can easily understand how love is presented in the New Testament as a *fruit* of the Spirit, indeed as the first of the many gifts listed by St. Paul: "The fruit of the Spirit is love, joy, peace, patience, kindness, goodness, faithfulness, gentleness, self-control" (Gal 5:22).

While correlating them, theological tradition distinguishes between the theological *virtues,* the *gifts* and the *fruits* of the Holy Spirit (cf. *CCC* 1830–1832). While the *virtues* are dispositions permanently conferred upon human beings in view of the supernatural works they must do, and the *gifts* perfect both the theological and the moral virtues, the *fruits* of the Spirit are virtuous acts which the person accomplishes with ease, habitually and with delight (cf. St. Thomas, *Summa Theol.,* I–II, q. 70 a. 1, *ad* 2). These distinctions are not contrary to what Paul says, speaking in the singular of the *fruit* of the Spirit. In fact, the Apostle wished to point out that the fruit *par excellence* is the same divine charity that is at the heart of every virtuous act. Just as sunlight is expressed in a limitless range of colors, so love is manifest in the multiple fruits of the Spirit.

In this regard, St. Paul says: "Above all these put on love, which binds everything together in perfect harmony" (Col 3:14). The hymn to love contained in the First Letter to the Corinthians (cf. ch. 13) celebrates this primacy of love over all the other gifts (cf. vv. 1–3), and even over faith and hope (cf. v. 13). The Apostle Paul says of it: "Love never ends" (v. 8).

Love of neighbor has a Christological connotation, since it must conform to Christ's gift of his own life: "By this we know love, that he laid down his life for us, and we ought to lay down our lives for the brethren" (1 Jn 3:16). Insofar as it is measured by Christ's love, it can be called a "new commandment" by which the true disciples may be recognized: "A new commandment I give to you, that you love one another, even as I have loved you, that you also love one another. By this all men will know that you are my disciples, if you have love for one another" (Jn 13:34–35). The Christological meaning of love of neighbor will shine forth at the second coming of Christ. Indeed at that very moment, it will be seen that the measure by which to judge adherence to Christ is precisely the daily demonstration of love for our neediest brothers and sisters: "I was hungry and you gave me food..." (cf. Mt 25:31–46). Only those who are involved with their neighbor and his needs concretely show their love for Jesus. Being closed and indifferent to the "other" means being closed to the Holy Spirit, forgetting Christ and denying the Father's universal love.

General audience of October 20, 1999

The Church's Preferential Love for the Poor

The Second Vatican Council underscored a specific dimension of charity that prompts us, following Christ's example, to reach out to those who are most poor: "Christ was sent by the Father 'to bring good news to the poor, to heal the contrite of heart' (Lk 4:18), 'to seek and to save what was lost' (Lk 19:10). Similarly, the Church encompasses with love all who are afflicted with human suffering, and in the poor and afflicted sees the image of its poor and suffering Founder. It does all it can to relieve their need and in them it strives to serve Christ" (*LG* 8). Today let us look closely at the teaching of Sacred Scripture about the reasons for the Church's preferential love of the poor.

It should first be noted that there is a development from the Old to the New Testament in evaluating the poor and their situation. In the Old Testament we often see the common human conviction that wealth is better than poverty and is the just reward for the upright and God-fearing person: "Blessed is the man who fears the Lord, who greatly delights in his commandments.... Wealth and riches are in his house" (Ps 112:1, 3). Poverty is considered a punishment for those who reject the instruction of wisdom (cf. Prv 13:18).

However, from another perspective, the poor become the object of special attention as victims of perverse injustice. The prophets' invectives against the exploitation of the poor are famous. The prophet Amos (cf. 2:6–15) includes oppression of the poor among his accusations against Israel: "They sell the righteous for silver and the needy for a pair of shoes — they trample the head of the poor into the dust of the earth and turn aside the way of the afflicted" (2:6–7). The connection between poverty and injustice is also stressed in Isaiah: "Woe to those who decree iniquitous decrees and the writers who keep writing oppression, to turn aside the needy from justice and to rob the poor of my people of their right, that widows may be their spoil and that they may make the fatherless their prey" (10:1–2). This connection also explains why there were many laws defending the poor and those who were socially the weakest: "You shall not afflict any widow or orphan. If you do afflict them and they cry out to me, I will surely hear their cry" (Ex 22:22–23; cf. Prv 22:22–23; Sir 4:1–10). To defend the poor is to honor God, Father of the poor. Generosity to them is therefore justified and recommended (Dt 15:1–11; 24:10–15; Prv 14:21; 17:5).

In the developing reflection on the theme of poverty, the latter acquires a religious value. God speaks of "his" poor (cf. Is 49:13) who are identified with the "remnant of Israel," described as a humble and lowly people by the prophet Zephaniah (cf. 3:12). It is also said of the future Messiah that he will take the poor and the oppressed to heart, as Isaiah states in the famous text about the root that would sprout from the stump of Jesse: "With righteousness he shall judge the poor and decide equity for the meek of the earth" (Is 11:4).

This is why in the New Testament the good news of deliverance is announced to the poor, as Jesus himself stressed, applying to himself the prophecy of the Book of Isaiah: "The Spirit of the Lord is upon me, because he has anointed me to preach good news to the poor. He has sent me to proclaim release to the captives and recovery of sight to the blind, to set at liberty those who are oppressed, to proclaim the acceptable year of the Lord" (Lk 4:18; cf. Is 61:1–2).

To possess the "kingdom of heaven," it is necessary to have the interior attitude of the poor (cf. Mt 5:3; Lk 6:20). In the parable of the great feast, the poor, the crippled, the blind and the lame — in a word the most suffering and marginalized social categories — were invited to the banquet (cf. Lk 14:21). St. James would later say that God has "chosen those who are poor in the world to be rich in faith and heirs of the kingdom which he has promised to those who love him" (Jas 2:5).

"Evangelical" poverty always implies great love for the poorest of this world. We must rediscover God as the provident Father who has compassion on human suffering in order to relieve all who are afflicted. Our charity too must be expressed in sharing, and in human development understood as the integral growth of each person.

Throughout history Gospel radicalism has spurred many of Jesus' disciples to seek poverty to the point of selling their own goods and giving them as alms. Poverty here becomes a virtue that, besides alleviating the lot of the poor, becomes a spiritual path to true wealth, that is, to an unfailing treasure in heaven (cf. Lk 12:32–34). Material poverty is never an end in itself, but a means of following Christ, about whom Paul said: "Though he was rich, yet for your sake he became poor, so that by his poverty you might become rich" (2 Cor 8:9).

Here I can only stress again that the poor represent today's challenge especially for the wealthy peoples of our world, where millions of people are living in inhuman conditions and many are literally dying of hunger. We cannot proclaim God the Father to these brethren without the commitment to work together in Christ's name to build a more just society.

The Church, especially in her social Magisterium from *Rerum Novarum* to *Centesimus Annus,* has always striven to address the theme of the very poor. The Great Jubilee of the Year 2000 must be another opportunity for deep conversion of heart, so that the Spirit may raise up new witnesses to this cause. Christians, together with all people of good will, must contribute, by appropriate economic and political measures, to those structural changes that are so necessary for humanity to be freed from the plague of poverty (cf. *Centesimus Annus,* 57).

General audience of October 27, 1999

Reducing International Debt

"Come, O blessed of my Father, inherit the kingdom prepared for you from the foundation of the world; for I was hungry and you gave me food, I was thirsty and you gave me drink..." (Mt 25:34–35). These words of the Gospel help us to reflect on charity in practical terms, prompting us to focus, as suggested in *Tertio Millennio Adveniente* (cf. n. 51), on some forms of action that are particularly in keeping with the spirit of the Great Jubilee we are preparing to celebrate.

For this reason, it is appropriate to recall the biblical jubilee. As described in the Book of Leviticus, in certain respects it retraces and gives more complete expression to the role of the sabbatical year (cf. 25:2–7, 18–22), which was the year when the land was to remain uncultivated. The jubilee year occurred after forty-nine years. In this year, too, the soil was not to be cultivated (cf. 25:8–12), but the jubilee included two laws to the Israelites' advantage. The first concerned the return of land and buildings (cf. 25:13–17, 23–34); the second involved the freeing of Israelite slaves who had been sold because of debt to one of their compatriots (cf. 25:39–55).

The Christian jubilee, which was first celebrated by Boniface VIII in 1300, has its own specific features, but includes elements related to the biblical jubilee. As for the ownership of immovable property, the biblical jubilee's law is based on the principle that the "land is the Lord's" and is thus given for the benefit of the whole community. For this reason, if an Israelite had alienated his land, the jubilee year allowed him to repossess it. "The land shall not be sold in perpetuity, for the land is mine; for you are strangers and sojourners with me. And in all the country you possess, you shall grant a redemption of the land" (Lv 25:23–24).

The Christian jubilee refers in an increasingly explicit way to the social values of the biblical jubilee, which it interprets and reproposes in the contemporary context, reflecting on the demands of the common good and on the fact that the world's resources are meant for everyone. With this in mind, I proposed in *Tertio Millennio Adveniente* that the Jubilee be seen as "an appropriate time to give thought, among other things, to reducing substantially, if not canceling outright, the international debt, which seriously threatens the future of many nations" (n. 51).

In his Encyclical *Populorum Progressio,* Pope Paul VI said in regard to this problem, typical of many economically weak countries, that dialogue is needed between those who contribute wealth and those who benefit from it, in order to make "an assessment of the contribution necessary, not only drawn up in terms of the generosity and the available wealth of the donor nations, but also conditioned by the real needs of the receiving countries and the use to which the financial assistance can be put. Developing countries will thus no longer risk being overwhelmed by debts whose repayment swallows up the greater part of their gains" (n. 54). In the Encyclical *Sollicitudo Rei Socialis,* I had to note that changed circumstances both in the debtor nations and in the international financial market have unfortunately made financing itself a "counterproductive mechanism," because "the debtor nations, in order to service their debt, find themselves obliged to export the capital needed for improving or at least maintaining their standard of living. It is also because, for the same reason, they are unable to obtain new and equally essential financing" (n. 19).

The problem is complex and not easy to solve. It should be clear, however, that the problem is not only economic but involves fundamental ethical principles and should have a place in international law, in order to be addressed and adequately resolved in the middle and long term. A "survival ethics" should govern relations between creditors and debtors, so that debtors at risk are not put under unbearable pressure. It is a question of avoiding abusive speculation, of devising solutions so that lenders will be more confident and borrowers will feel obliged to make effective overall reforms at the political, bureaucratic, financial and social level in their countries.[1] Today, in the context of a "globalized" economy, the problem of the international debt has become even thornier, but "globalization" itself requires that the path of solidarity be taken, if we do not want to suffer a general catastrophe.

Precisely in the context of these considerations, we welcome the almost universal request we have received from recent synods, from many episcopal conferences or from individual brother bishops, as well as from many representatives of the religious, priests and laity, to make a heartfelt appeal for the partial or total cancellation of debts incurred at the international level. In particular, the demand for payments at exorbitant rates would impose political decisions that could reduce entire populations to hunger and distress.

The vision of solidarity, which I called attention to in *Centesimus Annus* (cf. n. 35), has become even more urgent in the world situation of recent years. The Jubilee can be an

---

1. Cf. Pontifical Commission for Justice and Peace, *At the Service of the Human Community: An Ethical Approach to the International Debt Question, II.*

appropriate occasion for goodwill gestures: may wealthier countries give signs of confidence in the economic recovery of poorer nations; may business leaders realize that in the dizzying process of economic globalization, one cannot be saved alone. May the goodwill gesture of canceling or at least reducing these debts be the sign of a new way of understanding wealth in terms of the common good.

General audience of November 3, 1999

Commitment to
Promoting Women's Dignity

Among the challenges of this historical moment on which the Great Jubilee spurs us to reflect, I drew attention in my Apostolic Letter *Tertio Millennio Adveniente* to the issue of respect for women's rights (cf. n. 51). Today I would like to recall certain aspects of the women's question, which I have spoken of on other occasions.

Sacred Scripture sheds great light on the theme of women's advancement, pointing out God's plan for man and woman in the two accounts of creation. The first one says: "God created man in his own image, in the image of God he created him; male and female he created them" (Gn 1:27). This statement is the basis of Christian anthropology, because it identifies the foundation of man's dignity as a person in his creation "in the likeness" of God. At the same time, the passage clearly says that neither man nor woman separately are the image of the Creator, but man and woman in their reciprocity. Both are equally God's masterpiece.

In the second account of creation, through the symbolism of the creation of woman from man's rib, Scripture stresses that humanity is not complete until woman is created (cf. Gn 2:18–24).

She is given a name whose verbal assonance in Hebrew indicates a relationship to man *(iš / ššiah)*. "God created man and woman *together* and willed each *for* the other" (*CCC* 371). That woman is presented as a "helper fit for him" (Gn 2:18) should not be interpreted as meaning that woman is man's servant — "helper" is not the equivalent of "servant," for the Psalmist says to God: "You are my help" (Ps 70:5; cf. Ps 115:9–11; Ps 118:7; Ps 146:5). Rather, the whole statement means that woman is able to collaborate with man because she complements him perfectly. Woman is another kind of "ego" in their common humanity, which consists of male and female in perfectly equal dignity.

There is good reason to rejoice that in contemporary culture, reflection on what it means to be feminine has led to a deeper understanding of the human person in terms of his "being for others" in interpersonal communion. Today, to think of the person in his self-giving dimension is becoming a matter of principle. Unfortunately it is often disregarded at the practical level. Thus, among the many assaults on human dignity, that widespread violation of woman's dignity manifested in the exploitation of her person and her body should be strongly condemned. All practices that offend woman's freedom or femininity must be vigorously opposed: so-called "sexual tourism," the buying and selling of young girls, mass sterilization and, in general, every form of violence to the other sex.

The moral law requires a very different attitude, for it proclaims the dignity of woman as a person created in the image of God-Communion! Today it is more necessary than ever to present the biblical anthropology of relationality, which helps us genuinely understand the human being's identity in his relationship to others, especially between man and woman. In the human person considered in his "relationality," we find a vestige of God's own mystery revealed in Christ as a substantial unity in the communion of three divine Persons. In the light of this mystery it is easy to understand the statement of *Gaudium et Spes* that the human being, "who is the only creature on earth which God willed for itself, cannot fully find himself except through a sincere gift of himself (cf. Lk 17:33)" (*GS* 24). The difference between man and woman calls for interpersonal communion, and meditation on the dignity and vocation of woman strengthens the concept of the human being based on communion (cf. *Mulieris Dignitatem,* 7).

Precisely this capacity for communion, which the feminine dimension strongly evokes, enables us to reflect on God's fatherhood, thus avoiding the imaginative projections of a patriarchal sort that are so challenged, and not without reason, in some currents of contemporary literature. It is a question of discerning the Father's face within the mystery of God as Trinity, that is, as perfect unity in distinction. The figure of the Father must be reconsidered in his relationship to the Son, who is turned toward him from all eternity (cf. Jn 1:1) in the communion of the Holy Spirit. It should also be stressed that the Son of God became man in the fullness of time and was born of the Virgin Mary (cf. Gal 4:4), and this too sheds light on the feminine dimension, showing Mary as the model of woman as willed be God. The greatest event in human history took place in her and through her. The fatherhood of God the Father is related not only to God the Son in his eternal mystery, but also to his Incarnation in a woman's womb. If God the Father, who "begets" the Son from all eternity, turned to a woman, Mary, to "beget" him in the world, thus making her *"Theotókos,"* Mother of God, this is not without significance for understanding woman's dignity in the divine plan.

Therefore, the Gospel message about God's fatherhood, far from restricting woman's dignity and role, serves instead as a guarantee of what the "feminine" humanly symbolizes, that is, to welcome and to care for the human person and to give birth to life. All this is rooted, in a transcendent way, in the mystery of the eternal divine "begetting." Certainly God's fatherhood is entirely spiritual. Nevertheless, it expresses that eternal reciprocity and relationality which are truly Trinitarian and are the origin of all fatherhood and motherhood, and the basis of the riches common to male and female. Reflection on woman's role and mission is particularly appropriate this year, which is dedicated to God the Father and spurs us to work with ever greater effort so that all the possibilities that are proper to woman in the Church and in society will be acknowledged.

General audience of November 24, 1999

Society Depends on Stable Families

The Christian community should be seriously committed to rediscovering the value of the family and marriage (cf. *TMA* 51). This is more urgent today, since this value is questioned at many levels of culture and society. Not only are challenges made to certain models of family life, which change under the pressure of social transformations and new working conditions. But the concept of the family itself, as a community founded on marriage between a man and a woman, is attacked in the name of ethical relativism, which is spreading in wide areas of public opinion and in civil legislation.

The crisis of the family becomes, in turn, a cause of the crisis in society. Many pathological phenomena — from loneliness to violence and drugs — arise when families lose their identity and purpose. Wherever the family falls apart, society loses its connective tissue. This brings disastrous consequences that affect individuals, especially the weakest: from children to adolescents, to the handicapped, to the sick and the elderly, etc.

It is therefore necessary to encourage a reflection that will help not only believers, but all people of good will to rediscover the value of marriage and the family. We read in the *Catechism of the Catholic Church:* "The family is the *original cell of social life*. It is the natural society in which husband and wife are called to give themselves in love and in the gift of life. Authority, stability and a life of relationships within the family constitute the foundations for freedom, security and fraternity within society" (n. 2207).

Reason itself can rediscover the family by listening to the moral law inscribed in the human heart. As a community "which is founded and given life by love" (cf. Apostolic Exhortation *Familiaris Consortio,* 18), the family draws its strength from the definitive covenant of love by which a man and a woman give themselves to each other, becoming together God's collaborators in the gift of life. On the basis of this fundamental relationship of love, the relationships that are established with and among the other family members must also be inspired by love and marked by affection and mutual support. Far from closing the family in on itself, genuine love opens it to all society, since the little domestic family and the great family of all human beings are not in opposition, but in a close and primordial relationship. At the root of all this is the very mystery of God, which the family evokes in a special way. Indeed, as I wrote a few years ago in my *Letter to Families,* "in the light of the New Testament it is possible to discern how the primordial model of the family is to be sought in God himself, in the Trinitarian mystery of his life. The divine 'We' is the eternal pattern of the human 'we,' formed by the man and the woman created in the divine image and likeness" (n. 6).

God's fatherhood is the transcendent source of all human fatherhood and motherhood. As we lovingly contemplate it, we feel impelled to rediscover that wealth of communion, procreation and life that characterize marriage and the family. In families, interpersonal relations develop in which each member is entrusted with a specific task, although without rigid patterns. I do not intend to refer here to those social and functional roles that are expressions of specific historical and cultural contexts. I am thinking, rather, of the importance, in the mutual conjugal relationship and the shared parental commitment, of man and woman as they are called to realize their natural characteristics in the context of a deep, enriching and respectful communion. "To this 'unity of the two' God has entrusted not only the work of procreation and family life, but the creation of history" (*Letter to Women,* 8).

Children, then, must be seen as the greatest expression of the communion between man and woman, or rather of their reciprocal receiving/giving, which is fulfilled and transcended in a "third," in the child himself. A child is a blessing from God who transforms husband and wife into father and mother (cf. *FC* 21). Both "come out of themselves" and express themselves in a person, which, although the fruit of their love, goes beyond them.

The ideal expressed in the priestly prayer of Jesus, in which he asks that his unity with the Father be extended to the disciples (cf. Jn 17:11) and to those who believe through their word (cf. Jn 17:20–21), applies to the family in a special way. Christian families, "domestic churches" (cf. *LG* 11), are especially called to achieve this ideal of perfect communion.

Let us rediscover the family in the light of the divine fatherhood. Our contemplation of God the Father prompts an urgent concern that is particularly in keeping with the challenges of this moment in history. Looking at God the Father means understanding the family as a place where life is welcomed and nurtured, a workshop of brotherhood where, with the help of Christ's Spirit, "a new fraternity and solidarity, a true reflection of the mystery of mutual self-giving and receiving proper to the Most Holy Trinity" (*EV* 76) is created among men. From the experience of renewed Christian families, the Church herself can learn how to foster among all the members of the community a more family-like dimension, by accepting and encouraging a more human and fraternal style of relationship (cf. *FC* 64).

General audience of December 1, 1999

Building a Civilization of Love

"Mindful of the Lord's saying: 'By this will all men know that you are my disciples, if you have love for one another' (Jn 13:35), Christians cannot yearn for anything more ardently than to serve the men of the modern world with mounting generosity and success" (*GS* 93). This task, which the Second Vatican Council gave us at the end of the *Pastoral Constitution on the Church in the Modern World,* responds to the fascinating challenge of building a world enlivened by the law of love, a *civilization of love,* "founded on the universal values of peace, solidarity, justice and liberty, which find their full attainment in Christ" (*TMA* 52). This civilization is based on recognition of the universal sovereignty of God the Father, the inexhaustible source of love. Precisely on the acceptance of this fundamental value, a sincere examination at the end of the millennium should be made for the Great Jubilee of the year 2000, in order to set out more promptly toward the future that awaits us.

We have seen the decline of ideologies which deprived so many of our brethren of spiritual reference points, but the baneful fruits of a secularism that breeds religious indifference continue to exist, especially in more developed regions. The return to a confused religiosity, caused by fragile compensatory needs and the search for a psycho-cosmic balance, which appears in many of the new religious paradigms that proclaim a religiosity without reference to a transcendent and personal God, is certainly not a valid response to this situation.

Instead, we must carefully analyze the reason for this loss of the sense of God and courageously proclaim the message of the Father's face, revealed by Jesus Christ in the light of the Spirit. This revelation does not diminish but exalts the dignity of the human person created in the image of God-Love.

In recent decades, the loss of the sense of God has coincided with the advance of a nihilistic culture that impoverishes the meaning of human life and, in the ethical fields, relativizes even the fundamental values of the family and of respect for life. This does not often occur visibly, but through a subtle methodology of indifference that makes all kinds of behavior seem normal, so that moral problems are no longer acknowledged. It is paradoxically demanded that the State recognize as "rights" many forms of conduct that threaten human life, especially the weakest and the most defenseless, not to mention the enormous difficulties in accepting others because they are different, inconvenient, foreign, sick or disabled. It is precisely this ever more prevalent rejection of others because of their otherness that challenges our conscience as believers. As I said in the encyclical *Evangelium Vitae:* "We are confronted by an even larger reality, which can be described as a veritable structure of sin characterized by the emergence of a culture which denies solidarity and in many cases takes the form of a veritable 'culture of death'" (n. 12).

In face of this death-loving culture, our responsibility as Christians is expressed in commitment to the "new evangelization," one of whose most important fruits is the civilization of love. "The Gospel, and therefore evangelization, are certainly not identical with culture and they are independent in regard to all cultures" (*EN* 20), but they possess a regenerating power that can have a positive influence on culture. The Christian message does not demean cultures by destroying their particular features; on the contrary, it acts within them, making the most of that original potential which their genius can express. The Gospel's influence on culture purifies and uplifts what is human, making the beauty of life, the harmony of peaceful coexistence and the originality that every people contributes to the human community shine resplendently. This influence finds its strength in a love that does not impose but proposes, relying on free assent in an atmosphere of respect and mutual acceptance.

The Gospel message of love liberates human needs and values, such as solidarity, the yearning for freedom and equality and respect for pluralism in forms of expression. The cornerstone of the civilization of love is recognition of the value of the human person and, concretely, of all human beings. Christianity's great contribution is recognized precisely in this area. In fact, the anthropological doctrine of the human person as a relational being developed gradually, precisely from reflection on the mystery of the Trinitarian God and on the person of the Word made flesh. This precious discovery gave rise to the idea of a society that has made the human person its starting point and goal. The Church's social teaching has also helped to base the laws of social coexistence on the rights of the person. The Christian vision of the human being as the image of God implies that the rights of the person, by their very nature, demand the respect of society, which does not create but merely recognizes them (cf. *GS* 26).

The Church realizes that this doctrine can remain a dead letter if social life is not enlivened by the influence of authentic religious experience, especially by a Christian witness continuously nourished by the Holy Spirit's creative and healing action. She knows that the crisis of society and of contemporary man is largely caused by the reduction of the human person's specific spiritual dimension.

Christianity makes its contribution to building a more human society precisely by providing it with soul and by proclaiming the demands of God's law, on which all social organization and legislation should be based if they intend to guarantee human advancement, liberation from every kind of slavery and true progress. The Church makes this contribution principally through the witness given by Christians, especially lay people, in their daily lives. Indeed, contemporary man accepts the message of love more from witnesses than from teachers, and if he does accept it from teachers, it is because they are authentic witnesses (cf. *EN* 41). This is the challenge to be met so that new horizons will be opened for the future of Christianity and of humanity itself.

General audience of December 15, 1999

Mary, the Father's Beloved Daughter

A few days after the opening of the Great Jubilee, I am pleased today to begin the first General Audience of 2000 by offering my most cordial wishes for the Jubilee Year to everyone here: may it truly be a special time of grace, reconciliation and interior renewal. This past year, the final one dedicated to immediate preparation for the Jubilee, we reflected together on the mystery of the Father. Today, at the end of that series of reflections and as a special introduction to the catecheses of the Holy Year, let us once again lovingly consider the person of Mary.

In her, the "beloved daughter of the Father" (*LG* 53), the divine plan of love for humanity was manifested. Destining her to become the mother of his Son, the Father chose her from among all creatures and raised her to the highest dignity and mission in the service of his people. The Father's plan began to be revealed in the "protoevangelium," when, after the fall of Adam and Eve, God announced that he would put enmity between the serpent and the woman: the woman's son will crush the serpent's head (cf. Gn 3:15). The promise began to be fulfilled at the annunciation, when Mary was given the proposal to become the Mother of the Savior.

"Rejoice, full of grace" (Lk 1:28). The first word that the Father spoke to Mary through his angel is a form of greeting which can be understood as an invitation to joy, an invitation that echoes the one addressed by the prophet Zechariah to the entire people of Israel: "Rejoice greatly, O daughter of Zion! Lo, your king comes to you" (Zech 9:9; cf. also Zeph 3:14–18). With this first word addressed to Mary, the Father reveals his intention to communicate true and definitive joy to humanity. The Father's own joy, which consists in having his Son beside him, is offered to everyone, but it is first entrusted to Mary so that it may spread from her throughout the human community.

For Mary, the invitation to rejoice is linked to the special gift she received from the Father: "full of grace." The Greek expression *kécharitôménê* is often translated, and not without reason, "filled with grace": it is an abundance that reaches the highest degree.

We can see that the expression sounds as if it were Mary's very name, the "name" given her by the Father from the beginning of her existence. From the moment of conception, in fact, her soul was filled with every blessing, enabling her to live in outstanding holiness throughout her earthly life. Mary's face reflects the mysterious face of the Father. The infinite tenderness of God-Love is revealed in the maternal features of Jesus' Mother.

Mary is the only mother who can say "my son" when speaking of Jesus, just as the Father says: "You are my Son" (Mk 1:11). For his part, Jesus calls the Father "Abba," "Dad" (cf. Mk 14:36), while he calls Mary "Mama," putting all his filial affection into this name. After leaving his mother in Nazareth, when he later meets her, he calls her "woman" to emphasize that he now takes orders from the Father alone, and to declare that she is not just a biological mother. She has a mission to fulfill as the "Daughter of Zion" and the mother of the people of the New Covenant. As such, Mary's goal is always to comply fully with the Father's will.

This was not the case with all of Jesus' family. The fourth Gospel reveals to us that his relatives "did not believe in him"

(Jn 7:5), and Mark says that "they went out to seize him, for they said, 'He is beside himself'" (Mk 3:21). We can be sure that Mary's inner thoughts were completely different. We are assured of this in the Gospel of Luke, in which Mary presents herself as the humble "handmaid of the Lord" (Lk 1:38). In this light we should understand Jesus' answer when "he was told: 'Your mother and your brethren are standing outside, desiring to see you'" (Lk 8:20; cf. Mt 12:46–47; Mk 3:32). Jesus replied: "My mother and my brethren are those who hear the Word of God and do it" (Lk 8:21). Mary is a model of listening to the Word of God (cf. Lk 2:19, 51) and of docility to it.

The Virgin maintained and perseveringly renewed the total willingness she had expressed at the annunciation. The immense privilege and sublime mission of being the Mother of God's Son did not change her humble submission to the Father's plan. Among the other aspects of this divine plan, she took up the educational task that her motherhood entailed. A mother not only gives birth, but is also actively involved in the formation and development of her child's personality. Mary's behavior certainly influenced Jesus' conduct. One can think, for example, that the act of washing feet (cf. Jn 13:4–5), left to the disciples as an example to follow (cf. Jn 13:14–15), reflects what Jesus himself had seen since childhood in Mary's behavior when she washed their guest's feet in a spirit of humble service.

According to the Gospel testimony, during the time he spent in Nazareth Jesus was "obedient" to Mary and Joseph (cf. Lk 2:51). He thus received from Mary a true education that shaped his humanity. On the other hand, Mary let herself be influenced and formed by her Son. In Jesus' gradual manifestation, she discovered the Father more and more profoundly and offered him homage with all the love of her daughterly heart. Her task now is to help the Church to walk in Christ's footsteps as she did.

General audience of January 5, 2000

Mary Cooperates in God's Saving Plan

Completing our reflection on Mary at the end of the series of catecheses devoted to the Father, today we want to stress her role in our journey to the Father. He himself desired Mary's presence in salvation history. When he decided to send his Son into the world, he wanted him to come to us by being born of a woman (cf. Gal 4:4). Thus he willed that this woman, the first to receive his Son, should communicate him to all humanity. Mary is found on the path that leads from the Father to humanity as the mother who gives the Savior Son to all. At the same time, she is on the path that human beings must take in order to go to the Father through Christ in the Spirit (cf. Eph 2:18).

To understand Mary's presence on our journey to the Father, we must recognize with all the Churches that Christ is "the way and the truth and the life" (Jn 14:6) and the only Mediator between God and men (cf. 1 Tim 2:5). Mary is involved in Christ's unique mediation and is totally at its service. Consequently, as the Council stressed in *Lumen Gentium:* "The maternal duty of Mary toward men in no wise obscures or diminishes this unique mediation of Christ, but rather shows his power" (n. 60). In no way do we state that Mary has a role in the Church's life apart from Christ's mediation or alongside it, as if it were a parallel or competing mediation.

As I expressly said in the Encyclical *Redemptoris Mater,* Mary's maternal mediation "is mediation *in* Christ" (n. 38). The Council explains: "For all the salvific influence of the Blessed Virgin on men originates, not from some inner necessity, but from the divine pleasure. It flows forth from the superabundance of the merits of Christ, rests on his mediation, depends entirely on it and draws all its power from it. In no way does it impede, but rather does it foster the immediate union of the faithful with Christ" (*LG* 60).

Mary, too, was redeemed by Christ and is indeed the first of the redeemed, since the grace granted to her by God the Father at the beginning of her existence is owed to "the merits of Jesus Christ, Savior of the human race," as affirmed by the Bull *Ineffabilis Deus* of Pius IX (*DS* 2803). All of Mary's cooperation in salvation is founded on Christ's mediation, which, as the Council clearly states, "does not exclude but rather gives rise to a manifold cooperation which is but a sharing in this one source" (*LG* 62).

Viewed in this way, Mary's mediation appears as the most sublime fruit of Christ's mediation and is essentially directed to bringing us into a more intimate and profound encounter with him: "The Church does not hesitate to profess this subordinate role of Mary. It knows it through unfailing experience of it and commends it to the hearts of the faithful, so that, encouraged by this maternal help, they may the more intimately adhere to the Mediator and Redeemer" (*LG* 62).

Mary does not want to draw attention to herself. She lived on earth with her gaze fixed on Jesus and the heavenly Father. Her greatest desire is to focus everyone's attention in the same direction. She wants to encourage a vision of faith and hope in the Savior sent to us by the Father. Her gaze of faith and hope was especially exemplary when, in the turmoil of her Son's passion, she kept in her heart a total faith in him and in the Father. While the disciples were bewildered by the events and their faith deeply shaken, Mary, although tried by sorrow, remained completely certain that Jesus' prediction would be filled: "The Son of Man...will be raised on the third day" (Mt 17:22–23). This certitude never left her, even when she held in her arms the lifeless body of her crucified son.

With this vision of faith and hope, Mary encourages the Church and believers always to fulfill the Father's will revealed to us by Christ. What she told the servants for the miracle at Cana reverberates for every generation of Christians: "Do whatever he tells you" (Jn 2:5). Her advice was followed when the servants filled the jars to the brim. Mary addresses the same invitation to us. She urges us to enter this new period of history with the intention of carrying out whatever Christ said in the Gospel on the Father's behalf, and now intimates to us through the Holy Spirit who dwells in us. If we do what Christ tells us, the millennium now begun can take on a new aspect, one more evangelical and authentically Christian, and thus fulfill Mary's deepest longing.

The words "Do whatever he tells you" direct us to Christ, but they also remind us that we are on our way to the Father. They coincide with the Father's voice heard on the mount of the Transfiguration: "This is my beloved Son...listen to him" (Mt 17:5). This same Father, through the word of Christ and the light of the Holy Spirit, calls us, guides us and waits for us.

Our holiness consists in doing everything the Father tells us, and this is the value of Mary's life: the fulfillment of God's will. Accompanied and supported by Mary, we gratefully receive the new millennium from the Father's hands and commit ourselves to responding to its grace with humble and generous devotion.

General audience of January 12, 2000

THE TRINITY

The Trinity:
Fountain of Love and Light

"O superessential Trinity, infinitely divine and good, guardian of the divine wisdom of Christians, lead us beyond all light and everything unknown to the highest summit of the mystical Scriptures, where the simple, absolute and imperishable mysteries of theology are revealed in the luminous darkness of silence." With this prayer of Dionysius the Areopagite, an Eastern theologian (*Mystical Theology,* I, 1), we begin a difficult but fascinating journey of contemplating the mystery of God. After having reflected in the past few years on each of the three divine Persons — the Son, the Spirit and the Father — in this Jubilee Year we intend to take a comprehensive look at the glory common to the Three who are one God "not in the unity of a single person but in the Trinity of one substance" *(Preface for the Solemnity of the Holy Trinity).* This choice corresponds to what was suggested in the Apostolic Letter *Tertio Millennio Adveniente,* which said that during the celebration phase of the Great Jubilee the aim would be "to give glory to the Trinity, from whom everything in the world and in history comes, and to whom everything returns" (n. 55).

307

Taking our inspiration from an image offered by the Book of Revelation (cf. 22:1), we could compare this journey to a pilgrimage along the banks of God's river, that is, of his presence and revelation in human history. As a brief sketch of this journey, today we will dwell on the two extremities of that river: its source and its mouth, joining them in a single horizon. The divine Trinity is at the very origins of existence and history and is present in their final goal. It constitutes the beginning and the end of salvation history. Between the two extremities, the Garden of Eden (cf. Gn 2) and the tree of life in the heavenly Jerusalem (cf. Rev 22), flows a long history marked by darkness and light, by sin and grace. Sin has separated us from the splendor of God's paradise; redemption brings us back to the glory of a new heaven and a new earth, where "death shall be no more; neither shall there be mourning nor crying nor pain any more" (Rev 21:4).

An initial view of this horizon is offered by the first page of Sacred Scripture, which indicates the moment when God's creative power made the world out of nothing: "In the beginning God created the heavens and the earth" (Gn 1:1). This view is deepened in the New Testament, going back to the very heart of the divine life, when John proclaims at the beginning of his Gospel: "In the beginning was the Word, and the Word was with God, and the Word was God" (1:1). Before creation and as its foundation, revelation has us contemplate the mystery of the one God in the Trinity of persons: the Father and his Word united in the Spirit.

The biblical author who wrote the creation text could not have suspected the depths of this mystery. Even less could mere philosophical reflection have attained it, since the Trinity is beyond the capacities of our understanding and can only be known through revelation.

Nevertheless, this mystery that infinitely transcends us is also the reality closest to us, because it is the very source of our being. For in God we "live and move and have our being" (Acts 17:28), and what St. Augustine says of God must be applied to all three divine Persons: he is *"intimior intimo meo"* (*Conf.*, 3, 6, 11). In the depths of our being, where not even our gaze can penetrate, the Father, Son and Holy Spirit, one God in three Persons, are present through grace. Far from being a dry intellectual truth, the mystery of the Trinity is the life that dwells in us and sustains us.

Our reflection will take its themes from this Trinitarian life, which precedes and grounds creation. The mystery of the origins from which all things flow, God appears to us as the One who is the fullness of being and communicates being, as the light that "enlightens every man" (cf. Jn 1:9), as the Living One and giver of life. He appears to us above all as Love, according to the beautiful definition in the First Letter of John (cf. 4:8). He is love in his inner life, where the Trinitarian dynamism is the very expression of the eternal love with which the Father begets the Son, and both give themselves to each other in the Holy Spirit. He is love in his relationship to the world, since the free decision to make it out of nothing is the fruit of this infinite love that radiates into the sphere of creation. If the eyes of our heart, enlightened by revelation, become pure and penetrating enough, they can by faith encounter this mystery in which everything that exists has its root and foundation.

But as we mentioned at the beginning, the mystery of the Trinity also lies before us as the goal to which we long. Our reflection on the Trinity, in the various realms of creation and history, will look at this goal, which the Book of Revelation very powerfully points to as the seal of history.

This is the second and final part of God's river, which we referred to a few moments ago. In the heavenly Jerusalem, the beginning and the end reconverge. For God the Father, who sits on the throne, appears and says: "Behold, I make all things new" (Rev 21:5). At his side is the Lamb — Christ — on his throne, with his light, with the book of life containing the names of the redeemed (cf. Rev 21:23, 27; 22:1, 3). At the end, in a gentle and intense dialogue, the Spirit who prays in us and with the Church, the Bride of the Lamb, says: "Come, Lord Jesus" (cf. Rev 22:17, 20).

At the end of this first sketch of long pilgrimage into the mystery of God, let us return then to the prayer of Dionysius the Areopagite, who reminds us of the need for contemplation: "It is really in silence that we learn the secrets of this darkness...which shines with dazzling light.... While remaining completely intangible and invisible, it fills minds that know how to close their eyes with the most beautiful splendors" (*Mystical Theology,* I, 1).

General audience of January 19, 2000

The Trinity Is
Mysteriously Present in Creation

"How greatly to be desired are all his works and how sparkling they are to see!... He has made nothing incomplete.... Who can have enough of beholding his glory? Though we speak much we cannot reach the end, and the sum of our words is: 'He is the all.' Where shall we find strength to praise him? He is greater than all his works..." (Sir 42:22, 24–25; 43:27–28). With these words full of wonder, Sirach, a biblical sage, contemplated the splendor of creation and sang God's praises. It is a tiny piece of the thread of contemplation and meditation which runs throughout Sacred Scripture, from the first lines of Genesis when creatures, summoned by the powerful Word of the Creator, spring from the silence of nothingness.

"God said, 'Let there be light'; and there was light" (Gn 1:3). In this part of the first account of creation the Word of God is already seen in action; John will say of him: "In the beginning was the Word...the Word was God...all things were made through him, and without him nothing came to be" (Jn 1:1–3). Paul will emphasize in the hymn in the letter to the Colossians that "in him [Christ] all things were created, in heaven and on earth, visible and invisible, whether thrones or dominions or principalities or authorities — all things were created through him and for him. He is before all things, and in him all things hold together" (Col 1:16–17). But at the very first moment of creation the Spirit also seems to be foreshadowed: "The Spirit of God was moving over the face of the waters" (Gn 1:2). The glory of the Trinity — we can say with Christian tradition — is resplendent in creation.

We can see in the light of revelation how the creative act is appropriated in the first place to the "Father of lights, with whom there is no variation or shadow due to change" (Jas 1:17). He shines resplendently over the whole horizon, as the Psalmist sings: "O Lord, our Lord, how glorious is your name over all the earth! You have exalted your majesty above the heavens" (Ps 8:2). God "has made the world firm, not to be moved" (Ps 96:10) and as he faces nothingness, symbolized by the chaotic waters which lift up their voice, the Creator arises, giving firmness and safety: "The floods have lifted up, O Lord, the floods have lifted up their voice, the floods lift up their roaring. Mightier than the thunders of many waters, mightier than the waves of the sea, the Lord on high is mighty" (Ps 93:3–4).

In Sacred Scripture creation is also often linked to the divine Word that breaks in and acts: "By the word of the Lord the heavens were made and all their host by the breath of his mouth.... He spoke and it came to be; he commanded and it stood forth.... He sends forth his command to the earth; his word runs swiftly" (Ps 33:6, 9; 147:15). In the wisdom literature of the Old Testament, divine Wisdom personified brings forth the universe, carrying out the plan God has in mind (cf. Prv 8:22–31). It has been said that in God's Word and Wisdom, John and Paul saw the foretelling of the action of Christ "from whom are all things and for whom we exist" (1 Cor 8:6), because it is "through [Christ] also [that God] created the world" (Heb 1:2).

At other times Scripture stresses the role of God's Spirit in the act of creation: "When you send forth your Spirit, they are created, and you renew the face of the earth" (Ps 104:30). The same Spirit is symbolically described as the breath of God's mouth. He gives life and consciousness to man (cf. Gn 2:7), and brings him back to life in the resurrection, as the prophet Ezekiel announces in an evocative passage where the Spirit is at work breathing life into dry bones (cf. 37:1–14). This same breath subdues the waters of the sea at Israel's exodus from Egypt (cf. Ex 15:8, 10). Again the Spirit regenerates the human creature, as Jesus will say in his nighttime conversation with Nicodemus: "Truly, truly, I say to you, unless one is born of water and the Spirit, he cannot enter the kingdom of God. That which is born of the flesh is flesh, and that which is born of the Spirit is spirit" (Jn 3:5–6).

So, in beholding the glory of the Trinity in creation, man must contemplate, sing and rediscover wonder. In contemporary society people become indifferent "not for lack of *wonders,* but for lack of *wonder"* (G. K. Chesterton). For the believer, to contemplate creation is also to hear a message, to listen to a paradoxical and silent voice, as the "psalm of the sun" suggests: "The heavens are telling the glory of God, and the firmament proclaims his handiwork. Day to day pours forth speech, and night to night declares knowledge. There is no speech, nor are there words; their voice is not heard; yet their voice goes out through all the earth, and their words to the end of the world" (Ps 19:1–5).

Nature thus becomes a gospel that speaks to us of God: "from the greatness and beauty of created things comes a corresponding perception of their Creator" (Wis 13:5). Paul teaches us that "ever since the creation of the world his [God's] invisible nature, namely, his eternal power and deity, has been clearly perceived in the things that have been made" (Rom 1:20). But this capacity for contemplation and knowledge, this discovery

of a transcendent presence in created things, must lead us also
to rediscover our kinship with the earth, to which we have been
linked since our own creation (cf. Gn 2:7). This is precisely the
goal that the Old Testament wished for the Hebrew Jubilee,
when the land was at rest and man ate what the fields spontaneously gave him (cf. Lv 25:11–12). If nature is not violated and
degraded, it once again becomes man's sister.

General audience of January 26, 2000

The Glory of the Trinity
Is Revealed in History

Our meeting today opened with the "Great Hallel," Psalm 136, which is a solemn litany for soloist and choir. It is sung to the *hesed* of God, that is, to his faithful love revealed through the events of salvation history, especially the deliverance from slavery in Egypt and the gift of the Promised Land. Israel's profession of faith in God (cf. Dt 26:5–9; Jos 24:1–13) proclaims God's actions in human history. The Lord is not an impassive emperor surrounded with a halo of light and relegated to the golden heavens; he sees the affliction of his people in Egypt, hears their cry and comes down to deliver them (cf. Ex 3:7–8).

Now we will try to explain God's presence in history in the light of the Trinitarian revelation that, although fulfilled completely in the New Testament, is already in some way anticipated and foreshadowed in the Old. We will begin then with the Father, whose features can already be glimpsed when God intervenes in history on behalf of the righteous who call upon him as a tender and loving father. He is "the father of orphans and the defender of widows" (Ps 68:6); he is also a father to his rebellious and sinful people.

prophetic texts, extraordinarily beautiful and intense, introduce a delicate soliloquy of God concerning his "degenerate children" (Dt 32:5). Through them God reveals his constancy and loving presence in the tangle of human history. In Jeremiah the Lord exclaims: "I am a father to Israel.... Is he not my favored son, the child in whom I delight? Often as I threaten him, I still remember him with favor; my heart stirs for him; I must show him mercy" (Jer 31:9, 20). The other wonderful confession by God can be read in Hosea: "When Israel was a child, I loved him, and out of Egypt I called my son.... It was I who taught Ephraim to walk; I took them up in my arms, but they did not know that I healed them. I led them with cords of compassion, with the bands of love; I fostered them like one who raises an infant to his cheeks, and I bent down to them and fed them.... My heart recoils within me, my compassion grows warm and tender" (Hos 11:1, 3–4, 8).

We must draw the conclusion from these biblical passages that God the Father is far from indifferent to what happens to us. Indeed, he even sends his Only-begotten Son into the heart of history, as Christ himself testified in his nighttime conversation with Nicodemus: "God so loved the world that he gave his only Son, that whoever believes in him should not perish but have eternal life. For God sent the Son into the world, not to condemn the world, but that the world might be saved through him" (Jn 3:16–17). The Son enters into time and space as the living and life-giving center that gives definitive meaning to the flow of history, saving it from dissipation and triviality. In particular, all humanity, with its joys and sorrows, its tormented history of good and evil, converges upon the cross of Christ, source of salvation and eternal life: "When I am lifted up from the earth, I will draw all men to myself" (Jn 12:32). The Letter to the Hebrews will proclaim Christ's perennial presence in history in one dazzling sentence: "Jesus Christ is the same yesterday and today and forever" (13:8).

To discover this hidden yet effective presence in the flow of events, to discern the kingdom of God that is now in our midst (cf. Lk 17:21), we must look beyond the outward appearances of historical dates and events. Here the *Holy Spirit* comes into action. Even if the Old Testament does not yet offer an explicit revelation of his person, certain saving initiatives can certainly be "appropriated" to him. It is he who spurs the judges of Israel (cf. Jgs 3:10), David (cf. 1 Sam 16:13), and the Messiah King (cf. Is 11:1–2; 42:1), but above all he pours himself out in the prophets, whose mission is to reveal the divine glory hidden in history, the Lord's plan underlying the events of our lives. The prophet Isaiah offers a most effective passage, which will be taken up by Christ in his programmatic address at the synagogue of Nazareth: "The Spirit of the Lord is upon me, because the Lord has anointed me to bring good tidings to the afflicted; he has sent me to bind up the brokenhearted, to proclaim liberty to the captives and the opening of the prison to those who are bound; to proclaim the year of the Lord's favor" (Is 61:1–2; Lk 4:18–19).

The Spirit of God not only reveals the meaning of history, but also instills the strength to cooperate with the divine plan that is fulfilled in it. In the light of the Father, the Son and the Spirit, history ceases to be a succession of events that fade into the abyss of death, but becomes a land made fruitful by the seed of eternity, a path leading to that sublime goal in which "God will be all in all" (1 Cor 15:28). The Jubilee, which calls to mind "the year of favor" announced by Isaiah and inaugurated by Christ, is intended to be the epiphany of this seed and this glory, so that everyone, sustained by God's presence, may hope in a new world which is more genuinely Christian and human.

May each of us then, in stammering something of the mystery of the Trinity at work in our history, make his own the adoring wonder of St. Gregory of Nazianzus, theologian and poet, when he sings: "Glory to God the Father and the Son,

King of the universe. Glory to the Spirit, worthy of praise and all holy. The Trinity is the one God who created and filled all things...giving life to all things by his Spirit, so that all creatures might sing praise to their wise Creator, the one cause of life and its duration. More than any other, may the rational creature always celebrate him as the great King and good Father" (*Dogmatic Poems, XXI, Hymnus alias: PG* 37, 510–511).

General audience of February 9, 2000

The Incarnation Reveals
the Glory of the Trinity

"One source and one root, one form shines out in threefold splendor. From the bright depths of the Father bursts forth the power of the Son, the wisdom that created the whole world, the fruit born of the Father's heart! And there blazes the unifying light of the Holy Spirit." So sang Synesius of Cyrene in *Hymn II* at the beginning of the fifth century, celebrating the divine Trinity, one in source and threefold in glory, at the dawn of a new day. This truth of the one God in three equal and distinct Persons is not relegated to heaven; it cannot be regarded as a sort of "heavenly mathematical theorem" with no implications for human life, as the philosopher Kant supposed.

In fact, as we heard in the Evangelist Luke's account, the glory of the Trinity becomes present in time and space and finds its manifestation in Jesus, his Incarnation and his history. Luke interprets the conception of Christ precisely in the light of the Trinity: this is attested by the angel's words to Mary, spoken inside the modest home in the Galilean village of Nazareth, which archaeology has brought to light. The transcendent divine presence is revealed in Gabriel's announcement: the Lord God — through Mary and in the line of David's descendants —

gives his Son to the world: "You will conceive in your womb and bear a son, and you shall call his name Jesus. He will be great, and will be called the Son of the Most High, and the Lord God will give to him the throne of his father David" (Lk 1:31–32).

Here the word "son" has a twofold sense, because the filial bond with the heavenly Father and the bond with the earthly mother are closely united in Christ. But the Holy Spirit also shares in the Incarnation, and indeed his action makes that conception unique and unrepeatable. "The Holy Spirit will come upon you and the power of the Most High will over-shadow you; therefore, the child to be born will be called holy, the Son of God" (Lk 1:35). The angel's words are like a short creed that sheds light on the identity of Christ in relation to the other Persons of the Trinity. Luke already places the Church's unanimous faith at the dawn of the saving fullness of time: Christ is the Son of the Most High God, the Great One, the Holy One, the King, the Eternal One, whose conception in the flesh takes place through the power of the Holy Spirit. There-fore, as John will say in his First Letter, "No one who denies the Son has the Father. He who confesses the Son has the Father also" (2:23).

At the center of our faith is the Incarnation, in which the glory of the Trinity and the Trinity's love for us is revealed: "And the Word became flesh and dwelt among us.... We have beheld his glory" (Jn 1:14). "God so loved the world that he gave his only Son" (Jn 3:16). "In this the love of God was made manifest among us, that God sent his only Son into the world, so that we might live through him" (1 Jn 4:9). Through these words of the Johannine writings, we can understand how the revelation of the Trinity's glory in the Incarnation is not a flash of light dispelling the darkness for a moment, but a seed of divine life sown in the world and in human hearts forever.

In this regard a statement by the Apostle Paul in his Letter to the Galatians is emblematic: "When the time had fully come,

God sent forth his Son, born of woman, born under the law, to redeem those who were under the law, so that we might receive adoption as sons. And because you are sons, God has sent the Spirit of his Son into our hearts, crying, 'Abba! Father!' So through God you are no longer a slave but a son, and if a son then an heir" (Gal 4:4–7; cf. Rom 8:15–17). The Father, the Son and the Spirit are present and active in the Incarnation in order to involve us in their life. "All men," the Second Vatican Council stressed, "are called to this union with Christ, who is the light of the world, from whom we go forth, through whom our whole life strains" (*LG* 3). And as St. Cyprian stated, the community of God's children is "a people made one with the unity of the Father, the Son and the Holy Spirit" (*The Lord's Prayer,* 23).

> To know God and his Son is to accept the mystery of the loving communion of the Father, the Son and the Holy Spirit into one's own life, which *even now* is open to eternal life because it *shares in the life of God.* Eternal life is, therefore, that life of God himself and at the same time the *life of the children of God.* As they ponder this unexpected and inexpressible truth which comes to us from God in Christ, believers cannot fail to be filled with ever new wonder and unbounded gratitude (*EV* 37–38).

In this wonder and acceptance we must adore the mystery of the Holy Trinity, which "is the central mystery of Christian faith and life. It is the mystery of God in himself. It is therefore the source of all the other mysteries of faith, the light that enlightens them" (*CCC* 234).

In the Incarnation we contemplate the Trinitarian love, which is revealed in Jesus, a love that does not remain closed in a perfect circle of light and glory, but shines forth in human flesh and in human history. It pervades man, giving him new birth as a son in the Son. For this reason, as St. Irenaeus said, the glory of God is the living man: *"Gloria enim Dei vivens homo, vita autem hominis visio Dei."* He is not so only because of his physical life, but also especially because "man's life consists in the vision of God" (*Adv. Haer.,* IV, 20, 7). And to see God is to be transfigured in him: "We shall be like him, for we shall see him as he is" (1 Jn 3:2).

General audience of April 5, 2000

The Holy Trinity Is
Revealed at Jesus' Baptism

Today we pause spiritually at the side of the Jordan River, which flows through the two biblical testaments, to contemplate the great epiphany of the Trinity on the day when Jesus was brought into the limelight of history, in those very waters, to begin his public ministry. Christian art personifies this river as an old man looking with awe at what is happening in his watery depths. For, as the Byzantine liturgy says, "Christ the Sun is washed" in it. This same liturgy, at Matins on the day of the Theophany or Epiphany of Christ, imagines a dialogue with the river: "What did you see, O Jordan, that disturbed you so deeply? I saw the Invisible One naked and I trembled. How can one not tremble and draw back before him? At his sight the angels trembled, the heavens leapt for joy, the earth shook, the sea turned back with all the visible and invisible beings. Christ appeared in the Jordan to bless all waters!"

The presence of the Trinity at that event is clearly affirmed in all the Gospel accounts of the episode. Matthew's account, the most complete one, includes a dialogue between Jesus and the Baptist. At the center of the scene we see the figure of

Christ, the Messiah who fulfills all righteousness (cf. Mt 3:15). He is the one who brings the divine plan of salvation to fulfillment, humbly showing his solidarity with sinners.

His voluntary humbling wins him a wondrous exaltation: the *Father's* voice from heaven resounds above him, proclaiming: "This is my beloved Son, with whom I am well pleased" (Mt 3:17). This statement combines two aspects of Jesus' messianism: the Davidic, by evoking a royal hymn (cf. Ps 2:7), and the prophetic, by citing the first song of the servant of the Lord (cf. Is 42:1). In this way Jesus' deep bond of love with the heavenly Father and his investiture as the Messiah are revealed to all humanity.

The *Holy Spirit* appears on the scene in the form of a dove "descending...and alighting" on Christ. Various biblical references can be cited to explain these images: the dove that indicates the end of the flood and the dawn of a new era (cf. Gn 8:8–12; 1 Pt 3:20–21), the dove in the Song of Songs, symbol of the beloved woman (cf. Song 2:14; 5:2; 6:9), the dove that is like a coat of arms to indicate Israel in several Old Testament passages (cf. Hos 7:11; Ps 68:14).

Also significant is an ancient Jewish comment on the passage in Genesis (cf. 1:2) which describes the Spirit moving over the primeval waters with motherly tenderness: "The Spirit of God was moving over the face of the waters like a dove that hovers over her little ones without touching them" (Talmud, *Hagigah* 15a). The Holy Spirit descends on Jesus as the power of superabundant love. Referring precisely to Jesus' baptism, the *Catechism of the Catholic Church* teaches: "The Spirit whom Jesus possessed in fullness from his conception comes to 'rest on him.' Jesus will be the source of the Spirit for all mankind" (n. 536).

The whole Trinity is therefore present at the Jordan to reveal this mystery, to authenticate and support Christ's mission, and to indicate that with him salvation history has entered its central and definitive phase. It involves time and space, human life and the cosmic order, but first of all the three divine Persons. The Father entrusts the Son with the mission of bringing "righteousness," that is, divine salvation, to fulfillment.

Chromatius, a fourth-century bishop of Aquileia, says in a homily on Baptism and the Holy Spirit: "Just as our first creation was the work of the Trinity, so our second is the work of the Trinity. The Father does nothing without the Son or the Holy Spirit, because the Father's work is also the Son's, and the Son's work is also the Holy Spirit's. There is but one and the same grace of the Trinity. Thus, we are saved by the Trinity, since in the beginning we were created by the Trinity alone" (*Sermon* 18A).

After Christ's baptism, the Jordan also became the river of Christian Baptism: in a tradition dear to the Eastern Churches, the water of the baptismal font is a miniature Jordan. This is shown by the following liturgical prayer: "To you we pray, O Lord, that the purifying action of the Trinity may descend upon the baptismal waters and give them the grace of redemption and the blessing of the Jordan in the power, action and presence of the Holy Spirit" (Great Vespers of the Holy Theophany of Our Lord Jesus Christ, *Blessing of the Waters*).

St. Paulinus of Nola also seems to have been inspired by a similar idea in some verses he composed as an inscription for the baptistry: "From this font, which gives life to souls in need of salvation, flows a living river of divine light. The Holy Spirit comes down from heaven upon this river and joins the sacred waters with the heavenly source; the stream teems with God, and from the eternal seed gives birth to holy offspring by its fruitful waters" (*Letter* 32, 5). Emerging from the regenerative waters of the *baptismal* font, the Christian begins his journey of life and witness.

General audience of April 12, 2000

The Promise of Tabor
Is Fulfilled at Easter

In the octave of Easter, which is considered one great day, the liturgy tirelessly repeats the message of the resurrection: "Jesus is truly risen!" This proclamation opens a new horizon to all humanity. All that was mysteriously foreshadowed in the Transfiguration on Tabor becomes a reality in the resurrection. At that time the Savior revealed to Peter, James and John the miracle of glory and light sealed by the voice of the Father: "This is my beloved Son!" (Mk 9:7).

On the feast of Easter these words appear to us in the fullness of their truth. The Father's beloved Son, Christ who was crucified and died, is raised for our sake. In his brightness we believers see the light and, "raised by the Spirit," as the liturgy of the Eastern Church says, "we praise the consubstantial Trinity forever and ever" *(Great Vespers of the Transfiguration of Christ)*. Our hearts filled with the joy of Easter, today we spiritually climb the holy mountain that dominates the plain of Galilee to contemplate the event that took place on its summit, in anticipation of the Easter events.

Christ is the center of the Transfiguration. Two witnesses of the Old Covenant appear with him: Moses, mediator of the law, and Elijah, a prophet of the living God. The divinity of Christ, proclaimed by the Father's voice, is also revealed by the symbols that Mark describes with picturesque touches. Indeed, there is light and whiteness, which represent eternity and transcendence: "His garments became glistening, intensely white, as no fuller on earth could bleach them" (Mk 9:3). Then there is the cloud, a sign of God's presence during Israel's Exodus and over the tent of the covenant (cf. Ex 13:21–22; 14:19, 24; 40:34, 38).

At Matins for the Transfiguration the Eastern liturgy again sings: "Immutable brightness of the Father's light, O Word, in your shining light on Tabor we have seen today the light that is the Father and the light that is the Spirit, a light that illumines all creation."

This liturgical text emphasizes the Trinitarian dimension of Christ's Transfiguration on the mountain. In fact, the Father's presence with his revealing voice is explicit. Christian tradition catches an implicit glimpse of the Holy Spirit's presence based on the parallel event of the baptism in the Jordan, when the Spirit descended upon Christ like a dove (cf. Mk 1:10). Indeed, the Father's command: "Listen to him" (Mk 9:7) presupposes that Jesus was filled with the Holy Spirit so that his words would be "spirit and life" (Jn 6:63; cf. 3:34–35).

It is possible, then, to climb the mountain in order to pause, to contemplate and to be immersed in the mystery of God's light. Tabor represents all the mountains that lead us to God, according to an image dear to mystics. Another text of the Eastern Church invites us to make this ascent to the summit and the light: "Come, peoples, follow me! Let us climb the holy and heavenly mountain; let us spiritually pause in the city of the living God and contemplate in spirit the divinity of the Father and the Holy Spirit, which is resplendent in the Only-begotten Son" (Troparion at the conclusion of the *Canon of St. John Damascene*).

In the Transfiguration we not only contemplate the mystery of God, passing from light to light (cf. Ps 36:10), but we are also invited to listen to the divine word that is addressed to us. Above the word of the law in Moses and the prophecy in Elijah, the voice of the Father can be heard referring to the voice of the Son, as I have just mentioned. In presenting his "beloved Son," the Father adds the invitation to listen to him (cf. Mk 9:7). In commenting on the Transfiguration scene, the Second Letter of Peter emphasizes the divine voice: Jesus Christ "received honor and glory from God the Father, and the voice was borne to him by the majestic glory: 'This is my beloved Son, with whom I am well pleased'; we heard this voice borne from heaven, for we were with him on the holy mountain. And we have the prophetic word made more sure. You will do well to pay attention to this as to a lamp shining in a dark place, until the day dawns and the morning star rises in your hearts" (1:17–19).

Seeing and hearing, contemplating and obeying are the ways that lead us to the holy mountain on which the Trinity is revealed in the glory of the Son. "The Transfiguration gives us a foretaste of Christ's glorious coming, when he 'will change our lowly body to be like his glorious body' (Phil 3:21). But it also recalls that 'it is through many persecutions that we must enter the kingdom of God' (Acts 14:22)" (*CCC* 556).

The liturgy of the Transfiguration, as the spirituality of the Eastern Church suggests, presents a human "triad" in the three Apostles Peter, James and John, who contemplate the divine Trinity. Like the three young men in the fiery furnace of the Book of Daniel (3:51–90), the liturgy "blesses God, the Father and Creator, praises the Word who comes down to help them and changes the fire into dew, and exalts the Holy Spirit who gives life to all forever" *(Matins of the Feast of the Transfiguration)*.

Let us now pray to Christ transfigured in the words of the *Canon of St. John Damascene:* "You have allured me with desire for you, O Christ, and have transformed me with your divine love. Burn away my sins with your spiritual fire and deign to fill me with your sweetness, so that leaping with joy I may exalt all your manifestations."

General audience of April 26, 2000

Christ's Passion Reveals
the Glory of the Trinity

At the end of the Gospel account of Christ's death, the voice of the Roman centurion rings out, anticipating the Church's profession of faith: "Truly this man was the Son of God" (Mk 15:39). During the last hours of Jesus' earthly life, the supreme manifestation of the Trinity took place in darkness. The Gospel account of Christ's passion and death records that his intimate relationship with the heavenly Father continued even in the abyss of pain.

Everything began on the evening of the Last Supper inside the quiet walls of the upper room where, however, the shadow of betrayal already loomed. John has preserved for us those farewell discourses that wonderfully stress the deep bond and reciprocal immanence between Jesus and the Father: "If you had known me, you would have known my Father also.... He who has seen me has seen the Father.... The words that I say to you I do not speak on my own authority, but the Father who dwells in me does his works. Believe me that I am in the Father and the Father is in me" (Jn 14:7, 9–11).

In saying this, Jesus is repeating the words he had spoken a little earlier when he declared concisely: "I and the Father are one...the Father is in me and I am in the Father" (Jn 10:30, 38). And in the prayer that seals the discourses in the upper room, he addressed the Father in contemplation of his glory, saying: "Holy Father, keep them in your name, which you have given me, that they may be one, even as we are one" (Jn 17:11). With this perfect trust in the Father, Jesus prepared to make his supreme act of love (cf. Jn 13:1).

In the passion the bond that unites him to the Father is manifested in a particularly intense and, at the same time, dramatic way. The Son of God lived his humanity to the full, penetrating the obscurity of suffering and death that are part of our human condition. In Gethsemane, during a prayer similar to an "agony," Jesus addressed the Father with an Aramaic term expressing filial intimacy: "Abba, Father! All things are possible to you; remove this cup from me; yet not what I will, but what you will" (Mk 14:36).

Shortly afterward, when human hostility was unleashed against him, he reminded Peter that this hour of darkness is part of the Father's divine plan: "Do you think that I cannot appeal to my Father and he will at once send me more than twelve legions of angels? But how then should the Scriptures be fulfilled, that it must be so?" (Mt 26:53–54).

At his trial the dialogue with the high priest was also transformed into a revelation of the messianic and divine glory that surrounds the Son of God. "The high priest said to him, 'I adjure you by the living God, tell us if you are the Christ, the Son of God.' Jesus said to him, 'You have said so. But I tell you, hereafter you will see the Son of man seated at the right hand of Power and coming on the clouds of heaven'" (Mt 26:63–64).

When he was on the cross, the spectators sarcastically reminded him of his declaration: "He trusts in God; let God deliver him now, if he desires him; for he said, 'I am the Son of God'" (Mt 27:43). But at that hour the Father was silent in Jesus' regard, so that he could show his full solidarity with sinners and redeem them. As the *Catechism of the Catholic Church* teaches: "Jesus did not experience reprobation as if he himself had sinned. But in the redeeming love that always united him to the Father, he assumed us in the state of our waywardness of sin" (n. 603).

On the cross Jesus actually continued his intimate dialogue with the Father, living it with the full force of his lacerated and suffering humanity, never losing the trusting attitude of the Son who is "one" with the Father. On the one hand, there was the Father's mysterious silence, accompanied by cosmic darkness and pierced by the cry: "*'Eli, Eli, lema sabachthani?'* — 'My God, my God, why have you forsaken me?'" (Mt 27:46). On the other hand, Psalm 22, quoted here by Jesus, ends with a hymn to the sovereign Lord of the world and of history; this aspect is highlighted in Luke's account, in which the last words of the dying Christ are a clear citation of a psalm, to which is added an invocation to the Father: "Father, into your hands I commend my spirit" (Lk 23:46; cf. Ps 31:6).

The Holy Spirit also takes part in this continual dialogue between the Father and the Son. We are told this by the Letter to the Hebrews, when it describes Christ's sacrificial offering in a somewhat Trinitarian formula, stating that "through the eternal Spirit [he] offered himself to God" (9:14). In his passion, Christ fully opened his anguished human existence to the action of the Holy Spirit, who gave him the necessary force to make his death a perfect offering to the Father.

For its part, the fourth Gospel closely links the gift of the Paraclete with Jesus' "departure," that is, with his passion and death, when it recounts these words of the Savior: "Nevertheless, I tell you the truth: it is to your advantage that I go away, for if I do not go away, the Counselor will not come to you, but if I go, I will send him to you" (Jn 16:7). After Jesus' death on the cross, the water that flows from his pierced side (cf. Jn

19:34) can be seen as a symbol of the gift of the Spirit (cf. Jn 7:37–39). The Father then glorifies his Son, giving him the capacity to communicate the Spirit to all human beings.

Let us contemplate the Trinity, which is also revealed on the day of pain and darkness, as we reread the words of the spiritual "testament" of St. Teresa Benedicta of the Cross (Edith Stein): "It is not human activity alone which can help us, but Christ's passion: my true desire is to take part in it. From now on I accept the death that God has destined for me, in perfect union with his holy will. Accept, O Lord, my life and my death for the intentions of the Church, to your glory and your praise. May the Lord be welcomed among his own, and may his kingdom come to us in glory" *(The Power of the Cross)*.

General audience of May 3, 2000

The Trinity Is Present
in Christ's Resurrection

The final destination of Christ's journey through life is not the darkness of the tomb, but the shining heaven of the resurrection. Christian faith is based on this mystery (cf. 1 Cor 15:1–20), as the *Catechism of the Catholic Church* reminds us: "The resurrection of Jesus is the crowning truth of our faith in Christ, a faith believed and lived as the central truth by the first Christian community; handed on as fundamental by Tradition; established by the documents of the New Testament; and preached as an essential part of the paschal mystery along with the cross" (n. 638). A sixteenth century Spanish mystical writer said: "In God new seas are discovered the more one sails" (Friar Louis de León). We now intend to navigate the immensity of this mystery, toward the light of the Trinitarian presence in the Easter events. This presence extends throughout the fifty days after Easter.

Unlike the apocryphal writings, the canonical Gospels do not present the resurrection event in itself, but rather the new and different presence of the risen Christ among his disciples. Precisely this newness characterizes the first scene on which we would like to reflect. It is the apparition which takes place in a Jerusalem still bathed in the pale light of dawn: a woman, Mary Magdalene, and a man meet in a cemetery. At first the woman does not recognize the man who has approached her: yet he is that Jesus of Nazareth whom she had listened to and who had changed her life. To recognize him she needs another source of knowledge than reason and the senses. The way of faith is opened to her when she hears herself called by name (cf. Jn 20:18).

Let us focus our attention on that scene, on the words of the Risen One. He says: "I am ascending to my Father and your Father, to my God and your God" (Jn 20:17), thus revealing the heavenly Father. In saying "my Father," Christ emphasizes his special, unique bond with the Father, different from that between the Father and the disciples: "your Father." In Matthew's Gospel alone Jesus calls God "my Father" seventeen times. The fourth evangelist will use two different Greek words, one — *hyios* — to indicate Christ's full and perfect divine sonship, the other — *tekna* — to refer to our being children of God in a real but derivative way.

The second scene takes us from Jerusalem to a mountain in northern Galilee. There another Christophany takes places in which the Risen One reveals himself to the apostles (cf. Mt 28:16–20). It is a solemn event of revelation, recognition and mission. In the fullness of his saving powers, he gives the Church the mandate to preach the Gospel, to baptize, and to teach the nations to live according to his commandments. The Trinity emerges in those words, which are also repeated in the formula of Christian Baptism, as it will be administered by the Church: "Baptize them [all nations] in the name of the Father and of the Son and of the Holy Spirit" (Mt 28:19). An ancient Christian writer, Theodore of Mopsuestia (fourth to fifth century), comments: "The words, *in the name of the Father and of the Son and of the Holy Spirit,* show who it is who gives us the blessings of Baptism: new birth, renewal, immortality, incorruptibility, impassability, immutability, deliverance from death, slavery and all evil, enjoyment of freedom and participation in future and sublime benefits. This is why we are baptized! The Father, the Son and the Holy Spirit are invoked so that you know the source of the blessings of Baptism" (*Homily II, On Baptism,* 17).

So we come to the third scene we would like to recall. It takes us back in time to when Jesus still walked the roads of the Holy Land, speaking and acting. During the Jewish autumn feast of Booths, he proclaimed: "If anyone thirsts, let him come to me and drink. He who believes in me, as the Scripture has said, 'Out of his heart shall flow rivers of living water'" (Jn 7:37–38). The Evangelist John interprets these words precisely in the light of the glorious Easter and the gift of the Holy Spirit: "This he said about the Spirit, which those who believed in him were to receive; for as yet the Spirit had not been given, because Jesus was not yet glorified" (7:39). The glorification of Easter would come, and with it the gift of the Spirit of Pentecost, which Jesus would anticipate for his apostles on the very evening of the day of the resurrection. Appearing in the upper room, he would breathe on them and say: "Receive the Holy Spirit" (Jn 20:22).

Thus, the Father and the Spirit are united with the Son at the supreme moment of the redemption. Paul affirms this in an especially luminous passage in the Letter to the Romans, where he recalls the Trinity precisely in connection with the resurrection of Christ and of us all: "If the Spirit of him who raised Jesus from the dead dwells in you, he who raised Christ...from the dead will give life to your mortal bodies also through his Spirit who dwells in you" (8:11).

In the same letter, the Apostle reveals the condition for this promise to be fulfilled: "If you confess with your lips that Jesus is Lord and believe in your heart that God raised him from the dead, you will be saved" (10:9). The Trinitarian aspect of the profession of faith corresponds with the Trinitarian nature of the Easter event. In fact, "no one can say 'Jesus is Lord' except by the Holy Spirit" (1 Cor 12:3), and those who say it, confess it "to the glory of God the Father" (Phil 2:11).

Let us then accept the paschal faith and the joy that flows from it, making our own an Easter Vigil hymn of the Eastern Church: "All things are illumined by your resurrection, O Lord, and paradise is opened again. All creation blesses you and offers you a hymn each day. I glorify the power of the Father and of the Son; I praise the authority of the Holy Spirit, Godhead undivided, uncreated, consubstantial Trinity, who reigns forever and ever" (*Easter Canon of St. John Damascene,* Holy Saturday, third tone).

General audience of May 10, 2000

The Glory of the Trinity
in Christ's Ascension

The mystery of Christ's Passover involves the history of humanity, but at the same time, it transcends it. Thought itself and human language can in some way grasp and communicate this mystery, but do not exhaust it. For this reason, the New Testament, although speaking of "resurrection," as attested by the ancient Creed which Paul himself received and passed on in his First Letter to the Corinthians (cf. 15:3–5), also uses another expression to explain the meaning of Easter. Especially in John and Paul it is presented as the exaltation or glorification of the Crucified One. Thus, for the fourth evangelist, the cross of Christ is already the royal throne that stands on earth but penetrates the heavens. Christ is seated on it as the Savior and Lord of history.

Jesus exclaims in the Gospel of John: "I, when I am lifted up from the earth, will draw all men to myself" (12:32; cf. 3:14; 8:28). In the hymn inserted in the Letter to the Philippians, Paul, after describing the profound humiliation of the Son of God in his death on a cross, celebrates Easter in this way: "Therefore, God has highly exalted him and bestowed on him the name which is above every name, that at the name of Jesus every knee should bow, in heaven and on earth and under the earth, and every tongue confess that Jesus Christ is Lord, to the glory of God the Father" (2:9–11).

Christ's ascension into heaven, recounted by Luke as the seal to his Gospel and the beginning of his second work, the Acts of the Apostles, should be understood in this same light. It is Jesus' final appearance that "ends with the irreversible entry of his humanity into divine glory, symbolized by the cloud and by heaven" (*CCC* 659). Heaven is the sign of divine transcendence par excellence. It is the cosmic realm that lies above the earthly horizon within which human existence unfolds.

After walking the paths of history and entering even the darkness of death, the limits of our finitude and the wages of sin (cf. Rom 6:23), Christ returned to the glory that he shares from eternity (cf. Jn 17:5) with the Father and the Holy Spirit. He takes redeemed humanity with him. In fact, the Letter to the Ephesians says, "God, who is rich in mercy, out of the great love with which he loved us...made us alive together with Christ...and made us sit with him in the heavenly places" (2:4–6). This applies first to Mary, the Mother of Jesus, whose assumption is the first fruits of our ascension into glory.

We pause before the glorious Christ of the ascension to contemplate the presence of the whole Trinity. We know that Christian art, in the so-called *Trinitas in cruce,* has often depicted the crucified Christ with the Father leaning over him as if in an embrace, while the dove of the Holy Spirit hovers between them (for example, Masaccio in the Church of Santa Maria Novella in Florence). In this way the cross is a unifying symbol that joins humanity and divinity, death and life, suffering and glory.

In a similar way we can glimpse the presence of the three divine Persons in the ascension scene. On the last page of his Gospel, before presenting the Risen One who, as the priest of the New Covenant, blesses his disciples and is lifted up from the earth to be taken into heavenly glory (cf. Lk 24:50–52), Luke recalls Jesus' farewell discourse to the apostles. In it we see above all the saving plan of the *Father,* who in the Scriptures had foretold the death and resurrection of the *Son,* the source of forgiveness and liberation (cf. Lk 24:45– 47).

But in those same words of the Risen One we also glimpse the *Holy Spirit,* whose presence will be the source of strength and apostolic witness: "I send the promise of my Father upon you, but stay in the city until you are clothed with power from on high" (Lk 24:49). If in John's Gospel Christ promises the Paraclete, for Luke the gift of the Spirit is also part of a promise made by the Father himself.

The whole Trinity is therefore present when the time of the Church begins. Luke emphasizes this in the second account of Christ's ascension, in the Acts of the Apostles. Jesus exhorts his disciples "to wait for the promise of the *Father,*" that is, to "be baptized with the *Holy Spirit,*" at Pentecost which is now imminent (cf. 1:4–5).

The ascension, then, is a Trinitarian epiphany that indicates the goal to which personal and universal history is hastening. Even if our mortal body dissolves into the dust of the earth, our whole redeemed self is directed on high to God, following Christ as our guide. Sustained by this joyful certainty, we turn to the mystery of God the Father, the Son and the Spirit, which is revealed in the glorious cross of the risen Christ, with the adoring prayer of Bl. Elizabeth of the Trinity: "O my God, Trinity whom I adore, help me to forget myself entirely that I may be established in you as still and peaceful as if my soul were already in eternity.... Give peace to my soul; make it your heaven, your beloved dwelling and your resting place.... O my Three, my All, my Beatitude, infinite Solitude, Immensity in which I lose myself, I surrender myself to you...until I depart to contemplate in your light the abyss of your greatness" (*Prayer to the Blessed Trinity,* November 21, 1904).

General audience of May 24, 2000

Pentecost Involves the Three Divine Persons

The Christian Pentecost, a celebration of the outpouring of the Holy Spirit, presents various aspects in the writings of the New Testament. We will start with the one described in the passage from the Acts of the Apostles (2:1–41). It is the most obvious one in everyone's mind, in the history of art and in the liturgy itself.

In his second work, Luke situates the gift of the Spirit within a theophany, that is, a solemn divine revelation, whose symbols refer to Israel's experience at Sinai (cf. Ex 19). The roar, the driving wind and the lightning-like fire exalt the divine transcendence. In reality, the Father gives the Spirit through the intervention of the glorified Christ. Peter says so in his address: Jesus, "being therefore exalted at the right hand of God, and having received from the Father the promise of the Holy Spirit, has poured out this which you see and hear" (Acts 2:33). At Pentecost, as the *Catechism of the Catholic Church* teaches, the Holy Spirit is "manifested, given, and communicated as a divine person.... On that day, the Holy Trinity is fully revealed" (n. 731–732).

The whole Trinity is involved in the inbreaking of the Spirit, who is poured out upon the first community and upon the Church in every age as the seal of the New Covenant foretold by the prophets (cf. Jer 31:31–34; Ez 36:24–27), to support its witness and as a source of unity in plurality. In the power of the Holy Spirit, the apostles proclaim the Risen One, and all believers, in the diversity of their languages and thus of their cultures and historical events, profess the same faith in the Lord, "telling...the mighty works of God" (Acts 2:11).

It is significant to note that a Jewish commentary on Exodus, recalling chapter 10 of Genesis, which sketches a map of the seventy nations which were then thought to comprise humanity as a whole, leads them back to Sinai to hear the Word of God: "At Sinai the Lord's voice was divided into seventy languages, so that all the nations could understand" (*Exodus Rabbá,* 5, 9). So too in the *Lucan Pentecost,* the Word of God is addressed to humanity through the apostles, in order to proclaim "the mighty works of God" (Acts 2:11) to all peoples, even with their differences.

In the New Testament, however, there is another account that we could call the *Johannine Pentecost.* In the fourth Gospel, the outpouring of the Holy Spirit actually takes place on the evening of Easter and is closely connected to the resurrection. We read:

> On the evening of that day, the first day of the week, the doors being shut where the disciples were for fear of the Jews, Jesus came and stood among them and said to them, "Peace be with you!" When he had said this, he showed them his hands and his side. Then the disciples were glad when they saw the Lord. Jesus said to them again, "Peace be with you. As the Father has sent me, even so I send you." And when he had said this, he breathed on them, and said to them, "Receive the Holy Spirit. If you retain the sins of any, they are retained" (Jn 20:19–23).

The glory of the Trinity also shines out in this Johannine account: the glory of the *risen Christ,* who appears in his glorious body; of the *Father,* who is the source of the apostolic mission; and of the *Spirit* poured out as the gift of peace. This fulfills the promise which Christ had made between these same walls in his farewell discourse to the disciples: "But the Counselor, the Holy Spirit, whom the Father will send in my name, will teach you all things and bring to your remembrance all that I have said to you" (Jn 14:26). The Spirit's presence in the Church is intended for the forgiveness of sins, for remembering and carrying out the Gospel in life, for the ever deeper achievement of unity in love. The symbolic act of breathing is meant to recall the action of the Creator who, after forming man's body from the dust of the ground, "breathed into his nostrils" to give him "the breath of life" (Gn 2:7). The risen Christ communicates another breath of life, "the Holy Spirit." Redemption is a new creation, a divine work with which the Church is called to collaborate through the ministry of reconciliation.

The Apostle Paul does not offer us a direct account of the outpouring of the Spirit, but describes its fruits with such intensity that one could speak of a Pauline Pentecost, which is also marked by the Trinity. According to two parallel passages in the Letters to the Galatians and to the Romans, the Spirit is the gift of the Father, who makes us his adoptive children, giving us a share in the very life of the divine family. Paul therefore says: "For you did not receive the spirit of slavery to fall back into fear, but you have received the spirit of sonship. When we cry, 'Abba! Father!' it is the Spirit himself bearing witness with our spirit that we are children of God, and if children, then heirs, heirs of God and fellow heirs with Christ" (Rom 8:15–17; cf. Gal 4:6–7).

With the Holy Spirit in our hearts, we can address God with the familiar name *Abba,* the name Jesus himself used with his heavenly Father (cf. Mk 14:36). Like him, we must walk according to the Spirit in profound inner freedom: "The fruit of the Spirit is love, joy, peace, patience, kindness, goodness, faithfulness, gentleness, self-control" (Gal 5:22).

Let us end our contemplation of the Trinity at Pentecost with an invocation from the liturgy of the East: "Come, peoples, let us adore the Divinity in three Persons: the Father in the Son with the Holy Spirit. For the Father begets from eternity a coeternal Son, who lives and reigns with him, and the Holy Spirit is in the Father, glorified with the Son, one power, one substance, one divinity.... Holy Trinity, glory to you!" *(Vespers of Pentecost).*

General audience of May 31, 2000

Presence of the Trinity in Human Life

In our catechesis we have been reflecting with pleasure on the theme of the glorification of the Trinity. After contemplating the glory of the three divine Persons in creation, in history and in the mystery of Christ, our gaze now turns to man, to discern there the gleaming rays of God's action. "In his hand is the soul of every living thing, and the life breath of all mankind" (Jb 12:10). Job's evocative words reveal the radical link that unites human beings to the "Lord who loves the living" (Wis 11:26). Inscribed within the rational creature is an intimate relationship with the Creator, a fundamental bond established first by the gift of life. This gift is bestowed by the Trinity itself and includes two principal dimensions, as we will now seek to illustrate in the light of God's Word.

The first fundamental dimension of the life we have been given is physical and historical, that "soul" *(nefesh)* and that "breath" *(rûăh)* to which Job referred. The Father comes on the scene as the source of this gift at the very dawn of creation, when he solemnly proclaims: "Let us make man in our image, after our likeness.... So God created man in his own image; in the image of God he created him; male and female he created them" (Gn 1:26–27). With the *Catechism of the Catholic Church* we can draw this conclusion: "The divine image is present in every man. It shines forth in the communion of persons, in the likeness of the unity of the divine Persons among themselves" (n. 1702). In this communion of love and in the human couple's procreative capacity, there is a reflection of the Creator. In marriage man and woman continue God's creative work, sharing in his supreme fatherhood in the mystery which Paul invites us to contemplate when he exclaims: "one God and Father of us all, who is above all and through all and in all" (Eph 4:6).

The effective presence of God, whom the Christian prays to as *Father,* is already revealed at the beginning of every person's life and then expands throughout his days. This is attested by an extraordinarily beautiful strophe of Psalm 139, which can be rendered in the form closest to the original in this way: "Truly you have formed my inmost being; you knit me in my mother's womb.... Nor was my frame unknown to you when I was made in secret, when I was fashioned in the depths of the earth. Your eyes beheld my unformed substance *(golmî);* in your book they are all written; my days were limited before one of them existed" (vv. 13, 15–16).

The *Son* is also present at the Father's side as we come into existence, he who took on our own flesh (cf. Jn 1:14) to the point that he could be touched by our hands, be heard with our ears, and be seen and looked upon with our eyes (cf. 1 Jn 1:1). Indeed, Paul reminds us that "there is one God, the Father, from whom are all things and for whom we exist, and one Lord, Jesus Christ, through whom are all things and through whom we exist" (1 Cor 8:6). Every living creature, then, is also entrusted to the breath of God's *Spirit,* as the Psalmist sings: "When you send forth your Spirit, they are created" (Ps 104:30). In the light of the New Testament, we can read these words as foretelling the Third Person of the Most Holy Trinity. Therefore, at the source of our life there is a Trinitarian intervention of love and blessing.

As I have mentioned, there is another dimension to the life offered to the human creature. We can express it in three theological categories of the New Testament. First there is the *zoē aiōnios,* that is, "the eternal life" extolled by John (cf. 3:15–16; 17:2–3), to be understood as a sharing in the "divine life." Then there is the Pauline *kainē ktisis,* the "new creation" (cf. 2 Cor 5:17; Gal 6:15), produced by the Spirit who bursts into human creatureliness, transforming it and granting it a "new life" (cf. Rom 6:4; Col 3:9–10; Eph 4:22–24). This is the paschal life: "For as in Adam all die, so also in Christ shall all be made alive" (1 Cor 15:22). Finally, there is the life of the children of God, the *hyiothesia* (cf. Rom 8:15; Gal 4:5), which expresses our communion of love with the Father, through Christ in the power of the Holy Spirit: "The proof that you are sons is the fact that *God* has sent forth into our hearts the *Spirit* of his *Son* which cries out 'Abba!' ('Father!'). You are no longer a slave but a son! And the fact that you are a son makes you an heir by God's design" (Gal 4:6–7).

Through grace this transcendent life instilled in us opens us to the future, beyond the limits of our frailty as creatures. Paul says this in his Letter to the Romans, once again referring to the Trinity as the source of this paschal life: "If the *Spirit* of him who raised *Jesus* from the dead [that is, the *Father*] dwells in you, he who raised *Christ* from the dead will give life to your mortal bodies also through his *Spirit* who dwells in you" (8:11).

> Eternal life is therefore the life of God himself and at the same time the life of the children of God. As they ponder this unexpected and inexpressible truth which comes to us from God in Christ, believers cannot fail to be filled with ever new wonder and unbounded gratitude (cf. 1 Jn 3:1–2).... The dignity of this life is linked not only to its beginning, to the fact that it comes from God, but also to its final end, to its destiny of fellowship with God, in knowledge and love of him. In the light of this truth, St. Irenaeus qualifies and

completes his praise of man: "'The glory of God' is indeed 'man, living man,' but 'the life of man consists in the vision of God'" (*EV* 38; cf. Irenaeus, *Adv. Haer.,* IV, 20, 7).

Let us end our reflection with the prayer of an Old Testament sage to the living God who loves life: "You love all things that exist, and have loathing for none of the things which you have made, for you would not have made anything if you had hated it. How would anything have endured if you had not willed it? Or how would anything not called forth by you have been preserved? You spare all things, for they are yours, O Lord who loves the living. For your immortal Spirit is in all things" (Wis 11:24—12:1).

General audience of June 7, 2000

The Trinity in the Life of the Church

On her pilgrimage to full communion of love with God, the Church appears as "a people made one with the unity of the Father, the Son and the Holy Spirit." St. Cyprian's marvelous definition (*The Lord's Prayer,* 23; cf. *LG* 4) takes us into the mystery of the Church, which has been made a community of salvation by the presence of God the Trinity. Like the ancient People of God, she is guided on her new Exodus by the pillar of cloud by day and the pillar of fire by night, symbols of God's constant presence. In this perspective, let us contemplate the glory of the Trinity that makes the Church one, holy, catholic and apostolic.

First, the Church is *one.* The baptized are mysteriously united to Christ and form his Mystical Body by the power of the Holy Spirit. As the Second Vatican Council says: "It is a mystery that finds its highest exemplar and source in the unity of the Persons of the Trinity: the Father and the Son in the Holy Spirit, one God" (*UR* 2). Although in the past this unity has suffered the painful trial of many divisions, the Church's inexhaustible Trinitarian source spurs her to live ever more deeply that *koinonia,* or communion, which was resplendent in the first community of Jerusalem (Acts 2:42; 4:32).

Ecumenical dialogue draws light from this perspective, since all Christians are aware of the Trinitarian foundations of communion: we stress "the God-givenness of the *koinonia* and its Trinitarian character. The point of departure is the baptismal initiation into the Trinitarian *koinonia* by faith, through Christ in his Spirit. The Spirit-given means to sustain this *koinonia* are the Word, ministry, sacraments, charisms."[1] In this regard the Council reminds all the faithful that "the closer their union with the Father, the Word and the Spirit, the more deeply and easily will they be able to grow in mutual brotherly love" (*UR* 7).

The Church is also *holy*. In biblical language, even before being an expression of the moral and existential holiness of the faithful, the concept of "holy" refers to the consecration wrought by God through the election and the grace offered to his people. It is the divine presence, then, which "sanctifies" the community of believers "in the truth" (Jn 17:17, 19).

The loftiest sign of this presence is constituted by the liturgy, which is the epiphany of the consecration of God's people. In it there is the Eucharistic presence of the Body and Blood of the Lord, but also "our 'Eucharist,' that is to say, our giving God thanks, our praise of him for having redeemed us by his death and made us sharers in immortal life through his resurrection. This worship, given therefore to the Trinity of the Father and of the Son and of the Holy Spirit, above all accompanies and permeates the celebration of the Eucharistic liturgy. But it must fill our churches also" and the life of the Church (*Dominicae Cenae,* 3). And precisely, "For all of us, who are sons of God and constitute one family in Christ (cf. Heb 3:6), as long as we remain in communion with one another in mutual charity and in one praise of the most holy Trinity, are corre-

---

1. *Perspectives on Koinonia,* Report from the Third Quinquennium, 1985–89, of the Catholic-Pentecostal dialogue, n. 31.

sponding with the intimate vocation of the Church and partaking in foretaste the liturgy of consummate glory" (*LG* 51).

The Church is *catholic,* sent to proclaim Christ to the whole world in the hope that all leaders of the peoples will gather with the people of the God of Abraham (cf. Ps 47:9; Mt 28:19). As the Second Vatican Council says:

> The pilgrim Church is missionary by her very nature, since it is from the mission of the Son and the mission of the Holy Spirit that she draws her origin, in accordance with the decree of God the Father. This decree, however, flows from the "fount-like love" or charity of God the Father, who being the "principle without principle" from whom the Son is begotten and the Holy Spirit proceeds through the Son, freely creating us on account of his surpassing and merciful kindness and graciously calling us, moreover, to share with him his life and his glory, has generously poured out, and does not cease to pour out still, his divine goodness. Thus, he who created all things may at last be "all in all" (1 Cor 15:28), bringing about at one and the same time his own glory and our happiness (*AG* 2).

Lastly, the Church is *apostolic.* In accordance with Christ's command, his apostles must go and make disciples of all nations, baptizing them in the name of the Father and of the Son and of the Holy Spirit, and teaching them to observe all that he has commanded them (cf. Mt 28:19–20). This mission is extended to the whole Church, which through the Word is made living, luminous and effective by the Holy Spirit and the sacraments. Thus, "in this way and by this means, the plan of God is fulfilled — that plan to which Christ conformed with loving obedience for the glory of the Father who sent him, that the whole human race might form one People of God and be built up into one temple of the Holy Spirit" (*AG* 7).

The one, holy, catholic and apostolic Church is the People of God, the Body of Christ and the Temple of the Holy Spirit.

These three biblical images point to the Trinitarian dimension of the Church. In this dimension are found all disciples of Christ, who are called to live it ever more deeply and in an ever more intense communion. Ecumenism itself finds its solid foundation in this reference to the Trinity, because the Spirit "binds the faithful to Christ, the mediator of all salvific gifts, and who through him gives them access to the Father, whom they may invoke as 'Abba, Father,' in the same Spirit" (Lutheran-Roman Catholic Joint Commission, *Church and Justification,* n. 64). In the Church, then, we find a magnificent epiphany of Trinitarian glory. Let us therefore accept the invitation that St. Ambrose extends to us: "Rise, you who were lying fast asleep.... Rise and hurry to the Church: here is the Holy Spirit" (*Comm. on Luke,* VIII).

General audience of June 14, 2000

The Glory of the Trinity
in the Heavenly Jerusalem

"The Church, while on earth it journeys in a foreign land away from the Lord (cf. 2 Cor 5:6), is like an exile. It seeks and experiences those things which are above, where Christ is seated at the right hand of God, where the life of the Church is hidden with Christ in God until it appears in glory with its spouse (cf. Col 3:1–4)" (*LG* 6). These words of the Second Vatican Council describe the journey of the Church, which knows that she has "here no lasting city," but "seeks the city which is to come" (Heb 13:14), the heavenly Jerusalem, "the city of the living God" (Heb 12:22).

When we reach that final destination of history, as St. Paul tells us, we will no longer "see in a mirror dimly, but face to face.... Then I shall understand fully, even as I have been fully understood" (1 Cor 13:12). And John tells us again that "when [God] appears we shall be like him, for we shall see him as he is" (Jn 3:2).

Beyond the frontiers of history, then, the full, shining epiphany of the Trinity awaits us. In the new creation God will give us the intimate, perfect communion with him that the fourth Gospel calls "eternal life," the source of a "knowledge" which in biblical language is precisely a communion of love: "This is eternal life, that they know you, the only true God, and Jesus Christ whom you have sent" (Jn 17:3).

Christ's resurrection opens this horizon of light, which the First Testament had already extolled as a kingdom of peace and joy, in which "the Lord will wipe away the tears from all faces" (Is 25:8). Then, at last, "kindness and truth shall meet; justice and peace shall kiss" (Ps 85:11). But it is especially the last pages of the Bible, that is, the final glorious visions of Revelation, which reveal to us the city that is the ultimate goal of our pilgrimage, the heavenly Jerusalem.

First, we will meet the Father, "the Alpha and the Omega, the beginning and the end" of all creation (Rev 21:6). He will be fully manifest as Emmanuel, the God who dwells with humanity, wiping away tears and mourning, and making all things new (cf. Rev 21:3–5). But the Lamb, Christ, to whom the Church is joined in marriage, will also rise up in the midst of the city. From him she will receive the light of glory; with him she will no longer be intimately joined through a temple but in a direct and total way (cf. Rev 21:9, 22, 23). The Holy Spirit spurs us toward that city; he sustains the loving dialogue between the elect and Christ: "The Spirit and the Bride say, 'Come'" (Rev 22:17).

Our gaze turns to this full manifestation of the Trinity's glory, looking beyond the limits of our human condition, beyond the weight of misery and guilt that pervade our human existence. For this meeting we pray each day for the grace of continual purification, knowing that "nothing unclean shall enter" the heavenly Jerusalem, "nor anyone who practices falsehood, but only those who are written in the Lamb's book of life" (Rev 21:27). As the Second Vatican Council teaches, the liturgy we celebrate in the course of our days is a "taste" of that light, of that contemplation, of that perfect love: "In the earthly liturgy we take part in a foretaste of that heavenly liturgy which is celebrated in the holy city of Jerusalem toward which we journey as pilgrims, where Christ is sitting at the right hand of God, a minister of the holies and of the true tabernacle (cf. Rev 21:2; Col 3:1; Heb 8:2)" (*SC* 8).

Therefore, we already turn to Christ so that through the Holy Spirit he will help us to stand pure before the Father. This is what Simeon Metaphrastes asks us to do in a prayer which the liturgy of the Eastern Churches offers the faithful: "You, who by the descent of the Consoler Spirit made your holy disciples vessels of honor, make me a worthy dwelling for his coming. You, who will come again to judge the world in justice, allow me also to come before you, my Judge and my Creator, with all your saints, to praise you and sing to you eternally, with your eternal Father and with your all-holy, good and life-giving Spirit, now and forever" *(Communion Prayer)*.

Together with us, "the whole created world eagerly awaits the revelation of the sons of God...not without hope, because the world itself will be freed from its slavery to corruption and share in the glorious freedom of the children of God" (Rom 8:19–21). The Book of Revelation proclaims "a new heaven and a new earth," because the first heaven and the first earth will pass away (cf. 21:1). And in his Second Letter, Peter uses traditional apocalyptic images to stress the same idea: "The heavens will be kindled and dissolved, and the elements will melt with fire! But according to his promise we wait for new heavens and a new earth in which righteousness dwells" (3:12–13).

In expectation of this harmony and full praise, all creation must now sing with humanity a song of joy and hope. Let us do so as well in the words of a third-century hymn discovered in Egypt: "Together let none of God's marvelous creatures keep silent either morning or evening! Let none of the shining stars of the high mountains, or the depths of the seas, or the springs of the swift rivers keep silent as we sing our hymns to the Father, the Son and the Holy Spirit. Let all the angels of heaven respond: Amen! Amen! Amen!" (text published by A. Gastoné in *La Tribune de Saint Gervais,* September–October 1922).

General audience of June 28, 2000

God Always Goes in Search of Us

In his Letter to the Romans, the Apostle Paul quotes, not without surprise, a prophecy from the Book of Isaiah (cf. 65:1), in which God says through the mouth of the prophet: "I have been found by those who did not seek me; I have shown myself to those who did not ask for me" (Rom 10:20). After having reflected in our preceding catecheses on the glory of the Trinity manifested in the cosmos and in history, now we want to begin an inward journey, exploring the mysterious ways in which God comes to meet man in order to share his life and glory with him. For God loves the creature formed in his image and likeness. Like the caring shepherd in the parable (cf. Lk 15:4–7), he never tires of searching for him even when he appears indifferent or even hostile to the divine life, like the sheep that wanders from the flock and is lost in inaccessible and dangerous places.

Pursued by God, man already senses his presence, already basks in the light on his shoulders, and already hearkens to the voice calling him from afar. So he himself begins to search for the God who is searching for him: sought out, he begins to seek; loved, he begins to love. Today we will start to trace this stirring interaction between God's initiative and man's response, discovering it as a fundamental element of religious experience. In fact, an echo of this experience is also heard in some voices far removed from Christianity, a sign of the universal human desire to know God and to receive his kindness. Even an enemy of the biblical Israel, the Babylonian king Nebuchadnezzar, who had destroyed the holy city of Jerusalem in 587–586 B.C., addressed the Godhead in these words: "Without you, Lord, what would be the king whom you love and have called by name? You guide his name, you lead him by the right path!... By your grace, O Lord, which you richly share with everyone, your sublime majesty becomes mercy, and you make the feat of your divinity dwell in my heart. Give me what is good for you, since you have formed my life!" (cf. G. Pettinato, *Babilonia,* Milan 1994, p. 182).

Our Muslim brethren also express a similar belief by often repeating throughout their day the prayer that opens the Koran and precisely celebrates the way in which God, "the Lord of Creation the Compassionate, the Merciful," guides those upon whom he pours out his grace.

The great biblical tradition especially prompts the faithful to call often upon God to receive the necessary light and strength from him to do good. Thus the Psalmist prays in Psalm 119: "Instruct me, O Lord, in the way of your statutes, that I may exactly observe your law and keep it with all my heart. Lead me in the path of your commands, for in it I delight.... Turn away my eyes from seeing what is vain; by your way give me life" (vv. 33–35, 37).

In universal religious experience, especially in what is transmitted by the Bible, we thus find an awareness of God's primacy as he searches for man in order to lead him into the realm of his light and mystery. In the beginning there is the Word, which breaks through the silence of the void, the "favor" of God (Lk 2:14), who never abandons to themselves those he has created.

Certainly, this absolute beginning does not eliminate the need for human action or the human obligation to respond; man is called to let himself be touched by God and to open his life's door to him, but he also has the ability to turn down these invitations. In this regard, the Book of Revelation puts amazing words on Christ's lips: "Behold, I stand at the door and knock; if anyone hears my voice and opens the door, I will come in to him and eat with him, and he with me" (3:20). If Christ were not to travel the world's roads, we would be left alone within our narrow horizons. Still, we must open the door to him, so that we can have him at our table in a communion of life and love.

The journey of God's encounter with man will unfold under the banner of love. On the one hand, divine Trinitarian love goes before us, surrounds us and constantly opens the way for us to the Father's house. There the Father is waiting to embrace us, as in the Gospel parable of the "prodigal son," or better, of the "merciful Father" (cf. Lk 15:11–32). On the other hand, fraternal love is asked of us as a response to God's love: "Beloved," John admonishes us, "if God so loved us, we also ought to love one another.... God is love, and he who abides in love abides in God, and God abides in him" (1 Jn 4:11, 16). Salvation, life and eternal joy blossom from the embrace of divine love and human love.

General audience of July 5, 2000

God Satisfies Our
Longing for His Presence

"O that you would rend the heavens and come down!" Isaiah's great cry (63:19), which well summarizes the longing for God present especially in the history of the biblical Israel, but also in every human heart, was not in vain. God the Father crossed the threshold of his transcendence: through his Son, Jesus Christ, he set out on the paths of man, and his Spirit of life and love penetrated the hearts of his creatures. He does not leave us wandering far from his ways, nor does he let our hearts be hardened forever (cf. Is 63:17). In Christ, God draws near to us, particularly when our "face is sad," and then with the warmth of his word, as happened to the disciples at Emmaus, our hearts begin to burn within us (cf. Lk 24:17, 32). God's passage, however, is mysterious, and requires pure eyes and attentive ears to be perceived.

In this perspective, we want to focus today on two fundamental attitudes to be adopted toward the God-Emmanuel who decided to meet man both in space and time, and in the depths of his heart. The first attitude is that of waiting, well illustrated in a passage of Mark's Gospel (cf. 13:33–37). In the original Greek, we find three imperatives that mark this waiting. The

first is: "Take heed," literally, "Look out, be careful!" "Attention," as the word itself says, means to tend, to be directed
toward something with all one's soul. It is the opposite of
distraction, which unfortunately is almost our habitual state,
especially in a frenetic, superficial society such as ours today.
We find it difficult to focus on a goal, on a value, and to pursue
it with fidelity and consistency. We risk doing so even with
God, who came to us through his Incarnation to become the
lodestar of our lives.

The imperative to take heed is followed by "be alert,"
which in the Gospel's original Greek is the same as "stay
awake." There is a strong temptation for us to fall asleep, wound
in the coils of the dark night, which in the Bible is the symbol of
guilt, inertia and rejection of light. Thus we can understand the
Apostle Paul's exhortation: "You are not in darkness, brethren...for you are all sons of light and sons of the day; we are not
of the night or of darkness. So then let us not sleep, as others do,
but let us keep awake and be sober" (1 Thes 5:4 – 6). Only by
freeing ourselves from the obscure attraction of darkness and
evil can we meet the Father of lights, in whom "there is no
variation or shadow due to change" (Jas 1:17).

There is a third imperative expressed twice with the same
Greek verb: "Watch." It is the verb for the sentinel who must be
on guard, while he waits patiently for nighttime to pass in order
to see the light of dawn breaking on the horizon. The prophet
Isaiah vividly and forcefully describes this long wait by introducing a dialogue between two sentinels, which becomes a
symbol for the right use of time: "'Watchman, how much longer
the night?' The watchman replies, 'Morning has come, and
again night. If you will ask, ask; come back again'" (21:11–12).

We must question ourselves, be converted and go to meet
the Lord. Christ's three appeals: "Take heed, stay awake,
watch!" limpidly sum up the Christian watchfulness for meeting the Lord. The waiting must be patient, as St. James urges us

in his Letter: "Be patient until the coming of the Lord. See how the farmer awaits the precious yield of the soil. He looks forward to it patiently while the soil receives the winter and spring rains. You, too, be patient. Steady your hearts, because the coming of the Lord is at hand" (5:7–8). If an ear is to grow or a flower blossom, there are times which cannot be forced; for the birth of a human being, nine months are required; to write a book or a worthy piece of music, years must often be spent in patient searching. This is also the law of the spirit. "Everything that is rushed / will soon fade," a poet wrote (R. M. Rilke, *Sonnets to Orpheus*). To encounter the mystery takes patience, inner purification, silence and waiting.

We were speaking earlier of the two spiritual attitudes for discovering the God who approaches us. The second — after attentive and watchful waiting — is wonder, marvel. We must open our eyes to admire God, who both conceals and reveals himself in things and leads us into the realms of mystery. Technological culture and, even more, an excessive absorption in material realities often prevent us from discerning the hidden face of things. In reality, every thing, every event, for those who know how to read them in depth, bears a message, which, in the final analysis, leads to God. Thus, there are many signs that reveal God's presence. But if they are not to escape us, we must be as pure and simple as children (cf. Mt 18:3–4), who can admire, wonder at, be astonished and enchanted by God's acts of love and closeness in our regard. In a certain sense, we can apply to the fabric of daily life what the Second Vatican Council said about the fulfillment of God's great plan through the revelation of his Word: "…the invisible God (cf. Col 1:15; 1 Tim 1:17) out of the abundance of his love speaks to men as friends (cf. Ex 33:11; Jn 15:14–15) and lives among them (cf. Bar 3:38), so that he may invite and take them into fellowship with himself" (*DV* 2).

General audience of July 26, 2000

God Reveals Himself in Nature

"How greatly to be desired are all his works, and how sparkling they are to see!... Though we speak much we cannot reach the end, and the sum of our words is: 'He is the all'.... He is greater than all his works" (Sir 42:22; 43:27–28). These wonderful words sum up the hymn of praise, sung in every age and under every sky, to the Creator who reveals himself through the immensity and splendor of his works.

Although in still imperfect ways, many voices have recognized in creation the presence of its Author and Lord. An ancient Egyptian king and poet, addressing his sun god, exclaimed: "How manifold it is, what you have made! They are hidden from the face (of man). O sole god, like whom there is no other! You did create the world according to your desire, while you were alone."[1]

A few centuries later, a Greek philosopher also celebrated in a marvelous hymn the divinity manifest in nature and especially in man: "We are your offspring, and we have speech as a reflection of your mind, we alone of all the animate beings who

---

1. J. B. Pritchard, "The Hymn of Aton," *Ancient Near Eastern Texts,* 3rd ed. (Princeton: Princeton University Press, 1969), 369–371.

live and move on the earth" (Cleanthes, *Hymn to Zeus,* vv. 4–5). The Apostle Paul would take up this acclamation, citing it in his discourse at the Areopagus of Athens (cf. Acts 17:28).

The Muslim believer is also required to hear the word that the Creator has entrusted to the works of his hands: "O men, adore your Lord, who has created you and those who have gone before you: fear him who has made the earth a bed for you and the sky a dome, and has sent down water from the sky to bring forth fruits for your sustenance" (*Koran,* II, 21–23). The Jewish tradition, which flourished in the fertile soil of the Bible, would discover God's personal presence in every corner of creation: "Where I wander — you! Where I ponder — you! Only you, you again, always you!... Sky is you! Earth is you! You alone! You below! In every trend, at every end, only you, you again, always you!"[2]

Biblical revelation is set within this broad experience of religious awareness and human prayer, putting the divine seal upon it. In communicating the mystery of the Trinity to us, it helps us perceive in creation itself not only the marks of the Father, source of all life, but also those of the Son and the Spirit. The Christian's gaze now turns to the whole Trinity when he contemplates the heavens with the Psalmist: "By the word of the Lord" — that is, by his eternal Word — "the heavens were made; by the breath of his mouth" — that is, by his Holy Spirit — "all their host" (Ps 33:6). Thus, "The heavens declare the glory of God, and the firmament proclaims his handiwork. Day pours out the word to day, and night to night imparts knowledge. Not a word nor a discourse whose voice is not heard; through all the earth their voice resounds, and to the ends of the world, their message" (Ps 19:2–5).

---

2. M. Buber, *Tales of the Hasidim* (Milan: 1979), 256.

The ear of the heart must be free of noise in order to hear this divine voice echoing in the universe. Along with revelation properly so-called, contained in Sacred Scripture, there is a divine manifestation in the blaze of the sun and the fall of night. Nature too, in a certain sense, is "the book of God."

We can ask ourselves how it is possible in Christian experience for contemplation of the Trinity to be fostered through creation, discerning there not only the reflection of the one God in a generic sense, but also the marks of the individual divine persons. If it is true, in fact, that "the Father, the Son and the Holy Spirit are not three principles of creation but one principle" (Council of Florence, *DS* 1331), it is also true as well that "each divine person performs the common work according to his unique personal property" (*CCC* 258).

So when we contemplate with wonder the universe in its grandeur and beauty, we must praise the whole Trinity, but in a special way our thoughts turn to the Father from whom everything flows, as the source and fullness of being itself. If we then reflect on the order that governs the cosmos and admire the wisdom with which the Father created it, endowing it with laws that regulate its existence, we naturally think of the eternal Son, presented to us by Scripture as the Word (cf. Jn 1:1–3) and divine Word (cf. 1 Cor 1:24, 30). In the marvelous hymn sung by Wisdom in the Book of Proverbs, she says: "Ages ago I was set up, at the first, before the beginning" (Prv 8:23). Wisdom is present at the moment of creation "like a master workman" (Prv 8:30), ready to delight "in the sons of men" (cf. Prv 30–31). From these aspects Christian tradition has seen in Wisdom the face of Christ, "the image of the invisible God, the firstborn of all creation.... All things were created through him and for him. He is before all things, and in him all things hold together" (Col 1:15–17; cf. Jn 1:3).

In the light of the Christian faith, creation particularly calls to mind the Holy Spirit in the dynamism that marks the relations between things, within the macrocosm and the microcosm, and is apparent especially wherever life is born and develops. Because of this experience, even in cultures far removed from Christianity, the presence of God is perceived in a way as the "spirit" which gives life to the world. Virgil's words are famous in this regard: *"spiritus intus alit"* — *"the spirit nourishes from within"* (*Aeneid,* VI, 726).

The Christian knows well that this reference to the Spirit would be unacceptable if it meant a sort of *"anima mundi"* taken in a pantheistic sense. However, while excluding this error, it remains true that every form of life, activity and love refers in the last analysis to that Spirit who, as Genesis tells us, "was moving over the face of the waters" (1:2) at the dawn of creation, and in which Christians, in the light of the New Testament, see a reference to the Third Person of the Holy Trinity. Indeed, the biblical concept of creation "includes not only the call to existence of the very being of the cosmos, that is to say, *the giving of existence,* but also the presence of the Spirit of God in creation, that is to say, the beginning of God's salvific self-communication to the things he creates. This is true first of all concerning man, who has been created in the image and likeness of God" (*DViv* 12).

Before the unfolding of cosmic revelation, we proclaim God's work in the words of the Psalmist: "When you send forth your Spirit, they are created, and you renew the face of the earth" (Ps 104:30).

General audience of August 2, 2000

Jesus Is the Supreme Encounter of God and Man

In our previous reflections, we have followed humanity in its encounter with God who created it and walks on its paths to seek it out. Today we will meditate on the supreme encounter between God and man which took place in Jesus Christ, the divine Word who became flesh and dwelt among us (cf. Jn 1:4).The definitive revelation of God — as St. Irenaeus, Bishop of Lyons, observed in the second century — was accomplished "when the Word became man, making himself like man and man like him, so that man might become precious to God through his likeness to the Son" (*Adv. Haer.,* V, 16, 2). This intimate embrace of divinity and humanity, which St. Bernard compares to the kiss mentioned in the Song of Songs (cf. *Sermons on the Song of Songs,* II), expands from the person of Christ to those he touches. This encounter of love has various dimensions that we will try to illustrate.

This encounter takes place in everyday life, in time and in space. A passage of John's Gospel (cf. 1:35 – 42) is descriptive in this regard. There we find a precise chronological indication of the day and time, locality and house where Jesus was staying. There are people who lead a simple life and are transformed, even in name, through that meeting. In fact, to have Christ enter one's life means to see one's history and projects disrupted. When those fishermen of Galilee found Jesus at the lakeside and heard his call, "they left everything and followed him" (Lk 5:11). This is a radical turning point that allows no hesitation and sets one on a path fraught with difficulties, but very liberating: "If anyone would come after me, let him deny himself and take up his cross and follow me" (Mt 16:24).

When he crosses a person's life, Christ disquiets his conscience and reads his heart, as happened with the Samaritan woman when he told her "all that she ever did" (cf. Jn 4:29). Above all, he moved her to repentance and love, as occurred with Zacchaeus, who gave half of his goods to the poor and restored fourfold to anyone he may have defrauded (cf. Lk 19:8). This is also what happened with the repentant woman, whose sins were forgiven "because she loved much" (Lk 7:47), and the adulteress who was not judged but urged to lead a new and sinless life (cf. Jn 8:11). The encounter with Jesus is like a rebirth: it brings forth the new creature who is capable of true adoration, which consists in worshipping the Father "in spirit and truth" (Jn 4:23–24).

Encountering Christ on one's path through life often means finding physical healing. Jesus would entrust to his disciples themselves the mission of proclaiming God's kingdom, conversion and the forgiveness of sins (cf. Lk 24:47), and also of healing the sick, delivering people from every evil, giving comfort and support. For the disciples "preached that people should repent. And they cast out many demons, and anointed with oil many who were sick and healed them" (Mk 6:12–13). Christ came to seek, meet and save the whole person. As a condition of salvation, Jesus demands faith, by which a person abandons himself totally to God who acts in him. Indeed, Jesus said to the woman with a hemorrhage who had touched his garment as her last hope: "Daughter, your faith has made you well; go in peace, and be healed of your disease" (Mk 5:34).

The purpose of Christ's coming among us is to lead us to the Father. For "no one has ever seen God; the only Son, who is in the bosom of the Father, he has made him known" (Jn 1:18). This historical revelation accomplished by Jesus in his words and deeds touches us deeply, through the Father's interior action (cf. Mt 16:17; Jn 6:44–45) and the enlightenment of the Holy Spirit (cf. Jn 14:26; 16:13). For this reason, the risen Jesus pours him forth as the principle of the forgiveness of sins (cf. Jn 20:22–23) and the source of divine love within us (cf. Rom 5:5). Thus, we have a Trinitarian communion which already begins in earthly life and whose final goal is the fullness of vision, when "we shall be like him, for we shall see him as he is" (1 Jn 3:2).

Now Christ continues to walk beside us on the paths of history, as he promised: "Lo, I am with you always, to the close of the age" (Mt 28:20). He is present through his Word, "a Word who calls, who invites, who personally summons, as happened to the apostles. When a person is touched by the Word, obedience is born, that is, the listening which changes life. Every day...[the believer] is nourished by the bread of the Word. Deprived of it, he is as though dead and has nothing left to communicate to his brothers and sisters, because the Word is Christ" (*Orientale Lumen,* 10).

Christ is also present in the Eucharist, the source of love, unity and salvation. The words he spoke one day at the synagogue in the little town of Capernaum on Lake Tiberias echo constantly in our churches. They are words of hope and life: "He who eats my flesh and drinks my blood abides in me, and I in him.... He who eats my flesh and drinks my blood has eternal life, and I will raise him up at the last day" (Jn 6:54, 56).

General audience of August 9, 2000

God Continually Calls Us to Repentance

The Psalmist sings: "My wanderings you have counted" (Ps 56:9). This short, essential sentence contains the history of man wandering through the desert of solitude, evil and aridity. With sin he has destroyed the wonderful harmony of creation established by God in the beginning: "God saw everything that he had made, and behold, it was something very good and beautiful," as the well-known text in Genesis might be rendered (1:31). Yet God is never very far from his creature; on the contrary, he is always present deep within him, as St. Augustine perceived so well: "Where were you then and how distant from me? I was wandering far from you.... But you were higher than my highest and more inward than my innermost self" (*Conf.*, 3, 6, 11).

However, the Psalmist had already described man's vain flight from his Creator in a stupendous hymn: "Where can I go from your spirit? From your presence where can I flee? If I go up to the heavens, you are there; if I sink to the nether world, you are present there. If I take the wings of the dawn, if I say, 'surely the darkness shall hide me, and night shall be my light' — For you darkness itself is not dark, and night shines as the day. Darkness and light are the same" (Ps 139:7–12).

When God seeks out the rebellious son who flees far from his sight, he does so with particular insistence and love. God traveled the tortuous roads of sinners through his Son, Jesus Christ, who bursting onto history's stage, is presented as "the Lamb of God, who takes away the sins of the world" (Jn 1:29). Here are the first words he says in public: "Repent, for the kingdom of heaven is at hand!" (Mt 4:17). An important term appears which Jesus will repeatedly explain in words and deeds: "Repent," in Greek *metanoeite,* that is, make a *metanoia,* a radical change of mind and heart. It is necessary to turn away form evil and to enter the kingdom of justice, love and truth which is being established.

The trilogy of parables on divine mercy collected by Luke in chapter 15 of his Gospel is the most striking depiction of how God actively seeks out and lovingly awaits his sinful creature. Through his *metanoia* or conversion man returns, like the prodigal son, to embrace the Father who has never forgotten or abandoned him.

In commenting on this parable of the father who is prodigal with his love toward the son who was prodigal with his sin, St. Ambrose introduces the presence of the Trinity:

> Rise, run to the Church: here is the Father, here is the Son, here is the Holy Spirit. He runs out to meet you, for he hears you as you reflect within the secrecy of your heart. And while you are still at a distance, he catches sight of you and starts to run. He sees into your heart; he runs out so that no one will detain you, and, furthermore, he embraces you.... He throws his arms around your neck, to lift up what had been lying on the ground and to enable someone oppressed by the burden of sin and looking down at earthly things to turn his gaze again to heaven, where he should have been seeking his Creator. Christ throws his arms around your neck because he wants to remove the yoke of slavery and put a gentle yoke upon it (*Comm. on Luke,* VII, 229–230).

A person's encounter with Christ changes his life, as we are taught by the story of Zacchaeus. The same thing happened to sinful men and women when Jesus crossed their path. On the cross there was an extreme act of forgiveness and hope given to the evil-doer, who made his *metanoia* when he arrived at the final frontier between life and death, and said to his companion: "We are receiving the due reward for our deeds" (Lk 23:41). To the one who implored him: "Remember me when you come in your kingly power," Jesus replied: "Truly, I say to you, today you will be with me in paradise" (cf. Lk 23:42–43). Thus, Christ's earthly mission, which began with the invitation to repent in order to enter the kingdom of God, ends with a conversion and an entry into his kingdom.

The apostles' mission also began with a pressing invitation to conversion. Those who heard Peter's first address felt cut to the heart and anxiously asked, "What should we do?" He said: "Repent *(metanoēsate)* and be baptized, every one of you, in the name of Jesus Christ for the forgiveness of your sins, and you shall receive the gift of the Holy Spirit" (Act 2:37–38). Peter's answer was promptly accepted: "about three thousand souls" were converted that day (cf. Acts 2:41). After the miraculous healing of a crippled man, Peter exhorted them again. He reminded the residents of Jerusalem of their horrible sin: "You denied the Holy and Righteous One...and killed the author of life" (Acts 3:14–15). But he mitigated their guilt, saying: "Now, brethren, I know that you acted in ignorance" (Acts 3:17); he then called them to conversion (cf. 3:19) and gave them immense hope: "God sent him to you first, to bless you in turning every one of you from your wickedness" (3:26).

In a similar way, the Apostle Paul preached repentance. He said so in his address to King Agrippa, describing his apostolate as follows: "I declared to everyone, also to the Gentiles, that they should repent and turn to God and perform deeds worthy of their repentance" (Acts 26:20; cf. 1 Thes 1:9–10).

Paul taught that "God's kindness is meant to lead [us] to repentance" (Rom 2:4). In the Book of Revelation Christ himself repeatedly urges repentance. Inspired by love (cf. 3:19), the exhortation is vigorous and expresses all the urgency of repentance (cf. 2:5, 16, 21–22; 3:3, 19), but is accompanied by wondrous promises of intimacy with the Savior (cf. 3:20–21).

The door of hope is always open to every sinner. "Man is not left alone to attempt, in a thousand often frustrated ways, an impossible ascent to heaven. There is a tabernacle of glory, which is the most holy person of Jesus the Lord, where the divine and the human meet in an embrace that can never be separated. The Word became flesh, like us in everything except sin. He pours divinity into the sick heart of humanity, and imbuing it with the Father's Spirit, enables it to become God through grace" (*OL* 15).

General audience of August 30, 2000

The Way Christ Taught Is Demanding

The encounter with Christ radically changes a person's life, spurs him to *metanoia* or a profound conversion of mind and heart, and establishes a communion of life that becomes discipleship. In the Gospels, the following of Christ is expressed in two attitudes: the first consists in "going with" Christ *(akolouthein)*; the second, in "walking behind" the One who leads, following in his footsteps and direction *(erchesthai opiso)*. This gives rise to the figure of the disciple, which is realized in different ways. Some follow him in a still general and often superficial way, like the crowd (cf. Mk 3:7; 5:24; Mt 8:1, 10; 14:13; 19:2; 10:29). There are sinners (cf. Mk 2:14–15), and the women who support Jesus' mission with their practical service are mentioned several times (cf. Lk 8:2–3; Mk 15:41). Some receive a specific calling from Christ, and among them a special place is reserved for the Twelve.

The typology of those called is thus quite varied: people involved in fishing, tax collectors, the honest and sinners, the married and the single, the poor and the wealthy, such as Joseph of Arimathea (cf. Jn 19:38), men and women. There is even Simon the Zealot (cf. Lk 6:15), that is, a member of the anti-Roman revolutionary opposition. There were some who refused the invitation, like the rich young man who, at Christ's demanding words, was saddened and went away sorrowful, "for he had great possessions" (Mk 10:22).

The conditions for taking the same way as Jesus are few but fundamental. As the Gospel states, it is necessary to turn one's back on the past and make a clean break with it, a *metanoia* in the profound sense of the word: a change of mind and life. Christ proposes a narrow way that demands sacrifice and total self-giving: "If anyone would come after me, let him deny himself and take up his cross and follow me" (Mk 8:34). It is a way that includes the thorns of suffering and persecution: "If they persecuted me, they will persecute you...also" (Jn 15:20). It is one which makes missionaries and witnesses to Christ's word, but demands that his apostles take "nothing for their journey...no bread, no bag, no money in their belts" (Mk 6:8; cf. Mt 10:9–10).

Discipleship, then, is not an easy journey on a level road. It can include moments of hardship to the point that on one occasion "many of his disciples drew back and no longer went about with him" (Jn 6:66). On another occasion, when Peter himself rebelled against the prospect of the cross, he was abruptly rebuked in words that, according to the nuance of the original text, could be an invitation to get "behind" Jesus again, after trying to reject the goal of the cross. "Get behind me, Satan! For you are not on the side of God, but of men" (Mk 8:33).

The risk of betrayal will be lurking for Peter who in the end, however, would follow his Master and his Lord with the most generous love. Peter would make his profession of love on the shores of the Sea of Tiberias: "Lord, you know everything; you know that I love you." And Jesus will tell him "by what death he was to glorify God," adding twice, "Follow me!" (Jn 21:17, 19, 22). Discipleship is expressed in a special way in the beloved disciple, who entered into intimacy with Christ, received his Mother as a gift and recognized him after he had risen (cf. Jn 13:23–26; 18:15–16; 19:26–27; 20:2–8; 21:2, 7, 20–24).

The ultimate goal of discipleship is glory. The way is one of "imitating Christ," who lived in love and died for love on the cross. The disciple "must, so to speak, enter into Christ with all his own self, he must 'appropriate' and assimilate the whole of the reality of the Incarnation and redemption in order to find himself" (*RH* 10). Christ must enter into his ego to free him from selfishness and pride, as St. Ambrose says in this regard: "May Christ enter your soul, may Jesus dwell in your thoughts, to prevent sin from having any room in the sacred tent of virtue" (*Comm. on Psalm 118, letter "daleth,"* 26).

The cross, sign of love and of total self-giving, is therefore the emblem of the disciple called to be configured to the glorious Christ. A Father of the Eastern Church, who was also an inspired poet, Romanus the Melodist, challenges the disciple in this way: "You have the cross as your cane; rest all your youth on it. Bring it to the common table, bring it to your prayer, bring it to the common table, bring it with you to bed and everywhere, as your claim to glory.... Say to your spouse who is now joined to you: I throw myself at your feet. In your infinite mercy, give peace to your world, help to your Churches, concern to pastors and harmony to the flock, so that we may all sing of our resurrection forever" (Hymn 52, *To the Newly Baptized,* strophes 19, 22).

General audience of September 6, 2000

The Holy Spirit Gives
Life and Freedom to Christians

In the upper room, on the last evening of his earthly life, Jesus promised the gift of the Holy Spirit five times (cf. Jn 14:16–17; 14:26; 15:26–27; 16:7–11; 16:12–15). In the same place, the Risen One presents himself to the apostles on Easter evening and pours out the promised Spirit with the symbolic act of breathing on them and with the words: "Receive the Holy Spirit!" (Jn 20:22). Fifty days later, also in the upper room, the Holy Spirit bursts in with his power, transforming the hearts and lives of the first Gospel witnesses.

Since then, the deepest dynamics of the Church's history have been imbued with the presence and action of the Spirit, "given not by measure" to those who believe in Christ (cf. Jn 3:34). The encounter with Christ involves the gift of the Holy Spirit who, in the words of Basil, the great Father of the Church, "is poured out on everyone without being diminished in any way, is present to each one of those who is capable of receiving it as if it were for him alone, and on all, he pours sufficient and complete grace" (*On the Holy Spirit,* IX, 22).

In a passage of the Letter to the Galatians (cf. 5:16–18, 22–25), the Apostle Paul describes "the fruit of the Spirit" (5:22), listing a broad range of virtues that flow into the life of the faithful. The Holy Spirit is at the root of the experience of faith. In fact, it is precisely in Baptism that through the Spirit we become children of God: "Because you are sons, God has sent the Spirit of his Son into our hearts, crying, 'Abba! Father!'" (Gal 4:6). At the very source of Christian life, when we are born as new creatures, is the breath of the Spirit who makes us children in the Son and enables us to "walk" on the paths of justice and salvation (cf. Gal 5:16).

All the events of Christian life must, therefore, take place under the influence of the Spirit. When he presents Christ's words to us, the light of truth shines within us, as Jesus promised: "The Counselor, the Holy Spirit, whom the Father will send in my name, will teach you all things, and bring to your remembrance all that I have said to you" (Jn 14:26; cf. 16:12–15). The Spirit is beside us at the moment of trial, becoming our defender and our support: "When they deliver you up, do not be anxious how you are to speak or what you are to say; for what you are to say will be given to you in that hour; for it is not you who speak, but the Spirit of your Father speaking through you" (Mt 10:19–20). The Spirit is at the root of Christian freedom, which is removal from the yoke of sin. The Apostle Paul clearly says so: "The law of the Spirit of life in Christ Jesus has set me free from the law of sin and death" (Rom 8:2). Precisely because moral life is irradiated by the Spirit, as St. Paul reminds us, it produces fruits of "love, joy, peace, patience, kindness, goodness, faithfulness, gentleness, self-control" (Gal 5:22).

The Spirit enlivens the entire community of believers in Christ. Once again, the Apostle celebrates as a work of the Holy Spirit the multiplicity and riches, as well as the unity of the Church, through the image of the body. On the one hand

Paul lists the variety of charisms or special gifts which are offered to the Church's members (cf. 1 Cor 12:1–10); on the other, he asserts that "all these are inspired by one and the same Spirit, who apportions to each one individually as he wills" (1 Cor 12:11). Indeed, "by one Spirit we were all baptized into one body — Jews or Greeks, slaves or free — and all were made to drink of one Spirit" (1 Cor 12:13).

Lastly, we are indebted to the Spirit for the attainment of our destiny of glory. In this regard, St. Paul uses the images of the "seal" and the "guarantee": "you...were sealed with the promised Holy Spirit, who is the guarantee of our inheritance until we acquire possession of it, to the praise of his glory" (Eph 1:13–14; cf. 2 Cor 1:22; 5:5). To sum up, the whole of the Christian's life, from its origins to its final goal, is under the banner of the Holy Spirit and is his work.

I am pleased to recall during this Jubilee Year what I said in the encyclical dedicated to the Holy Spirit: "The Great Jubilee of the Year 2000 thus contains a message of liberation by the power of the Spirit, who alone can help individuals and communities to free themselves from the old and new determinisms, by guiding them with the 'law of the Spirit, which gives life in Christ Jesus,' and thereby discovering and accomplishing the full measure of man's true freedom. For, as St. Paul writes, 'where the Spirit of the Lord is, there is freedom'" (*DViv* 60).

Therefore, let us abandon ourselves to the liberating action of the Spirit, making our own the amazement of Symeon the New Theologian, who addresses the third divine Person in these words:

> I see the beauty of your grace; I contemplate its radiance;
> I reflect its light; I am caught up in its ineffable splendor;
> I am taken outside myself as I think of myself; I see how I
> was and what I have become. O wonder! I am vigilant,
> I am full of respect for myself, of reverence and of fear, as I

would be were I before you; I do not know what to do. I am seized by fear; I do not know where to sit, where to go, where to put these members which are yours; in what deeds, in what works shall I use them, these amazing divine marvels! (*Hymns,* II, verses 19–27: cf. *VC* 20).

General audience of September 13, 2000

The Gift of the Spirit

We have started our meeting under the sign of the Trinity, described incisively and clearly by the words of the Apostle Paul in his Letter to the Galatians (cf. 4:4–7). In pouring out the Holy Spirit into Christians' hearts, the Father brings about and reveals the adoption as sons obtained for us by Christ. Indeed, the Spirit is "bearing witness with our spirit that we are children of God" (Rom 8:16). Looking at this truth as at the polestar of the Christian faith, let us meditate on some existential aspects of our communion with the Father through the Son and in the Spirit.

The typically Christian way of contemplating God always passes through Christ. He is the Way, and no one comes to the Father except through him (cf. Jn 14:6). To the Apostle Philip who implored him: "Show us the Father and we shall be satisfied," Jesus said: "He who has seen me has seen the Father" (Jn 14:8–9). Christ, the beloved Son (cf. Mt 3:17; 17:5), is the revealer of the Father par excellence. The true face of God is revealed to us only by the One "who is in the bosom of the father." The original Greek expression in John's Gospel (cf. 1:18) indicates an essentially intimate and dynamic relationship of love, of life, between the Son and the Father. This relationship of the eternal Word involves the human nature he took on in the Incarnation. Therefore, in the Christian perspective the experience of God can never be reduced to a general "sense of the divine," nor can the mediation of Christ's humanity be surpassed, as has been shown by the great mystics, such as St. Bernard, St. Francis of Assisi, St. Catherine of Siena, St. Teresa of Avila and many lovers of Christ in our time, from Charles de Foucauld to St. Teresa Benedicta of the Cross (Edith Stein).

Various aspects of Jesus' witness with regard to the Father are reflected in every authentic Christian experience. First, he witnessed that his teaching originates in the Father: "My teaching is not mine, but his who sent me" (Jn 7:16). What he made known is exactly what he "heard" from the Father (cf. Jn 8:26; 15:15; 17:8, 14). Therefore, the Christian experience of God cannot develop except in total coherence with the Gospel.

Christ also witnessed effectively to the Father's love. In the wonderful parable of the prodigal son, Jesus presents the Father who is constantly waiting for man the sinner to return to his embrace. In John's Gospel, he insists on the Father who loves mankind: "God so loved the world that he gave his only Son" (Jn 3:16). And again, "if anyone loves me, he will keep my word, and my Father will love him, and we will come to him and make our home with him" (Jn 14:23). Those who truly experience God's love can only repeat with ever new emotion the exclamation in John's First Letter: "See what love the Father has given us, that we should be called children of God, and so we are" (3:1). In this light, we can address God with that tender, natural, intimate name: *Abba,* Father. It is constantly on the lips of the faithful who feel they are children, as St. Paul recalls in Galatians (cf. 4:4–7).

Christ gives us the very life of God, a life that goes beyond time and leads us into the mystery of the Father, into his joy and infinite light. The Evangelist John testifies to this, passing on Jesus' sublime words: "For as the Father has life in himself,

so he has granted the Son also to have life in himself
"This is the will of my Father, that everyone who sees the
and believes in him should have eternal life, and I will raise
him up at the last day.... As the living Father sent me, and I live
because of the Father, so he who eats me will live because of
me" (Jn 6:40, 57).

This participation in the life of Christ, which makes us
"sons in the Son," is made possible by the gift of the Spirit. The
Apostle presents to us our being children in God in close connection with the Holy Spirit: "All who are led by the Spirit of
God are sons of God" (Rom 8:14). The Spirit puts us in relation
to Christ and to the Father. "In this Spirit, who is the eternal
gift, the Triune God opens himself to man, to the human spirit.
The hidden breath of the divine Spirit enables the human spirit
to open in its turn before the saving and sanctifying self-open-
ing of God.... In the communion of grace with the Trinity,
man's 'living area' is broadened and raised up to the supernatural level of divine life. Man lives in God and by God: he lives
'according to the Spirit,' and 'sets his mind on the things of the
Spirit'" (*DViv* 58).

The fatherly face of God truly appears to Christians illumined by the grace of the Spirit. The Christian can turn to him
with trust, as St. Thérèse of Lisieux witnesses in this intense
autobiographical passage: "The little bird would like to fly
toward the shining sun which fascinates its eyes. It would like
to imitate the eagles, its sisters, whom it sees flying high to the
divine fire of the Trinity.... However, alas! all that it can do is to
flap its tiny wings, but taking off in flight is not one of its few
possibilities.... So with bold abandon it stays gazing at its divine sun; nothing will be able to instill fear in it, neither wind,
nor rain" (*Autobiographical Manuscripts,* Paris 1957, p. 231).

General audience of September 20, 2000

THE EUCHARIST
AND
THE KINGDOM

The Eucharist Is a Celebration of Divine Glory

According to the program outlined in *Tertio Millennio Adveniente,* this Jubilee Year, the solemn celebration of the Incarnation, must be an "intensely Eucharistic" year (n. 55). Therefore, after having fixed our gaze on the glory of the Trinity that shines on man's path, let us begin a catechesis on that great yet humble celebration of divine glory that is the Eucharist. Great, because it is the principal expression of Christ's presence among us "always, to the close of the age" (Mt 28:20); humble, because it is entrusted to the simple, everyday signs of bread and wine, the ordinary food and drink of Jesus' land and of many other regions. In this everyday nourishment, the Eucharist introduces not only the promise but also the "pledge" of future glory: *"futurae gloriae nobis pignus datur"* (St. Thomas Aquinas, *Office for the Feast of Corpus Christi*). To grasp the greatness of the Eucharistic mystery, let us reflect today on the theme of divine glory and of God's action in the world, now manifested in the great events of salvation, now hidden beneath humble signs that only the eye of faith can perceive.

In the Old Testament, the Hebrew word *kabód* indicates the revelation of divine glory and of God's presence in history and creation. The Lord's glory shines on the summit of Sinai, the place of revelation of the divine Word (cf. Ex 24:16). It is present in the sacred tent and in the liturgy of the People of God on pilgrimage in the desert (cf. Lv 9:23). It dominates in the temple, the place — as the Psalmist says — "where your glory dwells" (Ps 26:8). It surrounds all the chosen people as if in a mantle of light (cf. Is 60:1). Paul himself knows that "they are Israelites, and to them belong the sonship, the glory, the covenants..." (Rom 9:4).

This divine glory, which is manifest to Israel in a special way, is present in the whole world, as the prophet Isaiah heard the seraphim proclaim at the moment of receiving his vocation: "Holy, holy, holy is the Lord of hosts; the whole earth is full of his glory" (6:3). Indeed, the Lord reveals his glory to all peoples, as we read in the Psalter: "All the peoples behold his glory" (Ps 97:6). Therefore, the enkindling of the light of glory is universal, so that all humanity can discover the divine presence in the cosmos.

It is especially in Christ that this revelation is fulfilled, because he "reflects the glory" of God (Heb 1:3). It is also fulfilled through his works, as the Evangelist John testifies with regard to the sign of Cana: Christ "manifested his glory, and his disciples believed in him" (Jn 2:11). He also radiates divine glory through his word, which is divine: "I have given them your word," Jesus says to the Father, "the glory which you have given me, I have given to them" (Jn 17:14, 22). More radically, Christ manifests divine glory through his humanity, assumed in the Incarnation: "The Word became flesh and dwelt among us, full of grace and truth; we have beheld his glory, glory as of the only Son from the Father" (Jn 1:14).

The earthly revelation of the divine glory reaches its apex in Easter, which especially in the Johannine and Pauline writings, is treated as a glorification of Christ at the right hand of the Father (cf. Jn 12:23; 13:31; 17:1; Phil 2:6–11; Col 3:1; 1 Tim 3:16). Now the paschal mystery, in which "God is perfectly glorified" (*SC* 7), is perpetuated in the Eucharistic sacrifice, the memorial of the death and resurrection entrusted by Christ to the Church, his beloved spouse (cf. *SC* 47). With the command "Do this in remembrance of me" (Lk 22:19), Jesus assures the presence of his paschal glory in all the Eucharistic celebrations that will mark the flow of human history. "Through the Holy Eucharist the event of Christ's Pasch expands throughout the Church.... By communion with the Body and Blood of Christ, the faithful grow in that mysterious divinization which by the Holy Spirit makes them dwell in the Son as children of the Father."[1]

It is certain that today we have the loftiest celebration of divine glory in the liturgy: "Since Christ's death on the cross and his resurrection constitute the content of the daily life of the Church and the pledge of his eternal Passover, the liturgy has as its first task to lead us untiringly back to the Easter pilgrimage initiated by Christ, in which we accept death in order to enter life" (Apostolic Letter *Vicesimus Quintus Annus,* 6). This task is exercised first of all through the Eucharistic celebration, which makes present Christ's Passover and communicates its dynamism to the faithful. Thus, Christian worship is the most vivid expression of the encounter between divine glory and the glorification that rises from human lips and hearts. The way we "glorify the Lord generously" (Sir 35:8) must correspond to "the glory of the Lord that filled the tabernacle" (cf. Ex 40:34).

As St. Paul recalls, we must also glorify God in our bodies, that is, in our whole existence, because our bodies are temples

---

1. John Paul II and Moran Mar Ignatius Zakka I Iwas, *Joint Declaration,* June 23, 1984, n. 6: *Enchiridion Vaticanum, 9,* 842.

of the Spirit who is within us (cf. 1 Cor 6:19, 20). In this light one can also speak of a cosmic celebration of divine glory. The created world, "so often disfigured by selfishness and greed," has in itself a "Eucharistic potential": it is "destined to be assumed in the Eucharist of the Lord, in his Passover, present in the sacrifice of the altar" (*OL* 11). The choral praise of creation will then respond, in harmonious counterpoint, to the breath of the glory of the Lord that is "above the heavens" (Ps 113:4) and shines down on the world in order that "in everything God may be glorified through Jesus Christ. To him belong glory and dominion forever and ever. Amen!" (1 Pt 4:11).

General audience of September 27, 2000

The Eucharist:
Memorial of God's Mighty Work

Prominent among the many aspects of the Eucharist is that of "memorial," which is related to a biblical theme of primary importance. We read, for example, in the Book of Exodus: "God remembered his covenant with Abraham and Jacob" (2:24). Deuteronomy, however, says: "You shall remember what the Lord your God did..." (7:18). In the Bible, the remembrance of God and the remembrance of man are interwoven and form a fundamental element in the life of God's People. However, this is not the mere commemoration of a past that is no more, but a *zikkarôn,* that is, a "memorial." It "is not merely the recollection of past events but the proclamation of the mighty works wrought by God for men. In the liturgical celebration of these events, they become in a certain way present and real" (*CCC* 1363). The memorial recalls the bond of an unfailing covenant: "The Lord has been mindful of us; he will bless us" (Ps 115:12).

Biblical faith thus implies the effective recollection of the works of salvation. They are professed in the "Great Hallel," Psalm 136, which — after proclaiming creation and the salvation offered to Israel in the Exodus — concludes: "It is he who remembered us in our low estate, for his steadfast love endures forever, and rescued us.... He who gives food to all flesh, for his steadfast love endures forever" (Ps 136: 23–25). We find similar words in the Gospel on the lips of Mary and Zechariah: "He has helped his servant Israel, in remembrance of his mercy...to remember his holy covenant" (Lk 1:54, 72).

In the Old Testament, the "memorial" par excellence of God's works in history was the Passover liturgy of the Exodus. Every time the people of Israel celebrated the *Passover,* God effectively offered them the gifts of freedom and salvation. In the Passover rite, therefore, the two remembrances converge: the divine and the human, that is, saving grace and grateful faith. "This day shall be for you a memorial day, and you shall keep it as a feast to the Lord.... It shall be to you as a sign on your hand and as a memorial between your eyes, that the law of the Lord may be in your mouth; for with a strong hand the Lord has brought you out of Egypt" (Ex 12:14; 13:9). By virtue of this event, as a Jewish philosopher said, Israel will always be "a community based on remembrance" (M. Buber).

The interweaving of God's remembrance with that of man is also at the center of the Eucharist, which is the "memorial" par excellence of the Christian Passover. For "anamnesis," i.e., the act of remembrance, is the heart of the celebration: Christ's sacrifice, a unique event done *ephapax,* that is, "once for all" (Heb 7:27; 9:12, 26; 10:12), extends its saving presence in the time and space of human history. This is expressed in the last command, which Luke and Paul record in the account of the Last Supper: "This is my body, which is for you. Do this in remembrance of me.... This cup is the new covenant in my blood. Do this, as often as you drink it, in remembrance of me" (1 Cor 11:24–25; cf. Lk 22:19). The past of the "body given for us" on the cross is presented alive today, and as Paul declares, opens onto the future of the final redemption: "As often as you eat this bread and drink the cup, you proclaim the Lord's death until he comes" (1 Cor 11:26).

The Eucharist is thus the memorial of Christ's death, but it is also the presence of his sacrifice and the anticipation of his glorious coming. It is the sacrament of the risen Lord's continual saving closeness in history. Thus, we can understand Paul's exhortation to Timothy: "Remember Jesus Christ, risen from the dead, descended from David" (2 Tim 2:8). In the Eucharist this remembrance is alive and at work in a special way.

The Evangelist John explains to us the deep meaning of the "memorial" of Christ's words and events. When Jesus cleanses the temple of the merchants and announces that it will be destroyed and rebuilt in three days, John remarks: "When he was raised from the dead, his disciples remembered that he had said this, and they believed the Scripture and the word that Jesus had spoken" (2:22). This memorial, which produces and nourishes faith, is the work of the Holy Spirit, "whom the Father will send in the name" of Christ: "He will teach you all things, and bring to your remembrance all that I have said to you" (Jn 14:26). Thus, there is an effective remembrance: one that is interior and leads to an understanding of the Word of God, and a sacramental one, which takes place in the Eucharist. These are the two realities of salvation that Luke combined in his splendid account of the disciples of Emmaus, structured around the explanation of the Scriptures and the "breaking of the bread" (cf. Lk 24:13–55).

"To remember" is "to bring back to the heart" in memory and affection, but it is also to celebrate a presence. "Only the Eucharist, the true memorial of Christ's paschal mystery, is capable of keeping alive in us the memory of his love. It is, therefore, the secret of the vigilance of the Church: it would be too easy for her, otherwise, without the divine efficacy of this continual and very sweet incentive, without the penetrating power of this look of her Bridegroom fixed on her, to fall into forgetfulness, insensitivity and unfaithfulness" (Apostolic Letter *Patres Ecclesiae,* III: *Ench. Vat.,* 7, 33). This call to vigilance opens our Eucharistic liturgies to the full coming of the Lord, to the appearance of the heavenly Jerusalem. In the Eucharist, Christians nurture the hope of the definitive encounter with their Lord.

General audience of October 4, 2000

The Eucharist Is a
Perfect Sacrifice of Praise

"Through him, with him, in him, in the unity of the Holy Spirit, all glory and honor is yours, almighty Father." This proclamation of Trinitarian praise seals the prayer of the canon at every Eucharistic celebration. The Eucharist is the perfect "sacrifice of praise," the highest glorification that rises from earth to heaven, "the fount and apex of the whole Christian life," in which the faithful "offer the divine victim to God, and offer themselves along with it" (*LG* 11). In the New Testament, the Letter to the Hebrews teaches us that the Christian liturgy is offered by "a high priest, holy, blameless, unstained, separated from sinners, exalted above the heavens," who achieved a unique sacrifice once and for all by "offering up himself" (cf. 7:26–27). "Through him then," the Letter says, "let us continually offer a sacrifice of praise to God" (13:15). Today, let us briefly recall the two themes of sacrifice and praise that are found in the Eucharist, *sacrificium laudis*.

First, the *sacrifice* of Christ becomes present in the Eucharist. Jesus is really present under the appearances of bread and wine, as he himself assures us: "This is my body...this is my blood" (Mt 26:26, 28). But the Christ present in the Eucharist is the Christ now glorified, who on Good Friday offered himself on the cross. The words he spoke over the cup of wine emphasize this: "This is my blood of the covenant, which is poured out for many" (Mt 26:28; cf. Mk 14:24; Lk 11:20). If these words are examined in the light of their biblical import, two significant references appear. The first consists of the expression "blood poured out," which as the biblical language attests (cf. Gn 9:6), is synonymous with violent death. The second is found in the precise statement "for many," regarding those for whom this blood is poured out. The allusion here takes us back to a fundamental text for the Christian interpretation of Scripture, the fourth song of Isaiah: by his sacrifice, the servant of the Lord "poured out his soul to death," and "bore the sin of many" (Is 53:12; cf. Heb 9:28; 1 Pt 2:24).

The same sacrificial and redemptive dimension of the Eucharist is expressed by Jesus' words over the bread at the Last Supper, as Luke and Paul traditionally relate them: "This is my body which is given for you" (Lk 22:19; cf. 1 Cor 11:24). Here too there is a reference to the sacrificial self-giving of the servant of the Lord according to the passage from Isaiah already mentioned (53:12): "He poured out his soul to death.... He bore the sin of many, and made intercession for the transgressors." "The Eucharist is above all else a sacrifice. It is the sacrifice of the New Covenant, as we believe and as the Eastern Churches clearly profess: 'Today's sacrifice,' the Greek Church stated centuries ago [at the Synod of Constantinople against Sotericus in 1156–57], 'is like that offered once by the Only–begotten incarnate Word; it is offered by him (now as then), since it is one and the same sacrifice'" (DC 9).

As the sacrifice of the New Covenant, the Eucharist is the development and fulfillment of the covenant celebrated on Sinai when Moses poured half the blood of the sacrificial victims on the altar, the symbol of God, and half on the assembly of the children of Israel (cf. Ex 24:5–8). This "blood of the covenant" closely united God and man in a bond of solidarity. With the Eucharist the intimacy becomes total; the embrace between God and man reaches its apex. This is the fulfillment of that "New Covenant" which Jeremiah had foretold (cf. 31:31–34): a pact in the spirit and in the heart, which the Letter to the Hebrews extols precisely by taking the prophet's oracle and linking it to Christ's one definitive sacrifice (cf. Heb 10:14–17).

At this point we can illustrate the other affirmation: the Eucharist is a sacrifice of *praise.*

Essentially oriented to full communion between God and man, "the Eucharistic sacrifice is the source and summit of the whole of the Church's worship and of the Christian life. The faithful participate more fully in this sacrament of thanksgiving, propitiation, petition and praise, not only when they wholeheartedly offer the sacred victim, and in it themselves, to the Father with the priest, but also when they receive this same victim sacramentally" (Sacred Congregation of Rites, *Eucharisticum Mysterium,* n. 3e).

As the term itself originally says in Greek, Eucharist means "thanksgiving"; in it the Son of God unites redeemed humanity to himself in a hymn of thanksgiving and praise. Let us remember that the Hebrew word *todah,* translated "praise," also means "thanksgiving." The sacrifice of praise was a sacrifice of thanksgiving (cf. Ps 50:14, 23). At the Last Supper, in order to institute the Eucharist, Jesus gave thanks to his Father (cf. Mt 26:26–27 and parallels); this is the origin of the name of this sacrament.

"In the Eucharistic sacrifice the whole of creation loved by God is presented to the Father through the death and the resurrection of Christ" (*CCC* 1359). Uniting herself to Christ's sacrifice, the Church in the Eucharist voices the praise of all creation. The commitment of every believer to offer his existence — his "body," as Paul says — as a "living sacrifice, holy and acceptable to God" (Rom 12:1), in full communion with Christ, must correspond to this. In this way, one life unites God and man, Christ crucified and raised for us all, and the disciple who is called to give himself entirely to him.

The French poet Paul Claudel sings of this intimate communion of love, putting these words on Christ's lips:

Come with me, where I Am, in yourself,
and I will give you the key to life.
Where I Am, there eternally
is the secret of your origin....
Where are your hands that are not mine?
And your feet that are not nailed to the same cross?
I died and rose once and for all!
We are very close to one another....
How can you separate yourself from me
without breaking my heart? *(La Messe là-bas)*.

General audience of October 11, 2000

The Eucharist,
Banquet of Communion with God

"We have become Christ. For if he is the head we are the members; he and we together are the whole man" (Augustine, *On John,* 21, 8). St. Augustine's bold words extol the intimate communion that is created between God and man in the mystery of the Church, a communion that on our journey through history, finds its supreme sign in the Eucharist. The commands, "Take, eat.... Drink of it..." (Mt 26:26–27) — which Jesus gave his disciples in that room on the upper floor of a house in Jerusalem on the last evening of his earthly life (cf. Mk 14:15) — are rich in meaning. The universal symbolic values of the banquet offered in bread and wine (cf. Is 25:6) already suggest communion and intimacy. Other more explicit elements extol the Eucharist as a banquet of friendship and covenant with God. For, as the *Catechism of the Catholic Church* recalls, it is "at the same time, and inseparably, the sacrificial memorial in which the sacrifice of the cross is perpetuated and the sacred banquet of communion with the Lord's body and blood" (n. 1382).

Just as in the Old Testament the movable shrine in the desert was called the "tent of meeting," that is, of the encounter between God and his people and of the brethren in faith among themselves, the ancient Christian tradition called the Eucharistic celebration the "synaxis," i.e., "meeting." In it "the Church's inner nature is revealed, a community of those summoned to the synaxis, to celebrate the gift of the One who is offering and offered: participating in the holy mysteries, they become 'kinsmen' of Christ, anticipating the experience of divinization in the now inseparable bond linking divinity and humanity in Christ" (*OL* 10).

If we wish to reflect more deeply on the genuine meaning of this mystery of communion between God and the faithful, we must return to Jesus' words at the Last Supper. They refer to the biblical category of "covenant," recalled precisely through the connection between Christ's blood and the sacrificial blood poured out on Sinai: "This is my blood of the covenant" (Mk 14:24). Moses had said: "Behold, the blood of the covenant" (Ex 24:8). The covenant on Sinai, which united Israel to the Lord with a bond of blood, foretold the new covenant which would give rise — to use an expression of the Greek Fathers — to a kinship, as it were, between Christ and the faithful (cf. Cyril of Alexandria, *On the Gospel of John,* 11; John Chrysostom, *Homily on Matthew,* 82, 5).

It is especially in the Johannine and Pauline theologies that the believer's communion with Christ in the Eucharist is extolled. In his discourse at the synagogue in Capernaum, Jesus said explicitly: "I am the living bread which came down from heaven; if anyone eats of this bread, he will live forever" (Jn 6:51). The entire text of this discourse is meant to emphasize the vital communion that is established in faith between Christ, the bread of life, and whoever eats it. In particular, we find the Greek verb *menein,* "to abide, to dwell," typically used in the Fourth Gospel to indicate the mystical intimacy between Christ and the disciple: "He who eats my flesh and drinks my blood abides in me, and I in him" (Jn 6:56; cf. 15:4–9).

The Greek word for "communion," *koinonia,* is used in the reflection of the First Letter to the Corinthians, where Paul speaks of the sacrificial banquets of idolatry, calling them the "table of demons" (10:21), while expressing a valid principle for all sacrifices: "Those who eat the sacrifices are partners in the altar" (10:18). The Apostle applies this principle in a clear and positive way to the Eucharist: "The cup of blessing which we bless, is it not a participation *(koinonia)* in the blood of Christ? The bread which we break, is it not a participation *(koinonia)* in the body of Christ?... We all partake of the one bread" (10:16–17). "Sharing in the Eucharist, the sacrament of the New Covenant, is the culmination of our assimilation to Christ, the source of 'eternal life,' the source and power of that complete gift of self" (*VS* 21).

This communion with Christ thus produces an inner transformation of the believer. St. Cyril of Alexandria effectively describes this event, showing its resonance in life and in history: "Christ forms us in his image so that the features of his divine nature will shine in us through sanctification, justice and a good life in conformity with virtue. The beauty of this image shines in us who are in Christ, when we show ourselves to be good people through our deeds."[1] "By sharing in the sacrifice of the cross, the Christian partakes of Christ's self-giving love and is equipped and committed to live this same charity in all his thoughts and deeds. In the moral life the Christian's royal service is also made evident and effective" (*VS* 107). This royal service is rooted in Baptism and blossoms in Eucharistic communion. The way of holiness, love and truth is, therefore, the revelation to the world of our intimacy with God, expressed in the Eucharistic banquet.

---

1. *"Tractatus ad Tiberium Diaconum sociosque,"* II, *Responsiones ad Tiberium Diaconum sociosque,* in vol. 3, *In divi Johannis Evangelium* (Brussels: 1965), 590.

Let us express our desire for the divine life offered in Christ in the warm tones of a great theologian of the Armenian church, Gregory of Narek (tenth century): "It is not for his gifts, but for the Giver that I always long.... It is not glory to which I aspire, but the Glorified One whom I desire to embrace.... It is not rest that I seek, but the face of the One who gives rest that I implore. It is not for the wedding feast, but for desire of the Bridegroom that I languish" (*Prayer* 12).

General audience of October 18, 2000

The Eucharist,
"A Taste of Eternity in Time"

"In the earthly liturgy we take part in a foretaste of that heavenly liturgy" (*SC* 8; cf. *GS* 38). These limpid and essential words of the Second Vatican Council show us a fundamental dimension of the Eucharist: it is a *"futurae gloriae pignus,"* a pledge of future glory, as beautifully expressed by the Christian tradition (cf. *SC* 47). "This sacrament," St. Thomas Aquinas notes, "does not admit us at once to glory, but bestows on us the power of coming into glory and, therefore, is called *viaticum"* (*Summa Theol.,* III, 79, 2, *ad* 1). The communion with Christ that we enjoy now while we are pilgrims and wayfarers on the paths of history anticipates that supreme encounter on the day when "we shall be like him, for we shall see him as he is" (1 Jn 3:2). Elijah, who collapsed helplessly under a broom tree during his journey in the wilderness and was strengthened by a mysterious bread until he reached the summit of his encounter with God (cf. 1 Kgs 19:1–8), is a traditional symbol of the journey of the faithful. They find strength in the Eucharistic bread to advance toward the shining goal of the holy city.

This is also the profound meaning of the manna prepared by God on the steppes of Sinai, the "food of angels," providing every pleasure and suited to every taste, a manifestation of God's sweetness toward his children (cf. Wis 16:20–21). Christ himself will shed light on this spiritual significance of the Exodus event. He enables us to taste in the Eucharist the twofold savor of the pilgrim's food and the food of messianic fullness in eternity (cf. Is 25:6). To borrow a phrase from the Jewish Sabbath liturgy, the Eucharist is a "taste of eternity in time" (A. J. Heschel). Just as Christ lived in the flesh while remaining in the glory of God's Son, so the Eucharist is a divine and transcendent presence, a communion with the eternal, a sign that "the earthly city and the heavenly city penetrate one another" (*GS* 40). The Eucharist, memorial of Christ's Passover, is by its nature the bearer of the eternal and the infinite in human history.

This aspect, which opens the Eucharist to God's future while leaving it anchored to present reality, is illustrated by the words Jesus spoke over the cup of wine at the last supper (cf. Lk 22:20; 1 Cor 11:25). With these same words Mark and Matthew evoke the covenant in the blood of the sacrifices on Sinai (cf. Mk 14:24; Mt 26:28; Ex 24:8). Luke and Paul, however, reveal the fulfillment of the "New Covenant" foretold by the prophet Jeremiah: "Behold, the days are coming, says the Lord, when I will make a New Covenant with the house of Israel and the house of Judah, not like the covenant I made with their fathers" (Jer 31:31–32). Jesus, in fact, declares: "This cup is the New Covenant in my blood." In biblical language "new" usually means progress, final perfection.

Luke and Paul also stress that the Eucharist anticipates the horizon of glorious light belonging to the kingdom of God. Before the Last Supper, Jesus said: "I have earnestly desired to eat this Passover with you before I suffer; for I tell you I shall not eat it until it is fulfilled in the kingdom of God. And he took a cup, and when he had given thanks he said, 'Take this, and divide it among yourselves; for I tell you that from now on I shall not drink of the fruit of the vine until the kingdom of God comes'" (Lk 22:15–18). Paul explicitly recalls that the Eucharistic supper looks forward to the Lord's final coming: "As often as you eat this bread and drink the cup, you proclaim the Lord's death until he comes" (1 Cor 11:26).

The fourth evangelist, John, extols this orientation of the Eucharist toward the fullness of God's kingdom in the well-known discourse on the "bread of life" that Jesus gave at the synagogue in Capernaum. The symbol he used as a biblical reference was, as already mentioned, the manna God offered to Israel on its pilgrimage through the desert. Regarding the Eucharist, Jesus solemnly declared: "If anyone eats of this bread, he will live forever.... He who eats my flesh and drinks my blood has eternal life, and I will raise him up at the last day.... This is the bread which came down from heaven, not such as the fathers ate and died; he who eats this bread will live forever" (Jn 6:51, 54, 58). In the language of the fourth Gospel, "eternal life" is the divine life itself that transcends the bounds of time. Being a communion with Christ, the Eucharist is thus a sharing in God's life, which is eternal and conquers death. Therefore, Jesus says: "This is the will of him who sent me, that I should lose nothing of all that he has given me, but raise it up at the last day. For this is the will of my Father, that everyone who sees the Son and believes in him should have eternal life, and I will raise him up at the last day" (Jn 6:39–40).

In this light — as a Russian theologian, Sergei Bulgakov, evocatively said — "the liturgy is heaven on earth." For this reason, in the apostolic letter *Dies Domini* I quoted the words of Paul VI, urging Christians not to neglect "this encounter, this banquet which Christ prepares for us in his love. May our sharing in it be most worthy and joyful! It is Christ, crucified and glorified, who comes among his disciples, to lead them all together into the newness of his resurrection. This is the climax, here below, of the covenant of love between God and his people: the sign and source of Christian joy, a stage on the way to the eternal feast" (*Gaudete in Domino,* 58).

General audience of October 25, 2000

The Eucharist:
Sacrament of the Church's Unity

"O sacrament of devotion! O sign of unity! O bond of charity!" St. Augustine's exclamation in his commentary on the Gospel of John (*On John,* 26, 13) captures the theme and sums up the words that Paul addressed to the Corinthians: "Because there is one bread, we who are many are one body, for we all partake of the one bread" (1 Cor 10:17). The Eucharist is the sacrament and source of the Church's unity. This has been stressed since the beginnings of the Christian tradition and is based on the sign of the bread and wine. The *Didache,* a writing composed at the dawn of Christianity, states it thus: "Just as this broken bread was first scattered on the mountains, and after being harvested became one reality, so may your Church be gathered from the ends of the earth into your kingdom" (9, 1).

St. Cyprian, bishop of Carthage, echoed these words in the third century, saying: "The sacrifices of the Lord themselves highlight the unanimity of Christians strengthened by solid, indivisible charity. For when the Lord calls the bread formed of the union of many grains his body, and when he calls the wine pressed from many clusters of grapes and poured together his blood, in the same way he indicates our flock formed of a multitude united together" (*Ep. ad Magnum,* 6). This Eucharistic symbolism of the Church's unity returns frequently in the Fathers and Scholastic theologians. The Council of Trent summarized the doctrine, teaching that our Savior left the Eucharist to his Church 'as a symbol of her unity and of the charity with which he wanted all Christians to be closely united with one another'; and for this reason it is 'a symbol of that one *body* of which he is the *head.* '"[1] The *Catechism of the Catholic Church* sums it up very effectively: "Those who receive the Eucharist are united more closely to Christ. Through it Christ unites them to all the faithful in one body — the Church" (n. 1396).

This traditional doctrine is deeply rooted in Scripture. Paul develops it in the passage already cited from the First Letter to the Corinthians, taking *koinonia* as the basic theme, that is, the communion which is established between the faithful and Christ in the Eucharist: "The cup of blessing which we bless, is it not a participation *(koinonia)* in the blood of Christ? The bread which we break, is it not a participation *(koinonia)* in the body of Christ?" (10:16). This communion is more precisely described in John's Gospel as an extraordinary relationship of "mutual interiority": "he in me and I in him." Jesus says at the synagogue in Capernaum: "He who eats my flesh and drinks my blood abides in me, and I in him" (Jn 6:56).

This theme will also be underscored in the discourses at the Last Supper with the symbol of the vine: the branch is verdant and fruitful only if it is grafted onto the vine stem, from which it receives sap and support (Jn 15:1–7). Otherwise, it is just a withered branch to be thrown into the fire: *aut vitis aut ignis,* "either the vine or the fire," St. Augustine succinctly comments (*On John,* 81, 3). Here we see a unity, a communion, which is

---

1. Paul VI, *Mysterium Fidei: Ench. Vat.,* 2, 424; cf. Council of Trent, *Decree on the Most Holy Eucharist,* introd. and ch. 2.

realized between the faithful and Christ present in the Eucharist, on the basis of the principle that Paul expresses this way: "Those who eat the sacrifices are partners in the altar" (1 Cor 10:18).

Because this type of "vertical" communion-*koinonia* makes us one with the divine mystery, it produces at the same time a communion-*koinonia* we could call "horizontal," or ecclesial, fraternal, capable of uniting all who partake of the same table in a bond of love. "We who are many are one body," Paul reminds us, "for we all partake of the one bread" (1 Cor 10:17). The discourse on the Eucharist anticipates the great ecclesial reflection that the Apostle will develop in chapter 12 of the same letter when he will speak of the body of Christ in its unity and multiplicity. The well-known description of the Jerusalem Church that Luke offers in the Acts of the Apostles also outlines this fraternal unity of *koinonia,* connecting it with the breaking of bread, that is, the Eucharistic celebration (cf. 2:42). This communion is realized in concrete historical reality: "They devoted themselves to the apostles' teaching and fellowship *(koinonia),* to the breaking of bread and the prayers.... All who believed were together and had all things in common" (Acts 2:42–44).

The profound meaning of the Eucharist is thus denied when it is celebrated without taking into account the demands of charity and communion. Paul is severe with the Corinthians because when they meet together, "it is not the Lord's supper that you eat" (1 Cor 11:20), as a result of their divisions, injustices and selfishness. In this case, the Eucharist is no longer *agape,* that is, the expression and source of love. Whoever partakes of it unworthily, without making it bear fruit in fraternal charity, "eats and drinks judgment upon himself" (1 Cor 11:29). "Christian life is expressed in the fulfilling of the greatest commandment, that is to say, in the love of God and neighbor, and this love finds its source in the Blessed Sacrament, which is commonly called the sacrament of love" (*DC* 5). The Eucharist recalls, makes present and brings about this charity.

Let us then answer the appeal of the bishop and martyr Ignatius, who exhorted the faithful of Philadelphia in Asia Minor to unity: "One is the flesh of our Lord Jesus Christ, one is the chalice in the unity of his blood, one is the altar, just as one is the bishop" (*To the Philadelphians,* 4). And let us pray with the liturgy to God the Father: "Grant that we, who are nourished by his body and blood, may be filled with his Holy Spirit, and become one body, one spirit in Christ" *(Eucharistic Prayer III).*

General audience of November 8, 2000

The Word,
the Eucharist and Ecumenism

In the program for this Jubilee Year we could not omit the dimension of ecumenical and interreligious dialogue, as I had indicated earlier in *Tertio Millennio Adveniente* (cf. nn. 53, 55). The Trinitarian and Eucharistic line we developed in our previous catecheses now prompts us to reflect on this aspect, examining first the problem of restoring unity among Christians. We do so in light of the Gospel account of the disciples of Emmaus (cf. Lk 24:13 – 35), observing the way that the two disciples who were leaving the community were spurred to reverse their direction to rediscover it.

The two disciples turned their backs on the place where Jesus had been crucified, because the event had cruelly disappointed them. For this reason they were leaving the other disciples and returning, as it were, to individualism. "They were talking with each other about all these things that had happened" (Lk 24:14), without understanding their meaning. They did not realize that Jesus had died "to gather into one the children of God who are scattered" (Jn 11:52). They only saw the tremendously negative aspect of the cross, which had destroyed their hopes: "We had hoped that he was the one to redeem Israel" (Lk 24:21). The risen Jesus came up and walked beside them, "but their eyes were kept from recognizing him" (Lk 24:16), because from the spiritual standpoint they were in the darkest shadows. Then with wonderful patience, Jesus endeavored to bring them back into the light of faith through a long biblical catechesis: "Beginning with Moses and all the prophets, he interpreted to them in all the Scriptures the things concerning himself" (Lk 24:27). Their hearts began to burn (cf. Lk 24:32). They begged their mysterious companion to stay with them. "When he was at table with them, he took the bread and blessed and broke it, and gave it to them. And their eyes were opened and they recognized him, and he vanished out of their sight" (Lk 24:30–31). Thanks to the clear explanation of the Scriptures, they emerged from the gloom of incomprehension into the light of faith and were able to recognize the risen Christ "in the breaking of the bread" (Lk 24:35). The effect of this profound change was an impulse to set out again immediately and return to Jerusalem to join "the eleven gathered together and those who were with them" (Lk 24:33). The journey of faith had made fraternal union possible.

The connection between the interpretation of the Word of God and the Eucharist also appears in other parts of the New Testament. In his Gospel John links this word with Eucharist, when in the discourse at Capernaum he presents Jesus recalling the gift of manna in the wilderness and reinterpreting it in a Eucharistic key (cf. 6:32–58). In the Church of Jerusalem, diligent listening to the *didache,* that is, the apostolic teaching based on the Word of God, preceded participation in the "breaking of bread" (Acts 2:42).

At Troas, when the Christians gathered around Paul "to break bread," Luke relates that the gathering began with a long speech by the Apostle (cf. Acts 20:7), which was certainly intended to nurture their faith, hope and charity. It is clear from all this that unity in faith is the necessary condition for common participation in the Eucharist.

Citing St. John Chrysostom (*Homily on John,* 46), the Second Vatican Council reminds us that with the liturgy of the Word and the Eucharist:

> The faithful united with their bishop have access to God the Father through the Son, the Word made flesh, who suffered and has been glorified, and so in the outpouring of the Holy Spirit, they enter into communion with the most holy Trinity, being made "sharers of the divine nature" (2 Pt 1:4). Hence, through the celebration of the Holy Eucharist in each of these churches, the Church of God is built up and grows in stature, and through concelebration, their communion with one another is made manifest (*UR* 15).

This link with the mystery of divine unity thus produces a bond of communion and love among those seated at the one table of the Word and of the Eucharist. The one table is a sign and expression of unity. "Thus, Eucharistic communion is inseparably linked to full ecclesial communion and its visible expression" (*Directory for the Application of the Principles and Norms of Ecumenism,* 1993, n. 129).

In this light we can understand how the doctrinal divisions between the disciples of Christ grouped in the various Churches and ecclesial communities limit full sacramental sharing. Baptism, however, is the deep root of a basic unity that links Christians despite their divisions. Therefore, although Christians who are still separated are excluded from participation in the same Eucharist, it is possible to introduce into the Eucharistic celebration, in specific cases provided for in the *Ecumenical Directory,* certain signs of participation that express the unity already existing and move in the direction of the full communion of the Churches around the table of the Word and of the Lord's Body and Blood. Consequently, "on exceptional occasions and for a just cause, the bishop of the diocese may permit a member of another Church or ecclesial community to take on the task of reader" during a Eucharistic celebration in the Catholic Church (n. 133). Likewise, "whenever necessity requires or a genuine spiritual advantage suggests, and provided that the danger of error or indifferentism is avoided," a certain reciprocity regarding the sacraments of Penance, the Eucharist and the Anointing of the Sick is lawful between Catholics and Eastern Christians (cf. nn. 123–131).

Nevertheless, the tree of unity must grow to its full extent, as Christ implored in his great prayer in the upper room (cf. Jn 17:20–26; *UR* 22). The limits to intercommunion at the table of the Word and of the Eucharist must become a call to purification, to dialogue and to the ecumenical progress of the Churches. These limits make us feel all the more strongly, in the Eucharistic celebration itself, the weight of our divisions and contradictions. The Eucharist is thus a challenge and a summons in the very heart of the Church to remind us of Christ's intense, final desire: "that they may be one" (Jn 17:11, 21).

The Church must not be a body of divided and suffering members, but a strong, living organism that moves onward, sustained by the divine bread as prefigured in Elijah's journey (cf. 1 Kgs 19:1–8), to the summit of the definitive encounter with God. There, at last, will be the vision of Revelation: "And I saw the holy city, new Jerusalem, coming down out of heaven from God, prepared as a bride adorned for her husband" (21:2).

General audience of November 15, 2000

Love Binds All Christian Communities

Faith, hope and love are like three stars that rise in the sky of our spiritual life to guide us to God. They are the theological virtues par excellence; they put us in communion with God and lead us to him. They form a triptych, whose apex is found in love, the *agape* Paul excellently praises in a hymn of the First Letter to the Corinthians. It is sealed by the following declaration: "So faith, hope and love abide, these three, but the greatest of these is love" (13:13).

To the extent that they enliven the disciples of Christ, the three theological virtues spur them on toward unity, in accordance with Paul's words: "One body...one hope...one Lord, one faith...one God and Father" (Eph 4:4 – 6). Continuing to reflect on the ecumenical perspective discussed in the preceding catechesis, today we want to look more closely at the role of the theological virtues in the journey that leads to full communion with God, with the Trinity and with others.

In the passage quoted from the Letter to the Ephesians, the Apostle primarily extols the unity of *faith*. This unity has its source in the Word of God, which all the Churches and ecclesial communities consider a light for the steps of their journey in history (cf. Ps 119:105). Together the Churches and the ecclesial communities profess their faith in "one Lord," Jesus Christ, true God and true man, and in "one God and Father of us all" (Eph 4:5–6). This fundamental unity, together with that constituted by the one Baptism, is clearly apparent in the many documents of the ecumenical dialogue, even when there remain reasons for reservation on this or that point. Thus we read, for example, in a document of the World Council of Churches: "Christians believe that the 'only true God' who made himself known to Israel, was revealed in 'him whom you have sent,' Jesus Christ (Jn 17:3); that in Christ, God reconciled the world to himself (2 Cor 5:19) and that, through his Holy Spirit, God brings new and eternal life to all those who, through Christ, entrust themselves to him" (WCC, *Confessare una sola fede,* 1992, n. 6).

The Churches and ecclesial communities all have a common reference point in the ancient creeds and the definitions of the early ecumenical councils. However, certain doctrinal divergences remain to be overcome, so that the journey toward unity of faith can reach the fullness indicated by the promise of Christ: "They will heed my voice. So there shall be one flock, one shepherd" (Jn 10:16).

In the text of the Letter to the Ephesians that we have taken as the emblem of our meeting, Paul also speaks about one *hope* to which we have been called (cf. 4:4). This hope is expressed in our common commitment, through prayer and an actively consistent life, to the coming of the kingdom of God. Within this vast horizon, the ecumenical movement has been oriented toward basic goals that are interrelated as objectives of one hope: the unity of the Church, the evangelization of the world, liberation and peace in the human community. The ecumenical journey has also taken advantage of the dialogue with the earthly and humanistic hopes of our time, even with the hidden hope, apparently defeated, of the "hopeless." In the face of these many expressions of hope in our time, Christians, despite the tensions among them and the trial of division, have been impelled to discover and bear witness to "a common reason for hope" (WCC, Faith and Order Commission, *Sharing in One Hope,* Bangalore, 1978), recognizing in Christ the indestructible foundation. A French poet wrote: "To hope is difficult...to despair is easy and is the great temptation" (Charles Péguy, *Le porche du mystère de la deuxième vertu,* ed. Pléiade, p. 538). But for us Christians, St. Peter's exhortation to always account for the hope that is in us remains ever valid (cf. 1 Pt 3:15).

At the apex of the three theological virtues is *love,* which Paul compares in a way to a golden knot that holds all the Christian communities in perfect harmony: "And above all these put on love, which binds everything together in perfect harmony" (Col 3:14). In the solemn prayer for the disciples' unity, Christ reveals the profound theological basis: "That the love with which you, [O Father], have loved me may be in them, and I in them" (Jn 17:26). This very love, accepted and made to grow, composes the Church in a single body, as Paul again indicates: "Speaking the truth in love, we are to grow up in every way into him who is the head, into Christ, from whom the whole body, joined and knit together by every joint with which it is supplied, when each part is working properly, fosters the body's growth and upbuilds itself in love" (Eph 4:15–16).

The ecclesial goal of love, and at the same time its inexhaustible source, is the Eucharist, communion with the Body and Blood of the Lord, an anticipation of perfect intimacy with God. Unfortunately, as I recalled in our previous catechesis, in the relations between divided Christians, "due to disagreements in matters of faith, it is not yet possible to celebrate together the same Eucharistic liturgy. And yet we do have a burning desire to join in celebrating the one Eucharist of the Lord, and this desire itself is already a common prayer of praise, a single supplication. Together we speak to the Father, and increasingly we do so 'with one heart'" (*Ut Unum Sint,* 45). The Council has reminded us that "human powers and capacities cannot achieve this holy objective — the reconciling of all Christians in the unity of the one and only Church of Christ." We must, therefore, put all our hope "on the prayer of Christ for the Church, on our Father's love for us, and on the power of the Holy Spirit" (*UR* 24).

General audience of November 22, 2000

God the Father Offers
Salvation to All Nations

The great fresco offered to us in the Book of Revelation is filled not only with the people of Israel, symbolically represented by the twelve tribes, but also with that great multitude of nations from every land and culture, all clothed in the white robes of a luminous and blessed eternity. I begin with this evocative image to call attention to interreligious dialogue, a subject that has become very timely in our day.

All the just of the earth sing their praise to God, having reached the goal of glory after traveling the steep and tiring road of earthly life. They have passed "through the great tribulation" (Rev 7:14) and have been purified by the blood of the Lamb, "poured out for many for the forgiveness of sins" (Mt 26:28). They all share in the same source of salvation that God has poured out upon humanity. For "God sent the Son into the world not to condemn the world, but that the world might be saved through him" (Jn 3:17).

Salvation is offered to all nations, as was already shown by the covenant with Noah (cf. Gn 9:8–17), testifying to the universality of God's manifestation and the human response in faith (cf. *CCC* 58). In Abraham "all the families of the earth shall bless themselves" (Gn 12:3). They are on the way to the holy city in order to enjoy that peace which will change the face of the world, when swords are beaten into plowshares and spears into pruning hooks (cf. Is 2:2–5).

It is moving to read these words in Isaiah: "The Egyptians will worship [the Lord] with the Assyrians...whom the Lord of hosts has blessed, saying, 'Blessed be Egypt my people, and Assyria the work of my hands, and Israel my heritage'" (19:23, 25). "The princes of the peoples," the Psalmist sings, "are gathered together with the people of the God of Abraham. For God's are the guardians of the earth; he is supreme" (Ps 47:10). Indeed, the prophet Malachi hears, as it were, a sigh of adoration and praise rising to God from the whole breadth of humanity: "From the rising of the sun to its setting my name is great among the nations, says the Lord of hosts" (1:11). The same prophet wonders: "Have we not all one Father? Has not one God created us?" (2:10).

A certain form of *faith* thus begins when God is called upon, even if his face is "unknown" (cf. Acts 17:23). All humanity seeks authentic adoration of God and the fraternal communion of men and women under the influence of the "Spirit of truth operating outside the visible confines of the Mystical Body" of Christ (*RH* 6).

In this connection St. Irenaeus recalls that God established four covenants with humanity: in Adam, Noah, Moses and Christ (cf. *Adv. Haer.*, III, 11, 8). The first three aim in spirit at the fullness of Christ and mark the stages of God's dialogue with his creatures, an encounter of disclosure and love, of enlightenment and grace, which the Son gathers in unity, seals in truth and brings to perfection.

In this light the faith of all peoples blossoms in *hope*. It is not yet enlightened by the fullness of revelation, which relates it to the divine promises and makes it a "theological" virtue.

The sacred books of other religions, however, are open to hope to the extent that they disclose a horizon of divine communion, point to a goal of purification and salvation for history, encourage the search for truth, and defend the values of life, holiness, justice, peace and freedom. With this profound striving, which withstands even human contradictions, religious experience opens people to the divine gift of *charity* and its demands.

The interreligious dialogue that the Second Vatican Council encouraged should be seen in this perspective (cf. *NA* 2). This dialogue is expressed in the common efforts of all believers for justice, solidarity and peace. It is also expressed in cultural relations, which sow the seed of idealism and transcendence on the often arid ground of politics, the economy and social welfare. It has a significant role in the religious dialogue in which Christians bear complete witness to their faith in Christ, the only Savior of the world. By this same faith they realize that the way to the fullness of truth (cf. Jn 16:13) calls for humble listening, in order to discover and appreciate every ray of light, which is always the fruit of Christ's Spirit, from wherever it comes.

"The Church's mission is to foster 'the kingdom of our Lord and his Christ' (Rev 11:15), at whose service she is placed. Part of her role consists in recognizing that the inchoate reality of this kingdom can be found also beyond the confines of the Church, for example, in the hearts of the followers of other religious traditions, insofar as they live evangelical values and are open to the action of the Spirit" (*DP* 35). As the Second Vatican Council told us in the Declaration *Nostra Aetate,* this applies especially to the monotheistic religions of Judaism and Islam. In this spirit I expressed the following wish in the Bull of Indiction of the Jubilee Year: "May the Jubilee serve to advance mutual dialogue until the day when all of us together — Jews, Christians and Moslems — will exchange the greeting of peace in Jerusalem" (*IM* 2). I thank the Lord for having given me, during my recent pilgrimage to the Holy Places, the joy of this greeting, the promise of relations marked by an ever deeper and more universal peace.

General audience of November 29, 2000

All Are Called to Build God's Kingdom

In this Great Jubilee year, the basic theme of our catecheses has been the glory of the Trinity as revealed to us in salvation history. We have reflected on the Eucharist, the greatest celebration of Christ under the humble signs of bread and wine. Now we want to devote several catecheses to what we must do to ensure that the glory of the Trinity shines forth more fully in the world.

Our reflection begins with Mark's Gospel, where we read: "Jesus came into Galilee, preaching the gospel of God and saying, 'The time is fulfilled, and the kingdom of God is at hand; repent and believe in the gospel'" (1:14–15). These are the first words Jesus spoke to the crowd: they contain the heart of his Gospel of hope and salvation, the proclamation of God's kingdom. From that moment on, as the evangelists note, Jesus "went about all Galilee, teaching in their synagogues, preaching the gospel of the kingdom, and healing every disease and every infirmity among the people" (Mt 4:23; cf. Lk 8:1). The apostles followed in his footsteps and with them Paul, the Apostle to the Gentiles, called to "preach the kingdom of God" among the nations, even to the capital of the Roman Empire (cf. Acts 20:25; 28:23, 31).

The Gospel of the kingdom links Christ with the Sacred Scriptures that, using a royal image, celebrate God's lordship over the cosmos and history. We read in the Psalter: "Say among the nations, 'The Lord reigns! The world is established, it shall never be moved; he will judge the peoples'" (Ps 96:10). The kingdom is thus God's effective but mysterious action in the universe and in the tangle of human events. He overcomes the resistance of evil with patience, not with arrogance and outcry.

For this reason Jesus compares the kingdom of God to a mustard seed, the smallest of all seeds, but destined to become a leafy tree (cf. Mt 13:31–32), or to the seed a man scatters on the ground: "He sleeps and rises night and day, while the seed sprouts and grows, and he knows not how" (Mk 4:27). The kingdom is grace, God's love for the world, the source of our serenity and trust: "Fear not, little flock," Jesus says, "for it is your Father's good pleasure to give you the kingdom" (Lk 12:32). Fears, worries and nightmares fade away, because in the person of Christ the kingdom of God is in our midst (cf. Lk 17:21).

But man is not a passive witness to God's entrance into history. Jesus asks us "to seek" actively "the kingdom of God and his righteousness," and to make this search our primary concern (Mt 6:33). To those who "supposed that the kingdom of God was to appear immediately" (Lk 19:11), he prescribed an active attitude instead of passive waiting, telling them the parable of the ten talents to be used productively (cf. Lk 19:12–27). For his part, the Apostle Paul states that "the kingdom of God does not mean food and drink but righteousness" (Rom 14:17). Above all, he urges the faithful to put their members at the service of righteousness for sanctification (cf. Rom 6:13, 19).

The human person is thus called to work with his hands, mind and heart for the coming of God's kingdom into the world. This is especially true of those who are called to the apostolate and are, as St. Paul says, "fellow workers for the kingdom of God" (Col 4:11), but it is also true of every human person.

Those who have chosen the way of the Gospel Beatitudes and live as "the poor in spirit," detached from material goods, in order to raise up the lowly of the earth from the dust of their humiliation, will enter the kingdom of God. "Has not God chosen those who are poor in the world," James asks in his Letter, "to be rich in faith and heirs of the kingdom which he has promised to those who love him?" (2:5). Those who lovingly bear the sufferings of life will enter the kingdom: "Through many tribulations we must enter the kingdom of God" (Acts 14:22; cf. 2 Thes 1:4–5), where God himself "will wipe away every tear...and death shall be no more, neither shall there be mourning nor crying nor pain anymore" (Rev 21:4). The pure of heart who choose the way of righteousness, that is, conformity to the will of God, will enter the kingdom, as St. Paul warns: "Do you not know that the unrighteous will not inherit the kingdom of God? Do not be deceived; neither the immoral, nor idolaters, nor adulterers...nor the greedy, nor drunkards, nor revilers nor robbers will inherit the kingdom of God" (1 Cor 6:9–10; cf. 15:50; Eph 5:5).

All the just of the earth, including those who do not know Christ and his Church, who, under the influence of grace, seek God with a sincere heart (cf. *LG* 16), are thus called to build the kingdom of God by working with the Lord, who is its first and decisive builder. Therefore, we must entrust ourselves to his hands, to his Word, to his guidance, like inexperienced children who find security only in the Father: "Whoever does not accept the kingdom of God like a child," Jesus said, "shall not enter it" (Lk 18:17).

With this thought we must make our own the petition: "Thy kingdom come!" This petition has risen to heaven many times in human history like a great breath of hope: "May the peace of your kingdom come to us," Dante exclaimed in his paraphrase of the Our Father (*Purgatorio,* XI, 7). This petition turns our gaze to Christ's return and nourishes the desire for the final coming of God's kingdom. This desire, however, does not distract the Church from her mission in this world, but commits her to it more strongly (cf. *CCC* 2818), in waiting to be able to cross the threshold of the kingdom, whose seed and beginning is the Church (cf. *LG* 5), when it comes to the world in its fullness. Then, Peter assures us in his Second Letter, "there will be richly provided for you an entrance into the eternal kingdom of our Lord and Savior Jesus Christ" (1:11).

General audience of December 6, 2000

God Entrusted the
Earth to Our Stewardship

The Apostle Paul states that "our homeland is in heaven" (Phil 3:20), but he does not conclude that we can passively wait for our entry into this homeland; rather he urges us to be actively involved. "Let us not grow weary in doing good," he writes, "for in due season we shall reap, if we do not lose heart. So then, whenever we have an opportunity, let us do good to all people, especially to those who are of the household of faith" (Gal 6:9 –10).

Biblical revelation and the best philosophical wisdom agree in stressing that, on the one hand, humanity strives for the infinite and the eternal, but on the other, it is firmly planted on earth, within the coordinates of time and space. There is a transcendent goal to be reached, but along a path that unfolds on earth and in history. The words of Genesis are illuminating: the human creature is tied to the dust of the earth, but at the same time he has a "breath" that unites him directly to God (cf. 2:7).

Genesis also says that when man came forth from God's hands, he was put "in the garden of Eden, to cultivate it and care for it" (2:15). The two verbs in the original Hebrew text are used elsewhere to indicate "serving" God and "observing" his word, that is, Israel's commitment to the covenant with the Lord. This analogy seems to suggest that a primary covenant joins the Creator to Adam and to every human creature, a covenant that is fulfilled in the duty to fill the earth, subduing it and having dominion over the fish of the sea and the birds of the air, and every other living thing that moves upon the earth (cf. Gn 1:28; Ps 8:7–9).

Unfortunately, man often carries out this mission assigned to him by God not as a wise artisan but as an overbearing tyrant. In the end, he finds himself in a devastated and hostile world, in a shattered and divided society, as Genesis further teaches us in the great fresco of the third chapter, which describes the breaking of the harmony between man and his fellow human beings, the earth and the Creator himself. This is the result of original sin, that is, of the rebellion which occurred at the very beginning of the plan entrusted to humanity by God.

Therefore, with the grace of Christ the Redeemer, we must once again make our own the plan of peace and development, of justice and solidarity, of the transformation and wise use of earthly and temporal realities foreshadowed in the first pages of the Bible. We must continue humanity's great adventure in the field of science and technology, discovering nature's secrets. We must develop — through the economy, trade and social life — well-being, knowledge and victory over poverty and over every degradation of human dignity.

In a certain sense, God has delegated his creative work to man, so that it will continue both in the extraordinary feats of science and technology and in the daily commitment of workers, scholars and those who, with their minds and hands, seek to "cultivate and care for" the earth and to increase solidarity among men and women. God is not absent from his creation, but has "crowned man with glory and honor," making him, so to speak, his representative, through his autonomy and freedom, in the world and in history (cf. Ps 8:6–7).

As the Psalmist says, in the morning "man goes forth to his work and to his labor until the evening" (Ps 104:23). In his parables Christ also refers to this work of man and woman in fields and at sea, in homes and at meetings, in law courts and in the market place. He uses it to illustrate symbolically the mystery of the kingdom of God and of its gradual realization, although he knows that this work is often frustrated by evil and sin, by selfishness and injustice. The mysterious presence of the kingdom in history sustains and enlivens the Christian's commitment to his earthly tasks.

Involved in this work and in this struggle, Christians are called to cooperate with the Creator to build on earth a "home for man" in greater conformity with his dignity and the divine plan, a home in which "mercy and faithfulness shall meet, justice and peace shall embrace" (Ps 85:11).

In this light, I would once again like to offer for your meditation the passages in the Pastoral Constitution *Gaudium et Spes* (cf. chs. 3, 4) which the Second Vatican Council devoted to "man's activity in the universe" and to "the role of the Church in the modern world." "To believers," the Council teaches, "this point is settled: considered in itself, this human activity accords with God's will. For man, created to God's image, received a mandate to subject to himself the earth and all it contains, and to govern the world with justice and holiness" (*GS* 34).

The complexity of modern society makes ever more arduous the commitment to animate the political, cultural, economic and technological structures, which are often soulless. In this difficult but promising horizon, the Church is called to recognize the autonomy of earthly realities (cf. *GS* 36), and also to proclaim effectively "the priority of ethics over techniques, the primacy of the person over things, the superiority of the spirit over matter."[1] Only in this way will Paul's prediction be ful-

---

1. Congregation for Catholic Education, *Guidelines for the Study and Teaching of the Church's Social Doctrine in the Formation of Priests,* December 30, 1988, n. 44.

filled: "Creation waits with eager longing for the revealing of the sons of God...who subjected it in hope, because creation itself will be set free from its bondage to decay and obtain the glorious liberty of the children of God" (Rom 8:19–21).

General audience of December 13, 2000

God Made Man the Steward of Creation

In the hymn of praise proclaimed a few moments ago (Ps 148:1–5), the Psalmist summons all creatures, calling them by name. Angels, sun, moon, stars and heavens appear on high; twenty-two things move upon the earth, as many as the letters of the Hebrew alphabet, in order to give an impression of fullness and totality. The believer, in a sense, is "the shepherd of being," that is, the one who leads all beings to God, inviting them to sing an "alleluia" of praise. The psalm brings us into a sort of cosmic church, whose apse is the heavens and whose aisles are the regions of the world, in which the choir of God's creatures sings his praise.

On the one hand, this vision might represent a lost paradise and, on the other, the promised paradise. Genesis (ch. 2) puts the horizon of a paradisal universe at the very origins of the world. Not without reason, Isaiah (ch. 11) and the Book of Revelation (chs. 21–22) place it at the end of history. Thus, we see that man's harmony with his fellow beings, with creation, and with God is the plan followed by the Creator. This plan was and is continually upset by human sin, which is inspired by an alternative plan depicted in the same Book of Genesis (chs. 3–11), which describes man's progressive conflictual tension with God, with his fellow human beings, and even with nature.

The contrast between the two plans emerges clearly in the vocation to which humanity is called, according to the Bible, and in the consequences resulting from its infidelity to this call. The human creature receives a mission to govern creation in order to make all its potential shine. It is a delegation granted at the very origins of creation, when man and woman, who are the "image of God" (Gn 1:27), receive the order to be fruitful and multiply, to fill the earth and subdue it, and to have dominion over the fish of the sea, the birds of the air and every living thing that moves upon the earth (cf. Gn 1:28). St. Gregory of Nyssa, one of the three great Cappadocian Fathers, commented: "God made man capable of carrying out his role as king of the earth.... Man was created in the image of the One who governs the universe. Everything demonstrates that from the beginning his nature was marked by royalty.... He is the living image who participates by his dignity in the perfection of the divine archetype" (*De Hominis Opificio,* 4: *PG* 44, 136).

Man's lordship, however, is not "absolute, but ministerial: it is a real reflection of the unique and infinite lordship of God. Hence, man must exercise it with wisdom and love, sharing in the boundless wisdom and love of God" (*EV* 52). In biblical language "naming" the creatures (cf. Gn 2:19–20) is the sign of this mission of knowing and transforming created reality. It is not the mission of an absolute and unquestionable master, but of a steward of God's kingdom who is called to continue the Creator's work, a work of life and peace. His task, described in the Book of Wisdom, is to rule "the world in holiness and righteousness" (9:3).

Unfortunately, if we scan the regions of our planet, we immediately see that humanity has disappointed God's expectations. Especially in our time, man has without hesitation devastated wooded plains and valleys, polluted waters, disfigured the earth's habitat, made the air unbreathable, disturbed the hydrogeological and atmospheric systems, turned luxuriant areas into deserts, and undertaken forms of unrestrained industrialization, degrading that "flowerbed" — to use an image from Dante Alighieri (*Paradiso,* XXII, 151) — which is the earth, our dwelling place.

We must, therefore, encourage and support the "ecological conversion" that in recent decades has made humanity more sensitive to the catastrophe it has been heading toward. Man is no longer the Creator's "steward," but an autonomous despot, who is finally beginning to understand that he must stop at the edge of the abyss. "Another welcome sign is the growing attention being paid to the quality of life and to ecology, especially in more developed societies, where people's expectations are no longer concentrated so much on problems of survival as on the search for an overall improvement of living conditions" (*EV* 27). At stake, then, is not only a "physical" ecology that is concerned to safeguard the habitat of the various living beings, but also a "human" ecology that makes the existence of creatures more dignified, by protecting the fundamental good of life in all its manifestations, and by preparing for future generations an environment more in conformity with the Creator's plan.

In this rediscovered harmony with nature and with one another, men and women are once again walking in the garden of creation, seeking to make the goods of the earth available to all and not just to a privileged few, as the biblical jubilee suggests (cf. Lv 25:8–13, 23). Among those marvels we find the Creator's voice, transmitted by heaven and earth, by night and day: a language "with no speech nor words, whose voice is not heard" and that can cross all boundaries (cf. Ps 19:2–5).

The Book of Wisdom, echoed by Paul, celebrates God's presence in the world, recalling, "from the greatness and beauty of created things comes a corresponding perception of their Creator" (13:5; cf. Rom 1:20). This is also praised in the Jewish tradition of the Hasidim: "Where I wander — you! Where I ponder — you!... In every trend, at every end, only you, you again, always you!"[1]

General audience of January 17, 2001

---

1. M. Buber, *Tales of the Hasidim* (Milan: 1979), 256.

A Future More Worthy
of the Human Person

If we cast a glance at the world and its history, at first sight the banner of war, violence, oppression, injustice and moral decay seems to predominate. It seems, as in the vision of chapter 6 of Revelation, that horsemen are riding through the barren lands of the earth, bearing now the crown of victorious power, now the sword of violence, now the scales of poverty and famine, now death's sharp sickle (cf. 6:1–8).

Faced with the tragedies of history and rampant immorality, we feel like repeating the question the prophet Jeremiah posed to God, giving voice to so many suffering and oppressed people: "Righteous are you, O Lord, when I complain to you; yet I would plead my case before you. Why does the way of the wicked prosper? Why do all who are treacherous thrive?" (12:1). Unlike Moses, who beheld the Promised Land from the top of Mount Nebo (cf. Dt 34:1), we look out over a troubled world in which the kingdom of God struggles to make headway.

In the second century St. Irenaeus identified the reason for this in the freedom of man who, instead of following the divine plan of peaceful harmony (cf. Gn 2), severed his relationship with God, with man and with the world. Thus, the Bishop of Lyons wrote: "It is not God's art, which can raise children of Abraham from stones, that is at fault, but those who do not follow him are the cause of their own failed perfection. Indeed, it is not the light that fails through the fault of those who have been blinded, but those who have been blinded remain in darkness through their own fault, while the light continues to shine. The light does not subdue anyone by force, nor does God constrain anyone to accept his art" (*Adv. Haer.,* IV, 39, 3).

Thus, a continuous effort of conversion is needed to straighten humanity's course, so that it may freely choose to follow "God's art," that is, his plan of peace and love, of truth and justice. This art is fully revealed in Christ. The convert Paulinus of Nola made it his own with this touching plan of life: "My only art is faith, and my music is Christ" (*Carmen,* XX, 32).

With faith the Holy Spirit also plants the seed of hope in the human heart. For as the Letter to the Hebrews says, faith is "assurance of things hoped for, the conviction of things not seen" (11:1). Against a horizon that is often marked by discouragement, pessimism, choices of death, inertia and superficiality, Christians must be open to the hope that springs from faith. This is portrayed in the Gospel scene of the storm that broke out on the lake: "Master, Master, we are perishing!" the disciples cry. And Christ asks them: "Where is your faith?" (Lk 8:24–25). With faith in Christ and in the kingdom of God we are never lost, and the hope of tranquil calm reappears on the horizon. For a future worthy of man it is also necessary to reinvigorate the active faith that gives rise to hope. On this subject a French poet wrote: "Hope is the anxious waiting of the good sower; it is the longing of those who are candidates for heaven. Hope is the infinity of love" (Charles Péguy, *Le porche du mystère de la deuxième vertu*).

Love for humanity, for its material and spiritual well-being, for its authentic progress, must stir all believers. Everything done to create a better future, a more habitable land and a more fraternal society participates, even if indirectly, in building up God's kingdom. Precisely in the perspective of this kingdom, "man — living man — represents the primary and fundamental way for the Church" (*EV* 2; cf. *RH* 14). It is the way that Christ himself followed, while at the same time making himself man's "way" (cf. Jn 14:6).

On this way we are called first to dispel our fear of the future. This fear often grips the younger generation, prompting it to react with indifference, with resignation in the face of life's demands, with self-destruction through drugs, violence and apathy. We must show the joy of every child that is born (cf. Jn 16:21), so that he will be welcomed with love and given the chance to grow in body and mind. In this way we cooperate in the very work of Christ, who described his mission in this way: "I came that they may have life, and have it abundantly" (Jn 10:10).

At the start of this audience we heard the Apostle John's message to fathers and sons, to the elders and the young, that they should continue to struggle and hope together, in the certainty that evil and the devil can be overcome through the heavenly Father's effective presence. To restore hope is a fundamental task of the Church. In this regard, the Second Vatican Council has left us this illuminating comment: "We can justly consider that the future of humanity lies in the hands of those who are strong enough to provide coming generations with reasons for living and hoping" (*GS* 31). In this perspective, I would like to suggest to you once again the appeal to trust that I addressed to the United Nations Organization in 1995: "We must not be afraid of the future.... We have within us the capacities for wisdom and virtue. With these gifts, and with the help of God's grace, we can build in the next century and the next millennium a civilization worthy of the human person, a true culture of freedom. We can and must do so! And in doing so, we shall see that the tears of this century have prepared the ground for a new springtime of the human spirit" (*Insegnamenti*, XVIII/2 [1995], p. 744).

General audience of January 24, 2001

We Look to
New Heavens and a New Earth

The Second Letter of Peter uses the characteristic symbols of the apocalyptic language current in Jewish literature to describe the new creation as though it were a flower blossoming from the ashes of history and the world (cf. 3:11–13). This image seals the Book of Revelation, when John proclaims: "Then I saw a new heaven and a new earth; for the first heaven and the first earth had passed away, and the sea was no more" (21:1). The Apostle Paul describes creation as groaning under the burden of evil, but destined to "be set free from its bondage to decay and obtain the glorious liberty of the children of God" (Rom 8:21).

Thus, Sacred Scripture weaves a golden thread, as it were, through the weaknesses, miseries, violence and injustices of human history and leads to a messianic goal of liberation and peace. On these sound biblical foundations, the *Catechism of the Catholic Church* teaches that "the visible universe, then, is itself destined to be transformed, 'so that the world itself, restored to its original state, facing no further obstacles, should be at the service of the just,' sharing their glorification in the risen

Jesus Christ" (n. 1047; cf. St. Irenaeus, *Adv. Haer.,* V, 32, 1). Then at last, in a world made peaceful, "the earth shall be full of the knowledge of the Lord as the waters cover the sea" (Is 11:9).

This new human and cosmic creation was inaugurated with the resurrection of Christ, the first fruits of that transfiguration to which we are all destined, as Paul says: "Christ the first fruits, then at his coming those who belong to Christ. Then comes the end, when he delivers the kingdom to God the Father.... The last enemy to be destroyed is death...that God may be everything to everyone" (1 Cor 15:23–24, 26, 28).

Certainly, this is a faith perspective that can sometimes be tempted by doubt in those who live in history under the weight of evil, contradictions and death. The Second Letter of Peter had already considered this, reflecting the objections of those who are suspicious, skeptical or even "scoffers," and who ask themselves: "Where is the promise of his coming? For ever since the fathers fell asleep, all things have continued as they were from the beginning of creation" (3:3–4).

This is the disheartened attitude of those who renounce every effort regarding history and its transformation. They are convinced that nothing can change, that every effort is bound to be useless, that God is absent and in no way interested in this minuscule point in the universe that is the earth. In the Greek world, some thinkers had taught this viewpoint, and perhaps the Second Letter of Peter is reacting to this fatalistic view with its obvious practical implications. If, in fact, nothing can change, what is the sense of hoping? One can only sit on the sidelines of life, letting the repetitive movement of human events complete its perennial cycle. With this attitude many men and women have already fallen on the fringes of history, without confidence, indifferent to everything, unable to struggle or hope. But the Christian vision is clearly explained by Jesus when, "asked by the Pharisees when the kingdom of God was coming, he answered them: 'The kingdom of God is not coming with signs to be observed; nor will they say, "Lo, here it is!" or "There!" for behold, the kingdom of God is in the midst of you!'" (Lk 17:20–21).

The temptation of those who imagine apocalyptic scenes of the inbreaking of God's kingdom and who close their eyes, weighed down with the sleep of indifference, is opposed by Christ with the quiet coming of the new heavens and the new earth. This coming is similar to the hidden but vigorous growth of the seed sprouting from the ground (cf. Mk 4:26–29).

God, therefore, entered the world and human history and proceeds silently, waiting patiently for humanity with its delays and conditioning. He respects its freedom, supports it when it is gripped by desperation, leads it step by step, and invites it to collaborate in the kingdom's project of truth, justice and peace. Divine action and human effort must therefore be intertwined. "It is clear that men are not deterred by the Christian message from building up the world, or impelled to neglect the welfare of their fellows, but that they are rather more stringently bound to do these very things" (*GS* 34).

A theme of great importance, which has always engaged the Church's work and reflection, thus opens before us. Without falling into the opposite extremes of holy isolation or secularism, Christians must also express their hope within the structures of secular life. If the kingdom is divine and eternal, it is still sown in time and space: it is "in the midst of us," as Jesus says.

The Second Vatican Council forcefully stressed this close and deep connection: "The mission of the Church is not only to bring the message and grace of Christ to men, but also to penetrate and perfect the temporal order with the spirit of the Gospel" (*Apostolicam Actuositatem,* 5). The spiritual and temporal orders "although distinct, are so connected in the singular plan of God that he himself intends to raise up the whole world again in Christ and to make it a new creation, initially on earth and completely on the last day" (*AA* 5).

Heartened by this certainty, Christians walk courageously on the world's highways, seeking to follow in God's footsteps and to cooperate with him in giving birth to a horizon in which "steadfast love and faithfulness will meet; righteousness and peace will kiss each other" (Ps 85:11).

General audience of January 31, 2001

The Church,
a Bride Adorned for Her Husband

Just as in the Old Testament the holy city was denoted by the feminine image of "the Daughter of Zion," so in the Revelation of John the heavenly Jerusalem is described "as a bride adorned for her husband" (21:2). The feminine symbol represents the face of the Church in her various aspects as betrothed, bride and mother, thus stressing a dimension of love and fruitfulness.

Our thoughts turn to the words of the Apostle Paul, who traces the Church's features in a very intense passage in the Letter to the Ephesians: "glorious, without spot or wrinkle or any such thing, but holy and without blemish," loved by Christ and the model of all Christian married life (cf. Eph 5:25–32). The ecclesial community, "betrothed to her one husband" as a chaste virgin (cf. 2 Cor 11:2), is presented in continuity with an idea developed in the Old Testament in impassioned texts, such as those of the prophet Hosea (ch. 1–3), or Ezekiel (ch. 16), or in the joyful radiance of the Song of Solomon.

To be *loved* by Christ and *to love him* with spousal love is constitutive of the Church's mystery. At its source is a free act of love, which the Father pours out through Christ and the Holy

Spirit. This love forms the Church and is radiated to all creatures. In this light we can say that the Church is a sign raised among the nations to bear witness to the intensity of divine love revealed in Christ, especially in the gift he made of his own life (cf. Jn 10:11–15). Therefore, "all human beings — both women and men — are called through the Church to be the 'Bride' of Christ, the Redeemer of the world" (*MD* 25).

The Church must let this supreme love shine, reminding humanity — which often feels alone and abandoned on the wastelands of history — that it will never be forgotten or lack the warmth of divine tenderness. Isaiah declares in a touching way: "Can a mother forget her infant, be without tenderness for the child of her womb? Even should she forget, I will never forget you" (49:15).

Precisely because she is born of love, the Church pours out love. She does so by proclaiming the commandment to love one another as Christ has loved us (cf. Jn 15:12), that is, even to the gift of our lives: "He laid down his life for us, and we ought to lay down our lives for the brethren" (1 Jn 3:16). That God who "first loved us" (1 Jn 4:19) and did not hesitate to give his Son out of love (cf. Jn 3:16), spurs the Church to follow the way of love "to the end" (cf. Jn 13:1). And she is called to do so with the freshness of a couple who love each other in the joy of unreserved self-giving and daily generosity, whether the skies of life are springlike and clear, or the darkness and clouds of a spiritual winter loom ahead.

In this sense we can understand why the Book of Revelation — despite its dramatic depiction of history — is filled throughout with songs, music and joyful liturgies. In the landscape of the spirit, love is like the sun illuminating and transfiguring nature, which would remain gray and monotonous without its brightness.

Another fundamental dimension of the Church's spousal nature is *fruitfulness*. The love received and given is not confined to the marital relationship, but becomes creative and life-giving. In Genesis, which presents humanity as made in the "image and likeness of God," there is a significant reference to being "male and female": "God created man in his own image; in the image of God he created him; male and female he created them" (1:27).

The distinction and reciprocity of the human couple are a sign of God's love not only as the basis of a vocation to communion, but also for the purpose of procreative fruitfulness. Not by chance is the Book of Genesis already interspersed with genealogies, which are the fruit of procreation and give rise to the history in which God reveals himself. Thus, we can understand how the Church too, in the Spirit who enlivens her and unites her to Christ her Bridegroom, is endowed with an inner fruitfulness by which she constantly brings forth children of God in Baptism and enables them to grow to the fullness of Christ (cf. Gal 4:19; Eph 4:13).

These children form that "assembly of the firstborn who are enrolled in heaven," destined to inhabit "Mount Zion and the city of the living God, the heavenly Jerusalem" (cf. Heb 12:21–23). Not without reason the Book of Revelation's last words are an intense plea to Christ: "The Spirit and the Bride say, 'Come'" (22:17), "Come, Lord Jesus!" (22:20). This is the Church's ultimate goal as she journeys confidently on her pilgrimage through history, while often sensing at her side, according to the image in the same biblical book, the hostile and furious presence of another female figure, "Babylon," the "great harlot" (cf. Rev 17:1, 5), who embodies the "bestiality" of hatred, death and inner barrenness.

As the Church looks at her goal, she nurtures "the hope of the eternal kingdom that is brought about by participation in the life of the Trinity. The Holy Spirit, given to the apostles as the Counselor, is the guardian and animator of this hope in the heart of the Church" (*DViv* 66). Let us ask God, then, to grant his Church always to be in history the guardian of hope, shining brightly like the woman of Revelation, "clothed with the sun, with the moon under her feet, and on her head a crown of twelve stars" (12:1).

General audience of February 7, 2001

All Creation Will Be "Recapitulated" in Christ

God's saving plan, "the mystery of his will" (cf. Eph 1:9) for every creature, is described in the Letter to the Ephesians with a distinctive term: to "recapitulate" all things in heaven and on earth in Christ (1:10). The image could also refer to the roller around which was wrapped the parchment or papyrus scroll of the *volumen* with a written text: Christ gives a single meaning to all the syllables, words and works of creation and history.

The first person to take up this theme of "recapitulation" and develop it in a marvelous way was St. Irenaeus of Lyons, a great second-century Father of the Church. Against any fragmentation of salvation history, against any division of the old and new covenants, against any dispersion of God's revelation and action, Irenaeus extols the one Lord, Jesus Christ, who in the Incarnation sums up in himself the entire history of salvation, humanity and all creation: "He, as the eternal King, recapitulates all things in himself" (*Adv. Haer.,* III, 21, 9).

Let us listen to a passage in which this Father of the Church comments on the Apostle's words concerning the recapitulation of all things in Christ. The phrase "all things," Irenaeus says, includes man, who was touched by the mystery of the Incarnation when the invisible Son of God "became visible, the

447

incomprehensible became comprehensible, the impassible became passible, the Word became man. He recapitulated all things in himself, so that, just as the Word of God has primacy over heavenly, spiritual and invisible beings, so he does over visible and corporeal beings. Assuming this primacy in himself and giving himself as head to the Church, he draws all things to himself " (*Adv. Haer.,* III, 16, 6). This coming together of all being in Christ, the center of time and space, gradually takes place in history, as the obstacles, the resistance of sin and the evil one, are overcome.

To illustrate this movement, Irenaeus refers to the difference, already presented by St. Paul, between Christ and Adam (cf. Rom 5:12–21): Christ is the new Adam, that is, the Firstborn of faithful humanity, who lovingly and obediently welcomes the plan of redemption that God designed as the soul and goal of history. Therefore, Christ must cancel the work of devastation, the horrible idolatries, violence and every sin that rebellious Adam sowed in the age-old history of humanity and in the created realm. By his total obedience to the Father, Christ opens the era of peace with God and among men, reconciling dispersed humanity in himself (cf. Eph 2:16). In himself he "recapitulates" Adam, in whom all humanity can see itself, transforms him into a child of God and restores him to full communion with the Father. Through his brotherhood with us in flesh and blood, in life and death, Christ becomes "the head" of saved humanity. St. Irenaeus writes: "Christ has recapitulated in himself all the blood shed by all the just and by all the prophets who have lived since the beginning" (*Adv. Haer.,* V, 14, 1; cf. V, 14, 2).

Good and evil, then, are considered in the light of Christ's redemptive work. As Paul shows us, this involves all creation with the variety of its elements (cf. Rom 8:18–30). Indeed, nature itself, since it was subjected to the senselessness, degradation and devastation caused by sin, thus shares in the joy of the liberation achieved by Christ in the Holy Spirit.

Therefore, the full realization of the Creator's original plan emerges: that of a creation in which God and man, man and woman, humanity and nature are in harmony, in dialogue and in communion. Christ, who mysteriously but effectively carries it out in the present reality, waiting to bring it to fulfillment, restores this plan, upset by sin, in the most marvelous way. Jesus himself said he was the fulcrum and point of convergence of this saving plan when he said: "I, when I am lifted up from the earth, will draw all men to myself" (Jn 12:32). The Evangelist John presents this work precisely as a kind of recapitulation: "to gather into one the dispersed children of God" (Jn 11:52).

This work will reach its fullness at the end of time when — as Paul again recalls — "God will be all in all" (cf. 1 Cor 15:28).

The last page of the Book of Revelation depicts this goal in vivid colors. And as Paul puts it, the Church and the Spirit are waiting and praying for the moment when Christ will "deliver the kingdom to God the Father after destroying every rule and every authority and power.... The last enemy to be destroyed is death. 'For God has put all things in subjection under his [Son's] feet'" (1 Cor 15:24, 26–27).

At the end of this battle — described in the marvelous pages of the Book of Revelation — Christ will complete the "recapitulation." Those who are united with him will form the community of the redeemed, which "will not be wounded any longer by sin, stains, self-love, that destroy or wound the earthly community. The beatific vision, in which God opens himself in an inexhaustible way to the elect, will be the ever-flowing well-spring of happiness, peace, and mutual communion" (*CCC* 1045).

The Church, the loving Bride of the Lamb, with her gaze fixed on that day of light, raises the ardent prayer: *"Marana tha"* (1 Cor 16:22), "Come, Lord Jesus!" (Rev 22:20).

General audience of February 14, 2001

Mary,
Eschatological Icon of the Church

We began our meeting by listening to one of the most famous passages in John's Book of Revelation. In the woman with child, who is giving birth while a red dragon rages against her and the child she has conceived, Christian liturgical and artistic tradition has seen an image of Mary, the Mother of Christ. However, according to the sacred author's primary intention, if the child's birth represents the coming of the Messiah, the woman obviously personifies the People of God, both the biblical Israel and the Church. The Marian interpretation does not conflict with the ecclesial meaning of the text, since Mary is "a type of the Church" (*LG* 63; cf. St Ambrose, *Comm. on Luke,* II, 7).

The profile of the Mother of the Messiah is thus seen against the background of the believing community. The dragon, which evokes Satan and evil, rises up against Mary and the Church, as the symbolism of the Old Testament has already indicated; red is the sign of war, slaughter and bloodshed; the "seven heads" with diadems mean immense power, while the "ten horns" recall the impressive strength of the beast described by the prophet Daniel (cf. 7:7), which too is an image of the abusive power that rages in history.

Good and evil thus confront each other. Mary, her Son and the Church represent the apparent weakness and smallness of love, truth and justice. Against them is unleashed the monstrous, devastating energy of violence, deceit and injustice. But the song that closes the passage reminds us that the final verdict is entrusted to "the salvation and the power and the kingdom of our God, and the authority of his Christ" (Rev 12:10).

Certainly, in historical time the Church can be forced to seek refuge in the desert, like ancient Israel on its way to the Promised Land. Among other things, the desert is the traditional refuge of those pursued, the secret, tranquil place where divine protection is offered (cf. Gn 21:14–19; 1 Kgs 19:4–7). However, as the Book of Revelation stresses (cf. 12:6, 14), the woman remains in this refuge for only a limited period. The time of anguish, persecution and trial, then, is limited: in the end liberation will come and the hour of glory.

In contemplating this mystery in a Marian perspective, we can say that "Mary, at the side of her Son, is the most perfect image of freedom and of the liberation of humanity and of the universe. It is to her as Mother and Model that the Church must look in order to understand in its completeness the meaning of her own mission."[1]

Let us fix our gaze, then, on Mary, the icon of the pilgrim Church in the wilderness of history, but on her way to the glorious destination of the heavenly Jerusalem, where she will shine as the Bride of the Lamb, Christ the Lord. The Mother of God, as the Church of the East celebrates her, is the *Hodegetria,* she who "shows the way," that is, Christ, the only mediator for fully encountering the Father. A French poet sees her as "creation in its first honor and its final flowering, as it came forth

---

1. Congregation for the Doctrine of the Faith, *Libertatis Conscientia,* March 22, 1986, n. 97; cf. *Redemptoris Mater,* 37.

from God at the dawn of its original splendor" (P. Claudel, *La vierge à midi,* ed. Pléiade, p. 540).

In her Immaculate Conception, Mary is the perfect model of the human creature who, filled from the very beginning with that divine grace which sustains and transfigures the creature (Lk 1:28), always and freely chooses God's way. On the other hand, in her glorious Assumption into heaven Mary is the icon of the creature who is called by the risen Christ to attain, at the end of history, the fullness of communion with God in the resurrection for an eternity of bliss. For the Church, which often feels the weight of history and the assault of evil, the Mother of Christ is the shining emblem of humanity redeemed and enveloped by the grace that saves.

We will reach the ultimate goal of human life when "God will be all in all" (1 Cor 15:28), and — as the Book of Revelation foretells — "the sea [will be] no more" (21:1), that is, the sign of destructive chaos and evil will be destroyed at last. Then the Church will be presented to Christ as "a bride adorned for her husband" (Rev 21:2). That will be the moment of intimacy and unblemished love. But now, gazing precisely at the Virgin assumed into heaven, the Church already has a foretaste of the joy that will be fully hers at the end of time. Mary accompanies the Church on her pilgrimage of faith through history as "a model of ecclesial communion in faith, in charity and in union with Christ. Eternally present in the mystery of Christ, she is, in the midst of the apostles, at the very heart of the Church at her birth and of the Church of all ages. Indeed, the Church was congregated in the upper part (of the cenacle) with Mary, who was the Mother of Jesus, and with his brethren. We cannot, therefore, speak of the Church unless Mary, the Mother of the Lord, is present there, with the Lord's brethren."[2]

---

2. Congregation for the Doctrine of the Faith, *Communionis Notio,* May 28, 1992, n. 19; cf. Chromatius of Aquileia, *Sermon 30,* 1.

So let us sing our hymn of praise to Mary, the icon of redeemed humanity, the sign of the Church, which lives in faith and love, anticipating the fullness of the heavenly Jerusalem. "The poetic genius of St. Ephrem the Syrian, called the 'lyre of the Holy Spirit,' tirelessly sang of Mary, leaving a still living mark on the whole tradition of the Syriac Church" (*RMat* 31). It is he who describes Mary as an icon of beauty: "She is holy in her body, beautiful in her spirit, pure in her thoughts, sincere in her understanding, perfect in her sentiments, chaste, firm in her intentions, immaculate in her heart, eminent and filled with all virtues" (*Hymns to the Virgin Mary,* 1, 4; ed. Th. J. Lamy, *Hymni de B. Maria,* Malines: 1886, t. 2, col. 520). May this image shine brightly at the center of every ecclesial community as a perfect reflection of Christ and a sign raised among the peoples, like a "city set on a hill" and "a lamp put on a stand so that it gives light to all" (cf. Mt 5:14–15).

General audience of March 14, 2001

Index

A

H

M

S

Pauline
BOOKS & MEDIA

The Daughters of St. Paul operate book and media centers at the following addresses. Visit, call or write the one nearest you today, or find us on the World Wide Web, www.pauline.org

CALIFORNIA
   3908 Sepulveda Blvd, Culver City, CA 90230   310-397-8676
   5945 Balboa Avenue, San Diego, CA 92111   858-565-9181
   46 Geary Street, San Francisco, CA 94108   415-781-5180

FLORIDA
   145 S.W. 107th Avenue, Miami, FL 33174   305-559-6715

HAWAII
   1143 Bishop Street, Honolulu, HI 96813   808-521-2731
   Neighbor Islands call: 800-259-8463

ILLINOIS
   172 North Michigan Avenue, Chicago, IL 60601   312-346-4228

LOUISIANA
   4403 Veterans Memorial Blvd, Metairie, LA 70006   504-887-7631

MASSACHUSETTS
   Rte. 1, 885 Providence Hwy, Dedham, MA 02026   781-326-5385

MISSOURI
   9804 Watson Road, St. Louis, MO 63126   314-965-3512

NEW JERSEY
   561 U.S. Route 1, Wick Plaza, Edison, NJ 08817   732-572-1200

NEW YORK
   150 East 52nd Street, New York, NY 10022   212-754-1110
   78 Fort Place, Staten Island, NY 10301   718-447-5071

OHIO
   2105 Ontario Street, Cleveland, OH 44115   216-621-9427

PENNSYLVANIA
   9171-A Roosevelt Blvd, Philadelphia, PA 19114   215-676-9494

SOUTH CAROLINA
   243 King Street, Charleston, SC 29401   843-577-0175

TENNESSEE
   4811 Poplar Avenue, Memphis, TN 38117   901-761-2987

TEXAS
   114 Main Plaza, San Antonio, TX 78205   210-224-8101

VIRGINIA
   1025 King Street, Alexandria, VA 22314   703-549-3806

CANADA
   3022 Dufferin Street, Toronto, Ontario, Canada M6B 3T5   416-781-9131
   1155 Yonge Street, Toronto, Ontario, Canada M4T 1W2   416-934-3440

¡También somos su fuente para libros, videos y música en español!